Life After Death: A Strategy to Bring New Life to a Dead Church!

I0225276

By Tom Cheyney & Steve Sells

R

RENOVATE
Publishing Group

First published by Renovate Publishing Group in 4/10/2019.

ISBN: 978-0-578-49403-6

Printed in the United States of America

Dedication (Tom)

To Cheryl, my beloved!
My best friend, life companion, and one who challenges me every day to be the best I can for my Lord. You mean the world to me. There are so many things I truly admire about you as a person, as my best friend and as my wife. Your smile lights up my soul. As a Church Revitalizer's wife, you have been courageous to go even when the path seemed unclear and yet the hand of God was certain. You have given much and sacrificed more so others might see Jesus. To all of those Church Revitalizers serving in local churches asking God to do great things once more and revive their church once more: The course is not easy, but the need is great and our Master longs to see the church restored for future generations.

"For God has not given us a spirit of fearfulness, but one of power, love, and sound judgment"

2 Timothy 1:7 HCSB

To God be the glory forever and ever.

Dedication (Steve)

To my wife Shirley, the best helpmate God could ever give a man! The one who challenges me to be a better man and leader. The one who encourages me to never settle for mediocrity. The one who believes in me no matter what the circumstances. You are my best friend and partner in ministry. You exemplify true Christianity in all of your living. You are the love of my life and the Godly mother of our children. I love you with all of my heart.

I would also like to dedicate this work to the Board of Directors of Operation Transformation who have made it possible for me to participate in my passion, church revitalization. Lastly, to my dear friends Rev. & Mrs. Robert Tenery, for their constant support and encouragement goes my deepest thanks and appreciation.

RENOVATE
National Church
Revitalization Conference

Life After Death:
A Strategy to Bring New Life to a Dead Church!

Table of Contents

Acknowledgements

Tom: I am blessed to serve each day the Greater Orlando Baptist Association (GOBA). This is a network of churches that is changing the way we have done associational work across Southern Baptist churches. No longer bound by geography, GOBA has raised the bar by working with churches, networks, and partners to plant healthy churches, to revitalize those churches in need of renewal, and to develop leaders equipped for the ministry through the GOAL Leadership Development Training. The Renovate National Church Revitalization Conference is one of these new things that has impacted Christianity cross-denominationally. Spearheaded by the wonderful pastors and laity who have partnered with us for the work of the Lord may I say thank you.

To my many committed Church Revitalization Practioners who join with me annually to make the Renovate National Church Revitalization Conference the largest conference focused on helping declining churches, I thank you. Your gifts and your passion for hurting churches make my heart leap for such godly compassion. To those just beginning the journey, seek God's best and become the best daily so you become a vessel fully developed for the work of a Church Revitalizer.

Steve: My deepest appreciation goes to so many people who have left a mark on my life. The most important acknowledgement, however, is my Lord and Savior Jesus Christ without whom I would have never made it this far in life. He is the reason for all that I am and all that I do.

There are also many people who have been a real encouragement to me in this journey. To my late parents, J.V. and Hazel Sells, whose lives led me to a relationship with Jesus Christ. My parents were a constant encouragement as I grew and matured in the Lord. Their Love for Jesus Christ was contagious and bold and I am eternally grateful for them and their Christian example.

To the faithful pastors who taught me the word of God, loved me when I erred and supported me as I sought to live for Christ.

To the Board of Directors of Operation Transformation who have made it possible for me to participate in my passion, church revitalization. They have been an encouragement and support as we have developed this ministry to churches.

Lastly, a special thanks to my dear friends Rev. & Mrs. Robert Tenery who have been constant friends through many years of ministry. They are truly choice servants of God.

To God alone be glory, honor and praise!

What Others Are Saying About *Life After Death: A Strategy to Bring New Life to a Dead Church!*

Tom Cheyney knows churches. As a church leader himself and as an advisor to countless pastors, Tom has developed insights about church life and health which are valuable resources for all of us. In particular, Tom has a heart for church revitalization, which is one of the most pressing issues of our day. I am thankful for the investment Tom Cheyney and Steve Sells have made in helping pastors and other leaders breathe new life into dying and declining congregations.

Michael Duduit, Executive Editor of Preaching Magazine and founding Dean of the Clamp Divinity School at Anderson University in Anderson, SC.

During the years I spent as an Organizational Change Consultant, I observed first-hand the kind of impact that leaders can have when they embrace the role of change agent. In *Life After Death: A Strategy to Bring New Life to a Dead Church*, Tom Cheyney gives church leaders tools to take on that critical role. This book will help to increase your confidence to become the kind of catalyst leader needed to lead your church into the future.

Lee Kricher, Author
For a New Generation: A Practical Guide for Revitalizing Your Church

I am convinced that nobody and I mean nobody in America understands Church Revitalization like my friend, Dr. Tom Cheyney, founder of the Renovate National Church Revitalization Conference. He not only understands the intricacies of the revitalization process itself, but the dynamics required of the leaders who attempt this important work. Tom Cheyney is the seminal leader in the Church Revitalization Movement in America today. His vast experience as a church planter and revitalizer, coupled with his ability to communicate within both academia and to the church, uniquely qualifies him to write the official playbooks of revitalization strategies. In *Life After Death: A Strategy to Bring New Life to a Dead Church*, Cheyney and Sells have comprehensively identified and described the contemporary strategies for addressing church revitalization in the dying church. Church leaders, looking for guidance as they lead their churches into a revitalization process, will find this work to be an essential and invaluable tool to guide them in the strategy that best fits their settings.

Terry Rials
Church Revitalizer & Pastor of Crestview Baptist Church
Co-Author of *The Nuts and Bolts of Church Revitalization*

I don't know anyone who is more well-versed or written on church revitalization than Tom Cheyney. His advice is solid, practical, and helpful. This is one for your tool chest, pastors.

Ron Edmondson, Blogger
CEO Leadership Network
ron.edmondson@gmail.com

Tom Cheyney does it again! He addresses a critical need in Church Revitalization in a way that is both insightful and practical. In *Life After Death: A Strategy to Bring New Life to a Dead Church*, Dr. Cheyney, who is quickly becoming known as the father of the church revitalization movement, writes about this crucial role for Church Revitalizers. Let us never forget the obvious- that church revitalization requires significant change. Readers will discover that much more is being done in the area of church revitalization than previously realized. This book is for and about those whose job it is to lead churches to do what they are reluctant to do. Inspiring and hopeful, this is a must read for anyone who is concerned about the state of rural churches in North America.

Mark Weible, Director of Church Planting Greater Orlando Baptist Association

Tom Cheyney understands Church Revitalization like few others. He realizes the local pastor of the church in search of revitalization is the key. If my declining or plateaued church was struggling and in need of revitalization than I would want to first read *Life After Death: A Strategy to Bring New Life to a Dead Church*. Tom leads a growing multi-denominational church revitalization movement that impacts thousands of churches and pastors. He is the leader in the field and the voice that so many turn to when it comes to church revitalization and renewal. This book by Tom Cheyney and Steve Sells, will be a valuable asset to any pastor desiring to lead his church through the process of Revitalization. This is a book you want to read and want to read it now.

Larry Wynn, Co-author
Preaching Towards Church Revitalization and Renewal

Buy this book, the cost is small in dollars but large in impact. *Life After Death: A Strategy to Bring New Life to a Dead Church*, is about new paradigms for the declining church. Tom and Steve train revitalization pastors who take action and bring about healthy change. Cheyney is like few in this world on Church Revitalization. Tom helps me consistently become a more effective leader personally and with churches. He will do the same with you here. It is important to understand that there, are specific "skill sets" that are either learned or acquired by pastors as they walk down the paths of their ministries. Everybody brings something to the table when they arrive to pastor a rural church. However, if they arrive at the table with an inability to analyze, create and adapt, they are going to be in for a rough "Pastor-Life," experience. I have known Dr. Tom Cheyney for over forty years. *Life After Death: A Strategy to Bring New Life to a Dead Church*, is packed with valuable insights that he has gleaned through the "School of Hard Ministry Knocks." Tired of watching others succeed in changing their situations where you are too scared to lead? Read this book! Don't know how to move your rural church past an entrenched establishment that hasn't changed in years? Read this book! Starting out in ministry and looking to not have to "learn the hard way?" Read this book!

Greg Kappas
President, Grace Global Network
Vice President, The Timothy Initiative
Author *Five Stages for Multiplying Healthy Churches*

No one has worked harder, written more, or studied more in the arena of church revitalization than Tom Cheyney. I consider him THE expert on this vital topic for 21st Century church leaders. Tom tackles the task of restarting dead churches in his latest book, *Life After Death: A Strategy to Bring New Life to a Dead Church.* I believe it is a "must read" for anyone who finds themselves in the position of leading, helping, or attending a "dead" church.

Steve Holt
Church Revitalization Leader
Tennessee Baptist Mission Board

No one has researched and trained more church leaders in the area of church revitalization than Dr. Tom Cheyney. As you peruse the pages of this book, you will discover how God is calling you to help bring necessary change to your church. Both pastors and lay leaders will benefit greatly from the challenges here offered by Cheyney and Sells. May the Lord use this tool in your church's life as it moves toward life!

Joel Breidenbaugh
Author, *Preaching for Body Building*
Senior Pastor and Church Planter

Leading change is one of the most difficult disciplines in rural church revitalization, yet one that cannot be overlooked. In Tom Cheyney's most recent book, ***Life After Death: A Strategy to Bring New Life to a Dead Church***, he is going to help you understand those necessary principles that will help you be an effective pastor in your church setting. If you find yourself in a place where change is so desperately needed, this is a must have book for you. Through Cheyney's expertise and experience, you will develop an appreciation for the many ways that God can bring about health and vitality in the church. The stakes are high and the challenge is big, but with the perils of wisdom you find within this book, as a revitalization leader you will gain confidence and understanding for how you can see revitalization in your church, for the glory of God.

Dr. Michael Atherton, Pastor
First Baptist Church O'Fallon
Author of *The Revitalized Church*

A critical book for a critical time! ***Life After Death: A Strategy to Bring New Life to a Dead Church*** carries with it a sense of urgency. The topic of RESTART addresses the necessity to act immediately in a dying situation. Church Revitalization takes a lengthy period to bring new life to a declining church. But there are many churches that do not have the years needed to bring revitalization to fruition. Dr. Cheyney's latest book, *Life after Death* addresses the immediate call for radical spiritual intervention. While many churches do not want to die, Tom Cheyney and Steve Sells outline how a resurrection can come from a terminal condition. **Except a grain of wheat fall to the ground and die, it remains by itself, but if it dies, it brings forth much fruit** -John 12:24.

Dr. Jim Grant
Executive Director
Galveston Baptist Association

Experience matters. If you are desperately searching for someone to help you restart your church, then Tom and Steve are your guys. Their experience in revitalizing churches will arm you to face this challenging task, not with untested theories, but with a phase by phase plan steeped in practical knowledge. In this book you will learn from two men who passionately want you to be used of God to rebuild a witnessing church in your community.

Dr. Steve Smith, Church Equippers Ministries

Tom Cheyney has done it again! With *Life After Death: A Strategy to Bring New Life to a Dead Church*, Cheyney and coauthor Steve Sells have applied their wisdom and experience to the challenge of replanting a church in a meaningful way. The focus of the authors on what it takes and the steps needed to make a replant successful are particularly helpful for any minister who finds himself in this setting. Replanting is not for the faint of heart! Cheyney and Sells recognize this, and with this book add to the toolbox you will need to be effective in partnering with God on this Kingdom adventure.

Dr. J. David Jackson, State Director of Missions
Baptist Convention of New England
author of ReNEW: Traveling the Forgotten Path

Across America, once vibrant churches are closing. But even in death there is hope! Tom Cheyney and Steve Sells presents a proven strategy for restarting a dying church. They've done it, with God's help. So can you!

Dr. Dale Robertson, Pastor
Secretary Treasurer of the North Carolina Baptist Pastors
Conference for 25 years.

Living in a throw-a-way society the dying church has been discarded by the secular world and by some spiritual leaders of Christ's kingdom on earth. There are simply too many resources and spiritual legacies being lost each year as churches close their doors for the very last time. "*Life After Death*" shares with us both a strategy and the spiritual tools to bring new life to dying churches that souls might be saved, and God may be Glorified.

Dr. Burt Wilbur, Director of Missions,
Brushy Mountain Baptist Association, Wilkesboro NC

Introduction
Growing the Kingdom by Giving Up!

"And now I'm going to tell you who you are, really are. You are Peter, a rock. This is the rock on which I will put together my church, a church so expansive with energy that not even the gates of hell will be able to keep it out."[1]

It is no secret that the local New Testament church today is in a pickle! Memberships are souring and the ability to reclaim former members has become a thing of the past. The hard reality in North America is that most churches and most, if not all, denominations are in a state of decline. The membership within these churches and denominations has plateaued and what used to pass for involvement and activity within churches is deteriorating. While all of this is happening, the rank and file of the church appears powerless to assemble the strength that is needed to get the churches growing again. There are more churches that die annually than are planted. Many more are declining than are growing. A small church can be defined as one in which the number of active adult members and the total annual undesignated budget are inadequate relative to the church's current organizational needs and expenses. It is a church struggling to pay its minister, heat or cool its buildings, and find enough people to assume leadership responsibilities to take the church into the future.

In 1990 an editor for the *Wall Street Journal* Wade Clark Roof published an editorial article entitled, "The Episcopalian Goes the Way of the Dodo," where he argued the decline of mainline denominationalism and its effect on Christianity.[2]

---

[1] Eugene H. Peterson, *The Message: The Bible in Contemporary Language* (Colorado Springs, CO: NavPress, 2005), Mt 16:18.

2 Wade Clark Roof, "The Episcopalian Goes the Way of the Dodo," *Wall Street Journal*, July 20, 1990.

With the turn of the twenty-first century sustained growth within our churches has become an intermittent exception while decline seems to be more of the pronouncement. The mainline denominations to which Roof referred, are still in the midst of severe decline and serious deterioration. Stuck in the status quo, new wine cannot be poured into the same old wine skins of outdated mindsets. A new sense of urgency is required for lasting change. Change is required and the church in need of revitalization and renewal cannot escape change. Will we allow the church of America to become mirrors of the churches all across Europe that find themselves empty urns holding the obvious? We must not. Kevin Ezell, President of the North American Mission Board of the Southern Baptist Convention declares, "We must keep our denominations focused on the ministry of rebirth and redemption, not on the business of enforcing rules and rituals."[3]

The need for training today's minister with the tools and skill sets necessary to combat this rampant plateau and decline is crucial. Most ministers coming out of our seminaries today lack preparation for the challenge of church revitalization and renewal. If the estimates are accurate that, at a minimum, eighty percent or more of our churches are in need of revitalization, then it stands to reason that the majority of graduates from our seminaries are going to begin their ministries in the majority of these churches. Less than five percent of these graduates will actually be going to healthy churches. Existing ministers will pastor the healthy pool of churches that make up the twenty percent so the seminarian needs to prepare for the eventual challenge of revitalizing a plateaued or declining church.

---

3 David S. Dockery, Ray Van Neste, and Jerry Tidwell, *Southern Baptists, Evangelicals and the Future of Denominationalism* (Nashville: B&H Publishing Group, 2011), i.

According to *Leadership Journal*, 340,000 churches are in need of church revitalization today.[4] Ninety-five percent of churches in North America average 100 or less. Over 80 percent of American Churches are in decline or on a plateau. Each year approximately 3,500 churches die in North America.[5] Within my own Southern Baptist Convention the annual death rate averages between seven and nine hundred![6] Studies have shown that churches typically plateau in attendance by their fifteenth year, and by year 35 they begin having trouble replacing the members they lose."[7] Only 7.3 % of small churches are growing in North America currently. Of the churches that are fifty years old or older, only 9.2% are growing.

In North America, fifty to sixty churches close their doors every week. Among churches of all sizes, growing churches are rare! In fact, they only make up about "20 percent of our churches today. The other 80 percent have reached a plateau or are declining."[8] In a study of more than two thousand churches, David Olson revealed that 69 percent of our churches in America have reached a plateau or

---

4 http://www.ctlibrary.com/le/2005/fall/8.24.html (accessed 3/20/11).

5 Warren Bird, "More Churches Opened Than Closed in 2006," *Rev Magazine,* July-August 2007, 68.

6 *"Annual Change in the Number of Southern Baptist Churches 1973-2009"* Center for Missional Research, North American Mission Board, SBC. Alpharetta, Georgia.

7 *"Churches Die with Dignity" Christianity Today* Jan. 1991, Vol. 36.

8 Stetzer, Ed and Warren Bird, *Viral Churches: Helping Church Planters Become Movement Makers* (San Francisco: Jossey-Bass, 2010), 60.

even worse are declining.[9] Jim Tomberlin and Warren Bird declare that "80 percent of the three hundred thousand Protestant churches in the United States have plateaued or are declining, and many of them are in desperate need of a vibrant ministry."[10] The majority of these churches have fewer than two hundred people in attendance and a large portion have fewer than seventy-five weekly.[11]

Life After Death: A Strategy to Bring New Life to a Dead Church, is book is about how to go about restarting your church. Steve Sells and I write it as a key resource focused upon the seventh pillar of church revitalization and renewal. From the start, I would be the first to tell you that while difficult, a restart just might be your church's best chance to become a growing viable church once more. I have been working with churches and doing the work of restarting churches for more than twenty years now. It is not the easiest process but it is perhaps the one which affords you the greatest chance for complete turnaround and renewal. I am a Southern Baptist and as such I often share from what I am learning within my beloved denomination in the field of revitalization and renewal. Two men both passionate and compassionate towards seeing you and your church come to a place where have all of the tools required to implement a restart strategy for your church.

---

9 David T. Olson, *The American Church in Crisis* (Grand Rapids: Zondervan Publishing, 2008), 132.

10 Tomberlin, Jim and Warren Bird, *Better Together: Making Church Mergers Work* (San Francisco: Jossey-Bass, 2010), xvi.

11 "Fast Facts." Hartford Institute for Religion Research. Retrieved from http://hirr.hartsem.edu/research/fastfacts/fast_facts.html#sizecong (accessed 3/20/2011).

Growing the Kingdom by Giving Up

As church memberships become entrenched in a senior citizen-based population and few options remain to keep the church going, often they are left with few choices as to what they can do. Here are the basic set of choices when you have allowed your critical mass to decline to such a state as to threaten the possible closure of your church:

- You can make the transition towards a totally bi-vocational pastor and staff.
- You can move towards morning services only and rent out facility to a Church Planter in the evening.
- You can sell your land, which is in my opinion the worst thing you could do!
- You could begin to place a higher degree of responsibility on lay leadership to pick up the slack of not having a full-time pastor.
- You could try to keep doing the same thing you are doing while hoping things will change. Remember that if you do what you have always done you will get what you have always gotten.
- It is important to realize that if you wait too long to make necessary changes and the membership continues to decline to less than 50 adult active members which is known as *"Critical Mass,"* then you should deed the church over to the local association as a *Legacy Church* and allow such an organization to utilize the church for future ministries while assuming your bills and upkeep. This allows future restarts to win and keeps a missional presence in the geographical location of the former church.

A decision to close a church should never be made on the basis of any single sign above, but taken as a whole they can provide church leaders with helpful insights as to the future potential of a church. Giving up the facilities to a group that will restart the church honors those who have sacrificed so greatly in the past for the cause of Christ. You can grow the Kingdom of God by your willingness to give up trying to hold on until that last one passes on into eternity.

The restart-based church revitalization model is being used all across North America. Any group working in the area of church revitalization should have a restart strategy if it is going to be a wise steward. I never sought to write a step-by-step process for doing a church restart. Yet, so many have used these materials over the last twenty years that it has become such a process. Sometimes I get kind notes of encouragement thanking me for the bold stance and unwavering advice offered within this strategy. A few times frankly, I have been ripped apart by those not brave enough to consider such drastic steps to move their local church towards a new expression of health and vitality! Dying churches can be restarted when the congregation is willing to take the hard steps and make the necessary commitments. The idea of a church that is dying taking the necessary steps to provide it the best chance for survival is not an easy idea to consider. For those who have been part of the setback, admitting that they have hurt the church is hard indeed. Those who will take over also have a challenge in that it will be under their watch as they seek to change those traits, now embedded within the local church, for the betterment and opportunity to turn around a church that is in rapid decline.

It is amazing to me today that many individuals that attend a dying church see nothing wrong biblically with allowing their church to die along with them. It is as if there is a secret message, which reads: "The last one alive, remember to turn the lights out!" Humorous? Possibly! Tragic for sure because the local church is the very thing for which Christ Jesus gave His life and yet we treat his local church with such irreverence that it is no wonder churches are dying all across the world. This Restart Strategy is a vital piece for anyone working in church revitalization efforts and for those who possibly lead church planting efforts. If the two disciplines could somehow just join forces at this point perhaps it would be the local church that ultimately wins. Change is going to happen within the small rapidly declining church and this strategy offers an opportunity for a turnaround that is working, has been working for decades, and needs to be reconsidered in light of the advancing decline and plateauing of our churches today.

Pastors and denominational workers who want to see a difference in their churches, they must commit themselves to seeing change happen. It was Dr. Henry Blackaby who said, "If you are going to join God, you must change. You cannot stay the same and work with God at the same time."

Statistics are Our Friends in Restarting Churches

This Southern Baptist research arm within the denomination, LifeWay Christian Resources, in cooperation with the Center for Missional Research from the North American Mission Board, conducted a study based on churches' five-year change in total membership. The study reports that 28.1 percent of our Southern Baptist Convention churches are growing, 43.9 percent are in a state of plateau, and 28 percent are in decline.[12]

A more recent series of studies were conducted by Bill Day, Associate Director of the Leavell Center for Evangelism and Church Health, who serves the New Orleans Baptist Theological Seminary as the Gurney Professor of Evangelism and Church Health, in his sequential studies on church health

---

12 Annual Church Profile data, LifeWay Christian Resources, Nashville, TN. Compiled by: Center for Missional Research, North American Mission Board, Alpharetta, GA.

and growth from 2003, 2007, and 2010, where he reports that currently there are less than seven percent (6.8) of our SBC churches which are healthy growing churches. That means only 3,087 of our 45,727 SBC churches are healthy.[13] Leonard Sweet states that the declining mainline church has faced a "double whammy of postmodernity and post-Christendom."[14]

The Time Is Right Now!

If there is going to be revitalization in American churches in the twenty-first century, the initial step must be taken immediately. Revitalization of our churches is not an insurmountable task. While we must start with re-encountering the divine and realizing that any church that is revitalized or becoming revitalized is the work of our Lord God, we must do our part to provide tools and methodologies for today's ministers to assist them with new practices and approaches that can help today's declining churches. Our churches must not remain in stained glass, red bricked, spire castles giving out apologies for lack of renewal or mixed gestures towards revitalization efforts.

The time for revitalization and renewal is now; sick and declining churches are all across America. Will the people of God be led like days of old when the shepherds of God boldly served the church of God and led His people to remember why they exist and to whom they belong? With such an absence of missionary mandates from our missionary agencies, the challenge is for the theological institutions

---

13 Bill Day. *The State of the Church in the S.B.C.* (New Orleans: Leavell Center for Evangelism and Church Health, 1/3/2012), C.f. Appendix Two.

14 Leonard Sweet. *So Beautiful: Divine Design for Life and the Church* (Colorado Springs: David C. Cook, 2009), 20.

across the convention to pick up the slack and prepare the new army of Church Revitalizers.

Some church revitalization restarts originate from the decline of others due to failure to remain on the threshold of community transitions. Sometimes our memories of how things use to be hinder us from seeing what we could become. I know that death is painful yet Jesus Christ can bring something new out of the sorrow. One critical point from the start is a complete change of lay leadership and direction is a must for this model to be successful. When we are talking about a true "church revitalization restart," I am not referring to the typical small, struggling church that finds fresh life and growth, nor am I looking at mergers or relocation of existing churches. A church that is a candidate for a church revitalization restart has already sought advice from the local association leader or district leader about disbanding or is almost ready to disbanded. The church has dwindled down to about twenty or thirty survivors who are too tired to continue on. They no longer possess the critical mass necessary to get the church healthy once more. The leadership which remains is too tired, too ineffective, and too small in numbers to bring about the changes it will take to make the turn. Those left are at the end of their rope and often want to make decisions that are unwise or lack any chance of success.

A church in need of a restart is a church that must have leadership and resources from outside of itself. Within these churches God often uses the local Missions Leader or a District Superintendent to help bring back to life what I am calling a "church revitalization restart." These leaders will look for healthy churches to parent the restart for a time. When a parenting church or field partner seeks to aid a dying congregation with a solid revitalization strategy, reality must be squarely faced and decisions must be made that are often hard for the declining church. It is hard to admit sometimes but the concept of letting the declining or dying church die is huge if you are going to restart it and make it a growing new work. For good healthy change, there needs to be a spiritual death for that former church. There is mixed opinion in the area of whether a church revitalization restart should close up for a time or continue on. I believe a significant case could and should be made for closing if not for even a short time. Some, to be fair, say that a rebirth of vision is all that is needed. That may be too optimistic and in my individual experience too unrealistic as well.

The future of mainline churches is that they will be smaller and probably won't be able to afford a full-time pastor, which means that we are going to see more and more folks becoming "tent making" pastors who have a job outside of the church on top of their duties in the congregation. A lot of folks, including people coming out of our seminaries and current pastors, are not ready for this future. Mainline Protestants are used to having full-time pastors. Individuals who are pastors or are going to be pastors, expect that they will have a nice full-time job.

Not Every Church is a Candidate for a Restart

Interestingly, many laymen often ask me if I think that their church could be a candidate for a restart. Usually they share of the need for their church to be revitalized. A series of questions frequently follows of which I will answer each and every single one of them. Once they wear out in asking questions, I ask one. That question is: "How willing are you and your lay leadership willing to let go of the controls of the church for the next three years and allow someone else to make the decisions necessary to restart your church?" One of two things happen at this point.

No Need to Bleed

The first response is that the individual and his co-leaders see no need to make such a drastic decision. There is no real need to make those necessary decisions that will stop the bleeding of the exodus. After all, they have been leading the church for over twenty years and see no reason to make this change despite the decline they are facing. Failure to admit one's weakness and need for a restart is often the initial response. Their emphasis on former glories over present or future glories is a key to the polarization and stuckness they face.

As a layperson, you have more to do with the church in its present state then you often take credit. Whether the congregation in which you belong is thriving or declining, it is ultimately up to you and your fellow members and because of you and your fellow members. Pastors are called to equip the saints for the work of the ministry and they can teach, train, lead, and inspire! But when the rubber meets the road, your church's health is a function of how you and your fellow members relate to one another, to the community in which the church is located, and to how they respond to God's leading within their lives. John 10:10 remind us that Jesus said, "I came that you might have life, and have it abundantly." We need to be reminded that as laymen we are the church! When a local Church is spiritually journeying as a vibrant Church:

- Church members willingly work together!
- The community finds hope from the church!
- There is a sense of belonging and togetherness!
- Members easily and frequently forgive others!
- The laity find their individual and corporate sense of purpose!
- God's leading and direction is apparent to everyone!

Your pastor can be the greatest pastor and preacher, but his message only has the power to the extent that the people of God within the specific local church live it and practice it with each other!

Is There a Guide to Stop the Slide?

The other response is less common and that is when the leader asks how this could happen and who would assist them in considering such an option. The question was once asked this way, "Pastor is there a guide we can follow in order to stop the slide we are facing?" Some laymen desire to stop the near-death throes of their dying church and take the drastic steps necessary to help it become healthy and vibrant once more. They are more concerned about the future needs by allowing the Lord to bring about a resurrection of life the way God wants over what man has become comfortable in.

The church dying or in rapid decline must face the hard realities and wrestle with the biblical passages dealing with reinvention, realignment, and restarting. Scriptures speak of the message of death and resurrection, and for rapidly declining churches it is a testament that God can bring life out of something that was once dead. You do not begin in the Bible with new life. You begin with life, death, and being raised in newness of life. Rapidly declining churches often want to skip the journey and jump right to newness of life. Jesus is a fitting example of not missing the process necessary to embrace newness of life.

A Restart Church's Revitalization Lesson

When a local church refuses to trade its fear of closing the door for a desire to see life come back within the congregation, the church revitalization experience will end promptly as soon as the danger of death has been eliminated. What happens next may mean another recycle of decline until it is bad again. Churches only experience renewal when their people experience renewal! Unless a churches leadership wants renewal, it will not happen. There must be a commitment to lead the church towards revitalization. If not, nothing will be changed. Church renewal must shift from a few being interested to eventually a full effort of the entire congregation. Revitalization is not a secret journey but a public one.

Preachers of the Word are called by God and even with their giftedness, renewal will not happen unless the laity is willing to experience a new and better journey. If the laity refuse to change, refuse to repent of unconfessed sins which are keeping the church from experiencing God's blessings, and refuse to allow the shepherd to lead the flock, there will be no impetus for renewal.

When a church is more interested in self- conservation, it develops a barrier towards the community it is called to serve, which declares our needs are more important than your needs. Many a church is not interested in serving its community until it is in trouble and then it is done for survival reasons. People will see right through this approach and feel cheapened.

Final Church Revitalization Restart Observations

The desire to see the church grow once again is not the main reason churches seek assistance in church renewal! The main reason is that they fear the church is dying, near death, or the members have waited too long to do something about it! A reduction in the church's ability to offer ministries usually prompts its desire for a church revitalization restart. The desire to avoid the deathblow of a church compels many congregations to consider church revitalization efforts! Yet, most laity find it hard to allow someone to assist them and reveal the very things that caused their decline.

Living With Your Head in the Sand

Restart churches seek to lead you in removing your head from the sands of confusion and avoidance of facing current realities. When you are unwilling to face current realities:

- **The challenges and difficulties you face will only get worse.** All of us have challenges in our churches certainly. Yet keeping our head in the sand only causes the situation to become more difficult and harder to tackle.

- **Your children's children are forsaken by the church.** I ask people all the time in declining churches if they love their grandchildren enough to make the necessary changes required to restart their church. The response I often get has more to do with their own interests and their own wants and little to do with reaching future generations for Christ.

- **Most pastors have regrets about serving a group of individuals who opt out of making a difference for Christ.** Pastors want to reach people and change the world. They want the church to be relevant and as current as today's newspaper. Pastoral regrets surface often as a result of an unwillingness of the laity to want to do something highly significant for the Kingdom of God. When laity hide their heads in the sand it only furthers problematic situations not eliminates them.

- **Your membership becomes unwilling to work together as a team to restart your church.** Failure to focus the congregation together often brings a lack of connection and comradery to the task of restarting a church. Facing reality is the starting place.

- **Urgency is eliminated and there becomes a failure to launch and begin the effort to restart.** Change is all around us and yet the local church struggles with change often. We live in a day where the speed of change is accelerated and yet many churches decline to keep up. They are then shocked to realize in a few years just how irrelevant they have become.

- **You focus on the same old things with very little to show for it.** Such a maintenance mentality only fosters ongoing conflict and struggle. Keeping the status quo only hurts the church's ability to attract others. Your progressive church leaders become frustrated and eventually give up on you as the pastor leader and the church as a whole. When you have nowhere to go, all that is left is the ability for everyone to blame each other and no one do anything about it.

- **Disobedience becomes the norm.** Living in a mode of denial nurtures a lack of willingness to remain a witness to the world.

- **Mediocrity is allowed.** An emphasis on not making waves or rocking the boat of compliance causes churches that need to be restarted to instead tolerate flagrant sin for the good of the status quo. When sin is allowed to be accepted and even left unconfronted, the church is on a spiral decline that is meteoric at best.

- **The best and the most committed will take flight.** Strong church members who are committed to the Lord over an institution will leave once they sense that no one is going to address the real issues requiring a restart. The very members your church needs in order to restart it often sense that the church does not want to make such a turn and off they go to a more committed church telling them how unwilling you are to follow scripture.

- **You have become comfortable with being comfortable.** So many churches get into a rut of well

being and contentment. The ability to make the
changes necessary for revitalization becomes a blur
due to a lack of focus on becoming a healthy New
Testament church once more. Entrenched laity
unwilling to do anything more than show up hurt the
chances for a restart.

When you are unwilling to face current realities and live in a
cocoon of denial not seeking to handle surfacing problems,
you are faced with a clear reality that you might be closing
your doors to never open them again. That was not what
Christ had in mind nor the people who sacrificed greatly to
plan your church originally.

So how do you know if you are a dying church? Simply, a
dying church is a church that has been in decline for a
significant period of time; that is, its ministry has been
steadily diminishing in both quantity and quality. Leadership
has not been able to reverse this downward trend. Without
immediate and significant change, this church will close its
doors, its ministry will cease, its congregation will disband, its
corporate existence will be dissolved, and its assets will be
liquidated and redistributed.15

*Life After Death: A Strategy to Bring New Life to a Dead
Church!,* is a journey of hope for the local struggling church
that is facing hard decisions in light of its future and what it
will do to ensure a Gospel lighthouse remains in the
community where it was placed for many more years until
Jesus comes to take all of us to Glory. Take the journey with
those in your area who are working to revitalize churches for
the sake of Christ. Become willing to embrace the
opportunity for your church to survive rather than close

---

15 Priddy, Kenneth Earl. *Restarting the Dying Church* Doctor of
Ministry Dissertation, Reformed Theological Seminary, May 2001. Pgs. 7-
8.

down in failure. Allow the Lord God to bring forth a miracle for your church as He transforms the work of ministry within your midst. Restarting churches is a long-distance relay run by marathoners not sprinters. You must be willing to invest a minimum of 1000 days into church renewal. Anything less, do not get involved. Pray that the Lord will rise up a group of committed new leaders with the energy to work and turn your church around. Ask God to bring new families into your worship center that have never heard the gospel message and are now drawn to hear the glorious message of salvation in Christ Jesus. Seek transformation not stagnation. Ask the Lord to transform your church, each one of you as individual worshippers and Christ followers. Watch how God will transform your individual families and bring a new expression of "church" right where you live.

Until Jesus Comes,
Tom Cheyney, Founder & Directional Leader
Renovate National Church Revitalization Conference
Col. 4:6

Chapter One
To Close or Not to Close, that is the Biggest Question: Key Issues in Considering a Restart

"Now faith is confidence in what we hope for and assurance about what we do not see."[16]

Every congregation began at one time as a church plant. Some launch and love for a short time until the sponsor monies dry up. Others have long-term ministries but after a time due to failure of recognizing the cultural shifts in a local church's ministry area they too eventually face cessation. There are many churches which live on and on to the glory of the Lord. All three of these types of churches are vital to the Lord. No local church assembly was ever started for the purpose of making a marginal influence on its community. Every church wants to leave its mark on community and society. Leaving a legacy, however, means more than simply opening the doors on a Sunday morning. Some will look back to how the foundations of their church buildings were laid by great-grandparents, and how landmark events in their families' lives centered around a church building. There are a number of church facilities that are vacant all across the nation. Even protestant churches have been losing congregations since the late sixties. Closure of a church in its current state is more common than one might think. I am always amazed just how excited we get when a new church plant is launched yet we do very little to actually keep an existing church afloat. Saving a church through revitalization ought to be a thing of praise for the local church and the body of Christ. Within my own denomination of Southern Baptist our convention sees seventeen churches closing their doors each and every week.17 As churches close, people in

---

16 Hebrew 11:1.

17 Mark Hallock, *Replant Roadmap: How Your Congregation Can Help Revitalize Churches*, (Littleton, CO: Acoma Press, 2017), Pg. 28.

these communities lose immediate access to help, hope and the heartbeat of Christ. Involvement has displayed that some declining churches ignore the realities of the changing community surrounding the church and fail to develop ministries that will draw and impact their community. What happens next is the rise within the fellowship of a commuter membership that is out of touch with the community where the church is placed. After a time of such loss of participants, finances, and a willingness to minister to the community, the church is left with no choice but to close. There are characteristically include several indicators that a church should consider a restart. Here are the more prevalent indicators of a church needing a restart. Sunday church attendance has declined to fewer than fifty people. There has been persistent decline over the past decade. Baptisms have not only declined but have been non-existent for five years or more. Similarly, there have been no new professions of faith in the past five years. Supporting the local association mission partner has ceased. If you have begun to look at visitors as an income source to keep your church open, you are a viable candidate for a restart. But it does not have to remain that way. Restarting a church is indeed a viable option.

> For everything there is a season,
> and a time for every matter under heaven:
> a time to be born, and a time to die;
> a time to plant, and a time to pluck up what is planted; a time to kill, and a time to heal;
> a time to break down, and a time to build up;
> a time to weep, and a time to laugh;
> a time to mourn, and a time to dance.[18]

The decision to close or not to close a church is a real big choice and should be made after much prayer. Ed Stetzer, the

---

18 Ecclesiastes 3:1-4.

Billy Graham Professor of Church, Mission and Evangelism and executive director of the Billy Graham Center for Evangelism at Wheaton College, estimated that 3,700 Protestant churches in the United States closed in 2014.

To Close or Not to Close
(My Apologies to William Shakespeare)

To close or not to close that is the question:
Whether it is nobler for the church to continue to suffer
The decline and exodus of drifting members,
Or take to battle against the onslaught of dilemmas
And by remain in the battle. Or to die and cease,
To terminate; and by such conclusion we bid farewell.
The sadness and despair of hundreds of failures
That we ignored till it was too late
Devotion was our wish short lived;
Ours was a dream short lived, Yes that's the shocker
To cease the work, was it a dream,
Once this building lacks the echoes of salvation,
When the melodious sounds are never more,
We must stop a moment to reflect
The blessings of service to others.
For who would come after us and try again,
The evil one's continual assault,
Twinges of what could have been, of dreams interruption,
No, visitor returning nay prospects slim,
That makes us our sanctuaries bare
They fly to other churches without regret
And make deserters of us all,
With this inaction their impact dwindles
And we are left with what might have been.

Acknowledged I am not the incredible William Shakespeare and this dribble is far removed from the third act and scene one of Hamlet. But for the rapidly declining church that faces closure to remain open or to close is a huge question. There are many churches that are barely existing. Helping these churches should be part of anyone working in church revitalization and renewal. Restarting a church is different than replanting a church. One is about saving an existing and the other is about launching an entirely new one utilizing some former churches buildings. Making a determination as to whether or not you should restart a church is something to be entered into with much prayer and counsel. Your local Director of Missions or District Leader can help you and pray along with you in this decision. Having assisted churches in this endeavor since 1997, I am always thankful to the Lord for a church that will embrace the restart strategy over giving up and walking away from an area the Lord wants to reach with the gospel. During my twenty plus years of helping churches in need of a restart I have recognized the most relevant factors to consider when praying about closing or remaining open as a church via a restart. Here are the most critical factors to prayerfully contemplate:

Your Core Group Has Grown Lethargic

Perhaps the initial critical factor for every church considering whether to restart or try to plow on is related to the dwindling core group and their understanding as well as buy-in to the churches current mission. Defining the vitality and health of the remining core group of participants in a rapidly declining church is needed. Is the core group of participants able to articulate what it means to be on mission for the church? If you have a renewed pastor and a group of lay leaders who have experienced personal renewal, then you can handle the pain necessary to revitalize your church. But what do you do if there are not a robust number of strong leaders still left in the church? Has there become a sense that the congregation is growing lethargic and unwilling to do the work of ministry to save their church? If so, you have a congregation which is physically, spiritually, and mentally exhausted. Such a fatigue factor in a declining church points towards getting involved in a restart sooner not later. The longer a church waits the less likely it will be able to turn it around, so acting on the challenges promptly is advisable. Many local congregations turned inward to keep the attending participants content and lost site of the mission field around them. The long years of maintaining a facility beyond their means, of recycling the same leaders and of aging membership and loss takes their toll. It becomes arduous trying to elect new lay leader. Closing the church and getting ready for a restart is your best option. You need help so contact a viable revitalization organization for assistance.[19] When the warriors in the church grow weary and lose the energy to turn around a church, the best thing one could do is to give it to a revitalization organization and allow it to be restarted. As the declining church becomes sluggish the longer its leadership waits to take action the worse the damage will be to the Kingdom and the effort for Christ within that community.

The Church Embroiled in Conflict

It appears practically guaranteed that pastors, staff, and lay leaders will discover that they have become embroiled in conflict from time to time. If the church is to move forward in ministry, these conflicts must be addressed in both a healthy and Godly way to rid itself of the origins of this conflict. Normal disagreements will begin to intensify as years of accumulated resentment begins to boil over. That tiny group of antagonists will grow until it reaches a critical mass. Once that happens this group of antagonists will be so

---

19 There are three very strong restart organizations available to coach you and your church. These three are: RenovateConference.org; OperationTrnasformation.com; and ChurchEquippers.org. All three church revitalization organizations have a proven track record of helping restart declining or dying churches.

entrenched that they are able to initiate continual conflict. A history of church conflict may continue to impact churches long after the initial disputes or quarrels took place. It is not easy to circumnavigate such skirmishes and bring healing for the future of the church. I have noticed from my years of working in revitalization, that at any given time, about twenty-five percent of most churches have an ongoing battle between the pastor and the church membership. Then they wonder why no one wants to join their church. The intensity and duration of the conflict become important factors in this decision-making process. The more intense the conflict and the more long-term the conflict, the greater the chance the leadership will not invest in resources for revitalization. Conflict is going to come your way so learning how to handle it is vital.

Radical Transparent for All to See

Adversaries often meet in secret, sabotage the clergy, and then insist that further conversations be carried out in secret so as not to hurt the church. In reality this is a power grab or coup taking place by a group of individuals who hope the rest of the church does not find out. All secrecy does is isolate the clergy and give the power of intimidation to antagonists. It is healthier to go public with the conflict right away and to keep everyone fully informed. That gives them the opportunity to speak as well. When a backdoor group of people try to run off leaders for the good of the church, often what they are doing is trying to get the control back that they have lost and they are using any and all means possible, including destroying the church, to achieve their intended desires. That is always a big mistake.

Resolution is Preferred Over Termination

Seeking resolution is much more preferred than trying to blame a single party such as the pastor. Many a declining church membership fails to take responsibility for the state of demise they are in. Many pastors are terminated so the laity can feel good about themselves when in reality the Church Revitalizer was the very thing they needed. In many situations, termination of the pastor is a destructive resolution. It misrepresents the deeper nature of the conflict, it wounds those who disagree with antagonists' agenda, and it spreads bitter seeds of distrust and fear.

When it Gets Bad Get Counsel

It goes without say perhaps that trying to seek mutual settlement of conflict is the preferred destination. Remember in the area of conflict all of the main parties need help. I have seen such mean churches that the best thing a pastor could do is to find a counselor first and a lawyer second. A mediator is often required if it is allowed to go too far with fighting and outright destruction of reputations. Unless the conflicts are launched by a group of formerly empowered individuals which have lost their sting and are mad about it, so the leadership board may also need to seek professional advice. With matters as serious as employment, severance, blame and the inevitable unsubstantiated charges that will arise, it is foolish to proceed without adequate and dispassionate professional assistance.

As you appraise this area of conflict some questions to consider are: Have there been any church splits in your history? Have there been more than one? Are there various factions within the congregation? Is there a genuine spirit of acceptance of people who are not like you and are not from the families of the church? A history of church conflict may continue to impact churches long after the initial disagreement(s) took place. What is the makeup of the community? It is helpful to interview organizational leaders in the local community to help you better understand where the community is headed.[20]

Abusive Laity

We are living in a day where satanic forces are everywhere. Even the local church can become a place where evil individuals are allowed to run rampant. Matthew the Gospel writer records Jesus' words: *"Behold, I send you out as sheep in the midst of wolves; therefore be shrewd as serpents, and innocent as doves…Anyone who welcomes you welcomes me, and anyone who welcomes me welcomes the one who sent me."*[21] The hardest issue pastors face when trying to begin the work of revitalization is when abusive lay people seek to hurt their under-shepherd. There is within some churches an air of toxic DNA that surfaces when those who have been part of killing the church are not happy with the pastor who the Lord is using to revitalize the church. Pastor abusers seldom repent of their sins and seek to remain in power until someone with a stronger backbone removes them. As shepherds continue to be battered, they ask themselves, "When will the silent majority of godly church members join together and excommunicate these bullies?" Satan loves that the membership within the local church have not risen to expose and remove such individuals from destroying the church. God's shepherds are being destroyed by these abuses while the rest of the membership avoids dealing with these unhealthy situations in the church. I must admit to you that it

---

20 A great resource we use for determining the vitality of a community is a Precept Report. It can be found at http://www.perceptgroup.com. This organization makes available studies of your community, providing solid data to better understand who lives in your community, the challenges they are facing, and the religious practices of the people.

21 Matthew 10:16 & 40.

is not always the laity that are destroying the church. In the field of revitalization, mean spirited church members are destroying many churches which actually could be renewed if a few individuals would learn how to follow the under-shepherd that God has called to lead the church. In most churches the slaughter of their church's pastor goes unacknowledged. Dennis Maynard says, "The pain that the victim of sheep attacks experiences is complex. A pastor that has been driven to resign will be devastated. One of the most devastating of those emotions is the feeling that their identity and integrity have been maligned. Their very backbone of their authority to be a pastor has been splintered."[22] Ray Stedman said, "Some people for the sake of their point of view would destroy the unity of your church. How do you deal with them? Avoid them. We must keep our eye on them and turn away from them. In other words, we don't listen to them. We're never obligated to hear a person out when what they're saying is not consistent with Christian speech. If they are tearing down the church, tearing down the pastor, tearing down the leaders or Sunday School teachers or any believer, we should not listen. Because even out of a misguided sense of courtesy, our listening to them would make it seem that we agree, while what we're doing is giving them another chance to vent their verbal poison."[23]

Aging Leadership Fear Change

Change is all around us and yet for the Church Revitalizer, bringing about change could be one of the most enormous tasks he is ever called upon to accomplish. In church life there are some who will embrace change and

---

22 Dennis R. Maynard, *Healing for Pastor and People Following a Sheep Attack.* (Rancho Mirage, CA: Dionysus Publications, 2013) pg. 19.

23 From a sermon by Bob Joyce, *Paul's Missionary Heart,* 8/3/2011.

some who will not. The hard work of revitalization pays off in the future. Laziness pays off in the present. Certain groups are drawn to the adventure of change while at least one group is repelled by the idea of change. There is one group within most churches who will seek to avoid any effort towards change. I want us to consider as a Church Revitalizer the concept of helping the elderly learn to love that which they naturally hate. Simply, most elderly seniors are opposed to making the critical changes within a local church in order to bring about change. Change for most in this generation is an ugly word that should never be spoken of in a church setting. Yet spiritually and scripturally, the older generations should serve the younger generations and prepare them for the work of the Lord. Elderly based churches often have developed a structure where they over-manage, under-minister, and thwart mostly any real possibility of change. They prefer newcomers their own age and lesser generations such as their grandchildren that will not threaten the status quo they have constructed. In some rapidly declining churches, there is a sense that the stable patterns of the past be preserved for those who make up the church currently, although admittedly it is far smaller than it used to be. The elderly in many churches want a pastor leader certainly, but only on their terms. What they desire is someone who will do the errands they need done for the church when they want them completed. Instead of a pastor revitalizer they are actually seeking a church administrator who can function more as a purveyor of the status quo. It is imperative that both pastoral and lay leadership are strong in order to move a church that is immovable into a revitalized life of effectiveness. It takes leadership, commitment to the mission, and strong ability to lead people to change patterns that have been established over many years, and perseverance to lead through resistance that will come. Helping the elderly to embrace change requires a soft approach and not one that is shoving it down their throats. Navigating the process of change with the elder church member is paramount due to their inclination to live a slower and more docile life. Most elderly church memberships hold out for the preservation of their past and function more as tradition keepers over cultural connectors. The elderly need to understand that the church where they have given sacrificially still has a place for them in the future. The tougher the elderly's choice, the higher the level of ambivalence they will experience. Developing ongoing support groups for the elderly to ask questions and be heard during this process will prove to be helpful. Loss of mission means loss of membership. In truth, the average Christian in America is only attending one in four services a month. This makes it virtually impossible to gather the volunteers it takes to put together an organized worship gathering, especially in declining churches. Remember revitalization is a minimal investment of one thousand days and not a short sprint, so move slowly.

Lead in Spite of the Challenge

As the pastor you are called to lead the church but do not be surprised when you are looked at strangely because you are providing leadership for your church. It is my conviction that churches do not change because of committees or resources or even renewal consultants. It is because God brings a leader into the situation and equips that leader to do the job. It is God who chooses to bless the leadership abilities of that revitalization leader. Revitalization pastors function best when they are not driven by their fears:

Fear of being fired.
Fear of needing to find a new place to minister.
Fear of pleasing everyone.
Fear of splitting the church.
Fear of people leaving the church under your leadership.

Paul says: *"For God has not given us a spirit of fear, but of power and of love and of a sound mind."*[24] Fear causes us to stop and question what God has clearly told us to do. Many a leader is confident in their obedience until persecution comes. Then they doubt that they have heard God unmistakably and appropriately. A pastor must be open, honest, firm, straight forward, able to confront problems and manage conflict and loving towards everyone.

One Must Honor the Past to Move into the Future

Another critical factor in working with a church needing a restart is that of honoring the past. The Church Revitalizer must honor the past in order to move into the future. There have been many who have come before you that worked hard to bring the church into existence. A wise revitalizer will understand that even though there are things which challenge the life and vitality of this church, honoring the past while moving into the future is the better solution. Do not act like everything that was done in the past is bad or irrelevant. I was talking to a replant pastor recently at a large meeting in Dallas. He told me that what he tries to do is to get the church he wants to take over to see what a waste it has been to the Lord and their only option is to give it away to him as a church planter. Sadly, I asked him if he really believed what he was saying. He did. Where is the honor in belittling another in order to get what they want? That is why a restart is such a better option than a replant.[25] Let's face it: not every church wants to give away their property to a church planter. They are looking for a hand up not a hand off. These members may not be the coolest but they have sacrificed

---

24 2 Timothy 1:7.

25 For more on this be sure to read Chapter Thirteen on The Perils of Steeple Jacking in Revitalization and Renewal. This chapter focuses on what happens when church planters steel an existing church.

greatly for the cause of Christ and deserve the utmost respect. A church restart is a way to honor the past and bring life to the future. In his research project, "Restarting the Dying Church," revitalization and ministry consultant Ken Priddy appropriately described the restart leader: "The restart pastor must be able to move toward the future while dealing with the past. He must be able to create new ministry while rebuilding a broken congregation. He must be leading on the frontlines while taking care of the wounded back at camp. He must be able to connect with a new target community while connecting with an established congregation. He must have experience as a visionary and entrepreneur, as well as experience in problem solving, conflict resolution, and leading a reluctant group of people through change."[26]

Financial Sustainability

Let's face it: the elephant in the room for most restarts is the church's present financial situation. In working with churches here in central Florida as well as others around the nation, I see church after church not up to the task of a restart. They are in a precarious situation and yet appear unwilling to take the severe steps to save the Lord's church. Their finances are paralyzing them and holding them captive, leaving them unwilling to embrace the future. Many of these churches and their leadership would rather embrace the pain of long-term decline and eventual complete closure then to assume the short-term discomfort of risking it all financially for the opportunity to still live on through a restart. When this happens, those churches miss the opportunity to see the hand of the Lord demonstrate His power and protection in the miraculous. God has done some incredible things in the churches I have worked with that I could have never foreseen had we not been willing to take the journey towards a restart.

---

26 Kenneth Priddy, "Restarting the Dying Church," (D.Min. Dissertation, Reformed Theological Seminary, 2001), 100-101.

The financial drain of dying churches is hard to assess. The membership is burdened and are fearful of doing ministry because of the anxiety of what any such effort might cost. Across America many churches are struggling weekly to pay the bills. Electricity, gas, water, insurance, building loans, church upkeep are a few of the pressing monthly bills that are not optional. Without financial support the local church will not survive. The cost of not having a healthy Christian church in the community is always greater than the cost of keeping that church alive. Most restarts are left with a large majority of senior church members that fear whether or not they would be able to pay the bills required to do anything significant to save their church. The Renovate Group, when working with churches in rapid decline, strives to help the declining church make the tough calls while there is still time for the church. We seek to give them the tools necessary to make key decisions which will begin to form their future. Financial sustainability for a restart is defined by five types:

One, is the church providing an equitable salary to its pastor?

Two, is the church capable of paying its operational expenses?

Three, is the church able to maintain its buildings properly?

Four, is the church sending any of its money to a missional effort outside of itself?

Five, is the church able to pay it partnership costs to its association or denomination?

If these questions were responded to in the negative, it increases the possibility that leadership would consider closing the church. That is because there are often not enough active participants and monetary resources to fulfill the obligations of the church. Real wisdom is needed not just about what decision you make, but when you make it. Some churches have grasped that their charge and ministry is completed long before they run out of resources. They attempt to end well and bless others with their remaining resources. Other churches wait too long to close and end up not having enough resources left to respond to their obligations.

Condition of the Facility

Costly repairs can greatly affect dying churches. There is a church located in Massachusetts that is facing the hard reality of costly repairs. The church bought a formerly closed church in the middle of town that sat high on the hill. Recently, it was discovered that the church had an extreme mold issue due to poor construction over a hundred years ago. Their basement was infested with mold and it had spread all the way from the floor where it started to now it was in the walls and ceiling as well. These dear members are not able to handle the mold removal and structural repairs. These churches are faced with closure sooner over later. There are other churches that actually have facilities that would be an asset in a restart. The building is the best thing remaining in the church. It could be used in the future restart with a leader who can bring a new vision and mission.

These eight critical factors challenge the church in need of a restart. They are the most relevant factors to consider when praying about closing or remaining open as a church via a restart. Prayerfully consider these factors. Often the best opportunity to reach a population for the Lord Jesus is to restart the church with a catalytic Church Revitalizer who will lead the former church through becoming a revitalized church. Investing in the community by allowing a restart to bear new and exciting fruit for the Kingdom of God is rewarding. Your church can survive and live once more. A restart is a tremendous opportunity to do just that.

Wrapping it Up!

It is no secret that thousands of churches close every year. The closing of our churches in North America reflects the rapid weakening of the faith, an occurrence that is painful to both worshippers and those who see faith as a unifying influence in a disparate society. The decision to shift from survival mode is indeed a leap of faith. Parishioners do not like to think of death. They do not like to think of what can be perceived as ministry and mission failure, and it breaks our hearts because the local church is a gift given by the Lord to be a lighthouse in a specific community. It is to be light in a dark world. A decision to close a ministry should be made only after an extended time of prayer, study and conversation. Due to the seriousness of the action, this will require a called meeting of the congregation. Are there ever good reasons a church ought to close? Carey Nieuwhof shares five good reasons a church should close. He says that a church should close when:

1. The Real Mission Is Lost

2. The Church Cares More About Itself Than the People It's Called to Reach

3. Its Members Hate the World

4. Preserving the Past Is More Attractive Than Embracing the Future

5. The Money Isn't Remotely Tied to The Mission[27]

---

27 https://careynieuwhof.com/5-good-reasons-a-church-should-close/

There are congregations all over North America who are going through challenging times. It is conceivable that your flock of parishioners is in this group and you are faced with the challenging reality that the church you love has been slowly losing its capability to engage the community and sustain active ministry. Distinguishing the voice of God concerning the cessation of a church needs to be entered into with meekness. Personal agendas and pride should be set aside and a dependence on the Spirit's leading should guide the journey. For struggling churchgoers, the fight to stay alive is often seen as a badge of honor and an act of finishing well. These churches are characterized by becoming inward looking and making little difference in its surrounding community. They are quickly depleting any and all of its assets to pay for current expenses. These churches are faced with the inability to maintain its property. The way they operate is to keep cutting back on ministries which have an accompanying cost. These churches often will sell property in order to remain in existence a little while longer over facing the need to consider a restart. The tithes and offering of its membership will no longer sustain the ministry. The reason many congregations will close this week is due to an unwillingness to change, evolve, grow, expand, or be rebirthed. Most states require that an organization's assets be distributed to other charitable organizations or governmental bodies. These laws ensure that assets amassed for charitable or other nonprofit activities continue to be used for similar purposes. When the Lord announces a new direction for a dying church, it will call for faith in God to be put into action. Jesus is coming again and until then, God is still present with his people through the Spirit leading them to live as faithful witnesses of this victorious life that has overcome sin and death. Should your church close, do know that things will get better, life will be better, and God will continue to use your gifts and talents to serve others. A restart is a viable option if your church is facing the final stages of its life cycle. If you find yourself confronting this time of discernment, contact your Director of Missions, District Supervisor or the Renovate Group who can provide assistance to your congregation throughout the process.

Chapter 2
What it takes to be a Restart Church Revitalizer:
Qualities & Characteristics

"Jesus, undeterred, went right ahead and gave his charge:
"God authorized and commanded me to commission you: Go out
and train everyone you meet, far and near, in this way of life, marking
them by baptism in the threefold name: Father, Son, and Holy Spirit.
Then instruct them in the practice of all I have commanded you.
I'll be with you as you do this, day after day after day, right up to the
end of the age."[28]

There is an inexorable principle about leadership in the secular world that "the right person (leader), at the right time will almost always bring the right results." When you translate that into the church world it would read something like this, "God's man, in God's timing will always bring God's results." The fact is when a church gets to the point that "restart" is the only solution it will take a *specially gifted, God called* leader to, under the leadership of the Holy Spirit, bring new life to a dying church. This leader must be endowed with special personal qualities and characteristics.

What are those qualities and characteristics one must possess in order to become a Church restart pastor? Unlike other pastoral qualities, there are certain absolutes that a restart pastor must possess if he is to be successful. For all practical purposes it takes a special calling from God and special qualities and characteristics for a pastor to undertake the task of restarting a dead church. Because of the trauma involved in the death of the church and the difficult task of breaking ties with the past, transitioning the church into new life is quite difficult. Furthermore, it is especially difficult to regain the trust of the community once it has seen the steady

---

[28] Eugene H. Peterson, *The Message: The Bible in Contemporary Language* (Colorado Springs, CO: NavPress, 2005), Mt 28:18–20.

decline and death of a vital member of the community. Even though it does take a special spiritual leader to lead in a restart church revitalization process, God is calling gifted individuals to take on the task. Oswald Chambers said of this kind of unique leadership, "The Bible shows us that when God does find a person who is ready to lead, to commit to full discipleship and take on responsibility for others that person is used to the limit."[29]

Distinct Characteristics of a Restart Pastor

So, let's jump right in and talk about what it takes to be a restart pastor. There are at least six characteristics he must possess. These characteristics must be a part of the makeup of the restart pastor's personality and ministry style. These are distinct, important and nonnegotiable.

First and foremost, *the Gospel message should always take precedence over how church is done.* Our culture is in a constant state of flux. We must never be caught up in the trap of trying to please the culture, rather we must change the culture by teaching and preaching the unchanging Gospel. What the restart pastor preaches and teaches is much more important that the start-up model he uses. The message is the life changing factor not the method. You can have the latest and supposedly greatest church planting model there is and be void of the true message of the Gospel and the restart will fall flat and the churches legacy will be gone. The key is not a model but a Gospel strategy that seeks to win the present culture. That strategy should always be focused on things eternal and how to reach people and make an eternal difference in their lives. When this occurs in a church restart the church will begin to make a difference in the community

---

29 J. Oswald Sanders, *Spiritual Leadership* (Chicago, Moody Press, 1994), p. 17.

where it exists. The church becomes transformational in its approach to the community.

The reality is that when a restart becomes necessary it is because the church that died had long ago ceased to be transformational in its message and the community has suffered spiritually as a result. The restart pastor enters that community with a fresh strategy but most importantly, a fresh renewed zeal for the Gospel and the souls that need to hear it. Ed Stetzer writes about relevance and the Gospel in his Blog which says, "Solely pursuing cultural relevance is not the answer. Relevance is a tool; gospel proclamation is the goal. When we pursue relevance as the goal, it leads to an unhelpful pendulum swing in church culture."[30]

While the church is challenged to engage the various cultures, it must engage the culture with the never-changing Gospel. Matthew 28:19-20 is that engagement challenge and is known as the Great Commission. It says, "Go ye therefore, and teach all nations, baptizing them in the name of the Father, and of the Son, and of the Holy Ghost: Teaching them to observe all things whatsoever I have commanded you: and, lo, I am with you always, even unto the end of the world. Amen."[31] The "Go" is the engaging part and the "Teaching them...whatsoever..." is the Gospel part. The church restart pastor must engage the culture where he lives but it must be done with the clear and powerful Gospel of the Lord Jesus Christ.

Second, *the presence and power of the Holy Spirit is indispensable.* When a church closes its doors, it becomes

---

30 Ed Stetzer, *Engaging and Ever-Changing Culture with a Never-Changing Gospel*, The Exchange, Christianity Today, 2018, www.ChristianityToday.com.

31 Matt. 28:19-20 KJV.

obvious that an important element was missing. It is possible that at one time the church had the power but somewhere on their past journey they lost it. This becomes evident each time this writer leads in a restart process. The lost power became evident when a pastor I was helping with the process said to me as we walked through the deserted building, "You know…it is clear that they had everything they ever needed (talking about facilities, equipment, etc.) except the power of God." Somewhere along the way these broken churches lost the power to succeed. However, the Bible gives the most thrilling and sensational news of the availability of that needed power. Where did that power of Pentecost, the power to change a culture and the power to turn the world upside down, go?

A close study of the book of Acts reveals just how important the Holy Spirit is to church leadership and how, even more importantly, He is in restarting a dead church. In this age of methods, models and mechanics we seem to have lost the understanding that only the Holy Spirit can bring back real life. After all, the book of Acts shows clearly His life-giving ability. It is also filled with the wonderworking power of the Holy Spirit which speaks clearly of the role of the Holy Spirit in the call of God upon the leader's life.

For instance, consider Acts 13:2 which states, "As they ministered to the Lord, and fasted, the Holy Ghost said, separate me Barnabas and Saul for the work whereunto I have called them."[32] It is clear from this verse that the Holy Spirit is the avenue through which God the Father calls individuals into the work of church planting. This powerfully demonstrates the appointing of Paul and Barnabas to the missionary enterprise to which God had called them.

---

32 Acts 13:2 KJV.

Acts 13:4 is an extension of verse 2 and the calling upon Paul and Barnabas's lives. It reveals the fact that, not only did the Holy Spirit appoint them, but He directed them out as well. It explains, "So they, being sent forth by the Holy Ghost, departed unto Seleucia; and from thence they sailed to Cyprus."[33] The Holy Spirit is the directing agent of God who directs the one appointed into the field that God has prepared.

Then we see in Acts 13:9 the reality that the Holy Spirit gave the power to accomplish the missionary work that had been assigned. It declares, "Then Saul, filled with the Holy Ghost, set his eyes on him."[34] He fills the servant with his presence and power. What a wonder it is to see the operation of the Holy Spirit as He empowers the servant for the work of restarting churches and empowering him in bringing new life to dying congregations.

These few verses reveal how tremendously important the role of the Holy Spirit is in the work of any restart pastor. Without His presence and power there will be no success. The truth is, we can sing songs of Zion without the Holy Spirit. We can quote the Bible without the Holy Spirit. We can prepare sermons without the Holy Spirit. We can pray without the Holy Spirit. But you cannot change a culture with the Gospel without the presence and power of the Holy Spirit. A church without the presence of the Holy Spirit to guide, equip, use, and mobilize will cease to be a New Testament church.

Third, *the process of multiplication is essential.* The church must be structured to multiply itself. The restart pastor's objective should always be to multiply the work of the

---

33 Acts 13:4 KJV.

34 Acts 13:9 KJV.

Gospel so as many people as possible may hear and respond to the good news. This calls for a missional mindset on the part of the restart pastor. God blesses this kind of missionary attitude. Jesus instructed His disciples to, "Go therefore and make disciples of all nations" [35] The plan of God has always been the spreading of the Gospel into all the world. Proclaiming the Good News to every man, woman, boy or girl, giving them the opportunity to trust Jesus Christ as Lord and Savior. That is the task of the local church and that means multiplication of itself. Churches multiply when Christians from one church body establishes a new church made up of believers that will reach another segment of the culture. This should become the missionary cycle of every church. I use the term "multiplication" rather than "reproduction" because the concept of reproduction has the connotation that we simply clone who we are, but the concept of multiplication indicates that we are simply increasing the number of churches and they are not particularly like the original. This is important because when a church multiplies it is creating something new that meets the needs of the people in that particular area. It is not necessarily like the original in approach, but it has the same message. "Church history shows us that church multiplication is the *norm* for healthy churches. But we do not achieve it simply by spending money or consulting with professional missiologists. Nor do we get it from pricey, quick-start programs. Funds and good strategy help, but do not drive the movement."[36]

Fourth, *personal integrity is the most important character trait of any restart pastor.* According to The American Heritage

---

35 Matt. 28:19 KJV.

36 Patterson, George & Galen Currah, *Church Multiplication – Guidelines and Dangers.* Western Seminary: Global Missiology, October 2003, www.globalmissiology.net.

Dictionary of the English Language "integrity" means "a rigid adherence to a code of behavior." The Latin word for integrity means "completeness, purity."[37]

Every Christian must operate with the highest level of integrity, but it is an absolute in the life of a restart pastor because of the public examination that is always present. When a church dies and a restart takes place, the eyes of the community will be focused on the new church start as well as observing the life and behavior of the leader. If a Christian leader fails to have integrity it damages the Kingdom of God and not just the individual's personhood. The person of integrity lives the way they do because of who they are. There is no pretentious living on the part of the person of integrity. Job 2:3 says *"And the Lord said unto Satan, hast thou considered my servant Job, that there is none like him in the earth, a perfect and an upright man, one that feareth God, and escheweth evil? And still he holdeth fast his integrity, although thou movedst me against him, to destroy him without cause."*[38] Character and integrity are basically the same thing. It was pleasing to God that Job kept his integrity even in the midst of horrible testing and tempting of Satan. Warren Wiersbe says in "The Integrity Crises" that "Integrity is to personal or corporate character what health is to the body or 20/20 vision is to the eyes...People with integrity have nothing to hide and nothing to fear. Their lives are open books. They are integers."[39]

Fifth, a *clear commitment to Biblical authority and sound theology and doctrine* on the part of the restart pastor is a must.

---

37 The American Heritage Dictionary of the English Language: "Integrity," Fourth Edition (September 14, 2000).

38 Job 2:3 KJV.

39 Warren W. Wiersbe, *The Integrity Crises* (Nashville: Oliver Nelson, 1988) p. 20-21.

Christians in every century have always viewed the Scripture with a high view as "the" direct word from God. Christians have always accepted the Bible as the authoritative, inerrant and inspired word of God. Likewise, the Bible has always been viewed as the final authority in matters of faith and practice.

The beauty of the authority of the Word of God is found in the realization that it applies to all races and creeds, all cultures and ethnicities and to all men and women in every walk of life. The Bible reveals the mind of God to all generations, cultures, ethnicities and genders. This is why a flimsy and faulty view of the authority of the scripture and of theology will doom the restart to failure.

Timothy speaks to the authority of the Bible in 2 Timothy 3:16–17: *"All scripture is given by inspiration of God, and is profitable for doctrine, for reproof, for correction, for instruction in righteousness: That the man of God may be perfect, thoroughly furnished unto all good works."*[40] There has been an ongoing discussion on the authority of the Bible for decades and the reality and fact has always been that it is the inerrant and authoritative word of God. Because it is the authoritative Word of God it demands obedience. When obeyed it gives direction to our moral, ethical and decision-making lives. The truth is that we humans do not have the ability within ourselves to know what is true and right. There must be a higher, more astute, wiser purveyor of truth for us to know, understand and live out that truth. God gave His Word to us in the form of the Bible to be that purveyor. It is sufficient for helping us understand divine truth and live accordingly. Human experience cannot and will not give a clear understanding of truth. Human understanding will always lead in the wrong direction. Only the Word of God can lead to truth because at the very heart of the Bible is Jesus Christ. He came into this

---

40 2 Timothy 3:16-17 KJV.

world as the divine truth of God the Father. Jesus made that very clear in John 14: 6 when He said, *"I am the way, the truth and the life: no man cometh unto the Father, but by me."*

The sixth and final characteristic is *a clear understanding of Biblical leadership.* Biblical, transformational leadership will make or break a church restart. Transformational leadership is the most effective kind of leadership to guide a church, especially a restart church. The problem is that transformational Spirit-led leadership has been overtaken by a secular and worldly approach to leadership in the church. Biblical leadership is spiritual leadership and the true source of every transformational leader must be the Holy Spirit.

There is a vast difference between secular forms of leadership and Christian transformational leadership. Secular leadership seeks to influence people to work toward achieving a group's goals. Christian transformational leadership leads by life and example and seeks only to advance the mission and calling of Christ on earth while also leading others to do the same.

The Biblical foundation for transformational leadership is found in Mark 10:43-45. It says, *"... whosoever will be great among you, shall be your minister: And whosoever of you will be the chiefest, shall be servant of all. For even the Son of man came not to be ministered unto, but to minister, and to give his life a ransom for many."*[41]

A Spirit-led transformational leader leads people from where they are to where God wants them to be. They depend on the Holy Spirit because they know they are accountable to God. Their influence affects everyone around

---

41 Mark 10:43-45 KJV.

them, not just Christians, as they seek to accomplish God's agenda on earth and not their own.

Spiritual leadership must have a higher source because man does not have within himself the ability to be a "Biblical leader" or a "spiritual leader." J. Oswald Sanders emphasizes this when he wrote, "Spiritual leadership requires superior power, which can never be generated by the self. There is no such thing as a self-made spiritual leader. A true leader influences others spiritually only because the Spirit works in and through him to a greater degree than in those he leads."[42] It takes a special kind of leader to restart a church and that leader only leads through the presence and power of the Holy Spirit.

The transformational leader lives a life that is Spirit filled and Biblically saturated. He is fervent in prayer and understands his role as a servant. He is visionary in his ministry. The effective leader seeks to include everyone in the congregation to follow God's direction to help their Church live again. He leads a caring and compassionate life. The preparatory steps for becoming a transformational leader is a personal walk with God, being broken before His holiness, and surrendered to God's plan for his life. He depends on the power and guidance of the Holy Spirit to empower him in his ministry with troubled churches.

There are four principles of transformational leadership that are irrefutable. These principles are: *(1). His leadership exists only under the authority for Jesus Christ. (2). they must possess and live Godly character and values. (3). they must consistently practice spiritual lifestyle habits. (4). they must always put action their visions and dreams.* Transformational leadership, under the presence and power of the Holy Spirit, is the only kind of leadership

---

42 J. Oswald Sanders, *Spiritual Leadership* (Chicago, Moody Press, 1994), p. 28.

that will insure the success of a church restart and its pastor. These characteristics are prerequisites for any church restart pastor.

Fundamental Qualification and Qualities of a Church Restart Pastor

I have identified at least seven subsets of qualifications (values) for a church restart pastor and these seven translate to over 40 spiritual life qualities that are significant and should be present in any restart leader. These are:

Family Standards

Because the Bible speaks volumes about the family and the role of the family in society, it is probably the most important aspect of the church restart pastor's personal life. The importance of the family structure and commitment reveals itself in the task of leading a restart process. It is intrinsically important that we discuss family values because restarting a church is difficult, stressful and sometimes downright daunting. The pastor's family must be prepared for the task. Because of the very demanding and all-encompassing work of a church restart, the restart pastor's family life must be strong, healthy and stable. Even though it is a labor of love, it can still be taxing on the family unit, especially the husband and father, because of the demands upon his time and energy. However, the first and foremost responsibility the restart pastor has is to sacrificially love his wife and children as he leads a new church into the future. He can never neglect his family and still be blessed of God!

It is a fact that it is tedious and hard work to restart a church and it is equally demanding to maintain a healthy family life. The task of the restart pastor is to work diligently at making both his church and his family healthy and stable. Dr. Thomas F. Jones, Jr., writes "It is hard work to start a new church. It's difficult to sustain a healthy marriage. However, it's worth the effort to get both right. If our culture needs anything, it is God-honoring marriages that couples and young people in our communities can get up close to and say, "I want that kind of marriage." When new churches are led by couples with good marriages, they almost always grow. People are naturally attracted to good relationships. They are contagious."[43]

Here are the most important elements of a transformational leader's family life.

First, the restart pastor must understand the clear mandate to a *Biblical family life*. The only way to build a marriage is to build it around Biblical principles and teaching. The entire familial relationship is structured under a submissive framework. Every member of the family must submit first to the perfect and clear will of God for them in their particular role as a family member. Submission to God is the absolute essential. We must submit to his plan for the Christian marriage and home. Secondly, there must be a mutual submission within the family ranks for the family to succeed. The Bible is clear about such submission.

The concept of mutual submission is taught clearly in the Bible, however there is somewhat of a difference in the purpose and meaning of that submission. The Greek word for submit is "hupotassó" which means "I place under, subject to; I submit, put myself into subjection."[44] This word is often given a bad rap by those who misunderstand the whole Biblical concept of submission. It seems that some think that the word infers inferiority but that is not the

---

43 Dr. Thomas F. Jones, Jr., Church Planting: It's All About Relationships (Part 4: "A God-Honoring Marriage"): Stadia, Nov. 1, 2017.

44 Thayer's Greek Lexicon, Electronic Database. Copyright © 2011: Biblesoft, Inc.

emphasis of the word at all. The word in Ephesians 5: 22 that is translated "wives" (gunaikes - γυναικες) is used in the vocative case with the definite article which generalizes the statement. That means that this statement is generally true, but it does not rule out exceptions. For instance, there may be cases in which the husband is absent from the home for long periods of time such as Armed Services or occupations that require them to travel widely. There are also cases in which the husband may be disabled by some type of dementia, a debilitating disease, or a crippling accident which makes it impossible for him to exercise leadership in the family. In such cases, it is often necessary for the wife to assume the position of leadership. Used in this case, the phrase, "wives submit yourself to your own husbands as unto the Lord" must be understood as compared to the last two verses of the chapter which summarizes the truth that Paul is teaching when he said, "… I speak concerning Christ and the Church. Nevertheless, let everyone of you in particular so love his wife even as himself and the wife see that she reverences her husband." Taken together, these affirmations of Scripture carry with them the connotation of a deep devotion and loyalty of the wife to her husband. Bossiness is not implied in this passage. It is not difficult for a wife to submit to a husband who loves her in the same way that Christ loved the Church. That means that a wife is to love her husband because his great love for her would cause him to lay down his life in her behalf or to spend out his life for her and her offspring. This passage also affirms monogamous marriages. The relationship of husband and wife is compared to that of Christ and the Church. The relationship of Christ and His Church is permanent. The relationship of Christ and His Church will never end. The teaching is clear. The marriage of one man and one woman will never end on this earth until they are separated by death. The profound truth of the passage is that the relationship between husband and wife is to be a complementary one, with the husband in the place of leadership. That is a normal

Biblical marriage. In this context the word submission is a military term that simply means that in the family unit the husband and father will be the one who will ultimately give an account to God for the way he leads and guides his family on earth.

The Bible tells us that the *husband's form of submission* is that he should "love his wife as Christ loved His church." Christ loved that Church so much that He gave His life for it. That simply means he cares for his wife's needs and works hard to bring fulfillment to her life. At the same time the father is to "raise up a child in the way he should go." That is a form of devotion to his children. It does not mean that he submits to their will, but that he cares for their needs and future just as the husband cares for the wife.

The Bible is also very clear about *the submission of the wife to her husband.* It says that the wife is to "submit to her husband as unto the Lord." This does not in any way infer inferiority on the part of the wife. It is not an affront to womanhood. It simply places the woman in a position of following the loving leadership of the husband as God has ordained. This speaks to the absolute necessity of *a supportive wife.* If there is to be success in a church restart there must be support from the wife.

Likewise, the children are to *submit to the authority and leadership of the parents.* Children who understand their position in a caring Christian home are a blessing to the parents and everyone they associate with. Obedience to parents is commanded in the Ten Commandments where it says, "Honor your father and your mother, so that you may live long in the land the Lord your God is giving you." In the New Testament the Word of God very pointedly charges children to," …obey your parents in the Lord for this is right." (Ephesians 6: 15) Obedient children in the home of a restart pastor will be make life and ministry so much easier and exciting. It will enable the pastor to do the work of God without having to deal with the disobedience of the child.

Spiritual Building Blocks

The Restart pastor must live by some potent spiritual principles. I have identified five building blocks (principles) to success in the restart. Living a spiritually principled life is what gives direction and guidance to the journey. These leadership principles are derived from the Bible. This is not an exhaustive list, but it is a crucial list. These principles build one on the other:

The first building block is a *fervent and consistent prayer life.* The prayer life of the restart pastor must be dynamic and consistent. Involved in that prayer life are three basic elements. These elements are:

Asking God – seeking His will and leadership as he leads the church through the restart,

Listening to God – knowing when God speaks.

Obeying God – after he speaks simply being obedient to his word and leadership.

How the restart pastor prays is important but not nearly as important as how he listens after he prays. James 5:16b says, *"The effectual fervent prayer of a righteous man availeth much."*[45] James is speaking about the importance of passion in prayer as he considers the gracious God who hears the prayer. The eloquence of a prayer nor the person who prays have nothing to do with the effectiveness of a prayer. What makes prayer effective is the Holy God who hears and answers prayers. In

---

45 James 5:16 KJV.

John 10:27 Jesus said *"My sheep hear my voice, and I know them, and they follow me:"*[46]

The restart pastor must have a listening ear when the all-powerful God speaks. The fact is God desires to communicate with his children. He desires to lead us and give direction for living. He communicates with us in various ways. Daniel received visions from God. A donkey talked to Balaam. A bush spoke to Moses. God can use anything to speak to his leaders. The key is for the leaders to have listening ears. Today He speaks to us through other people, through His word, through preaching, through song and a multitude of other avenues. All God asks of the leader is to listen for His voice and He will communicate. Isaiah 30:18 says *"And therefore will the Lord wait, that he may be gracious unto you, and therefore will he be exalted, that he may have mercy upon you: for the Lord is a God of judgment: blessed are all they that wait for him."*[47] Then in verse 21 He says *"And thine ears shall hear a word behind thee, saying, this is the way, walk ye in it, when ye turn to the right hand, and when ye turn to the left."*[48] The restart pastor must constantly ask himself, "What is God saying to me? How should I be praying for this church?" Obedience to what God is saying will make or break the restart effort.

There was a news article that came out of the Chicago Tribune some years ago about an 81-year-old man who had to land a plane after his pilot friend died at the controls. The elderly man, Robert Kupfreschmid and his friend were flying from Indianapolis, Indiana to Muncie, Indiana. While in flight the pilot died at the controls and the plane began to nose dive.

---

46 John 10:27 KJV.

47 Isaiah 30:18 KJV.

48 Isaiah 30:21 KJV.

Not having a clue as to how to fly the plane Robert grabbed the controls and began to plead for help on the radio and finally two other pilots heard his plea and responded with instructions on how to take control of the plane and ultimately bring the plane to a landing. Robert listened attentively to every word the other pilots spoke as they instructed him on how to steer and land the plane. He circled the airport three times before gaining the courage to set the plane down on the runway. Emergency vehicles were dispatched to the runway in anticipation of a crash landing. Witnesses stood by and watched as the nose of the plane touched down and bounced several times before the tail hit the ground. To everyone's amazement the plane came to a stop and the 81-year man got out of the plane uninjured.[49]

What made the difference for Robert Kupfreschmid on that day? He carefully listened to the voice that gave him direction as to how to land a plane. He had never done it before but the pilots with the instruction had. His life depended on his listening. The very life of dead churches depends on the restart pastor seeking, listening and obeying God as he prays seeking the wisdom of God. Fervent prayer is the life line for restarting a church.

The second building block principle is *a personal walk with Jesus.* You must walk the walk and not just talk the talk. Greg Firzzsell in his book *How to Develop a Powerful Prayer Life* tells the parable of the football coach. "A huge high school student walked up to the football coach and told him he wanted to play football. The coach was thrilled and said, "Son, I'm so glad you want to play. We sure need a player your size." Then the coach told the young man to be at

---

49 Chicago Tribune: *Wings, A Prayer And 2 Nearby Fliers Help Non-pilot,* 81, Land, *June 18, 1998 | By From Tribune News Services.*

practice the following day and he would get a chance to play on the team. For the next three days the coach anxiously watched for the young man and he never showed up for practice."

The young man came back a week later and said to the coach "Coach I sure love football and I really want to be on the team." The coach responded "I'm glad to hear it, but you never came to practice. Son we really need you on our team but if you want to play football, you must come to practice." The young man assured the coach he would be at the next practice. But a whole week passed, and he never came to practice.

Later the young man saw the coach walking at a distance and he yelled for the coach to stop but the coach kept walking. The young man ran and stopped the coach and proclaimed his desire to play football and the coach interrupted him and said, "No son you really don't want to play football. I told you in order to play you must come to practice. The truth is, you had rather do other things than pay the price to be on the team. When you say you want to play, yet you won't come to practice, you are really just kidding yourself. Now excuse me while I go coach the boys who are waiting at practice. You see son, they do want to play football."[50]

Unlike that young football want-to-be, a church restart calls for the leader to be in the game. To be at practice. To walk with Jesus daily and not just talk about it. The restart leader must never allow peripheral things derail his personal walk with the Lord. There must be an everyday strong effort to spend time with God through His word and prayer. The

---

50 Gregory R. Frizzell, *How to Develop a Powerful Prayer Life* (Memphis: Bethany Press) p. 20-21.

restart pastor's personal spiritual life is the one element that will feed the work of the restart. It is true you can't be on a football team if you don't pay the price to practice and it is equally true that a leader cannot lead people to where he himself has never been. You cannot lead people to walk with Jesus if you are not walking with him. The leader can never depend on self to make a restart successful. It is only by spending quality time and walking daily with the Lord Jesus that the leader will be equipped to lead a successful restart. There is a slogan that says, "Just do it!" That's good advice to the leader who desires to have an intimate walk with Jesus, the Christ of God!

The third building block is *an extreme faith*. Hebrews 11:1 gives the basic definition of Faith it says, *"Now faith is the substance of things hoped for, the evidence of things not seen.'*[51] To lead in a church restart process takes not just faith but "extreme" faith. It takes a faith that, even when you can't see the way, the knowledge that God is in absolute control gives motivation and direction. The leader rests in the fact that God is working everything out according to His will.

The element of expectation is a real part of extreme faith. Leading with a sense of expectation reveals the heart of faith that is needed by the leader. The restart pastor cannot see what is around the next corner, but God already knows so he must live with the expectation that God is in control and is working His will and plan.

Extreme faith is not just a lot of words or talk, it shows up in how we work and lead. It is leaning on God even when the circumstances and situation around you seems difficult or even impossible. It shows up in our praying when we pray and trust God to accomplish the work in us that He has begun.

---

51 Hebrews 11:1 KJV.

Extreme faith has a "no-fear" factor built into it. A good example of this is the account of Abraham and Isaac in Genesis 22:2-3. God made a very fearful and difficult request of Abraham. He instructed Abraham to take his only son Isaac to Mt. Moriah to offer him up as a burnt sacrifice. What a demand of God! What a challenge to faith! What a fearful request. The command of God called for a kind of faith that no human can have within themselves. It called for "extreme" faith.

We see in the scripture that Abraham loaded fire wood on his donkey, gathered the instruments of sacrifice and his son and began to make the long journey of extreme faith. When they reached the mountain, Isaac pointed out to his father that he saw the wood, and everything needed for the sacrifice except the sacrifice itself. Abraham simply replied that the Lord would provide the sacrifice. Abraham built an alter and readied his son for the sacrifice. Abraham had a "no fear" kind of faith that called for absolute obedience to God. Of course, we know that God stopped the sacrifice of Isaac by providing a ram that was caught in the bush. But God saw in Abraham what He wanted to see...the kind of faith that it would take for his future work and life. This is the kind of extreme faith that a church restart pastor must have!

The fourth building block is *a passion and hunger for souls.* Matthew 9:36-38 says *"But when he saw the multitudes, he was moved with compassion on them, because they fainted, and were scattered abroad, as sheep having no shepherd. Then saith He unto his disciples, The harvest truly is plenteous, but the laborers are few; Pray ye therefore the Lord of the harvest, that he will send forth laborers into his harvest."*[52] Jesus was gazing at the multitudes that had

---

52 Matt. 9:36-38 KJV.

gathered around him because of the miracles that he had performed. When He saw the helpless and the hopeless, He had compassion on them because they were as sheep without a shepherd. He cared for the condition of the lost around Him. The church restart pastor will not get very far without a passion and compassion for the souls of lost people.

How does that passion reveal itself? The first thing that must be present in the heart is a firm conviction that souls are valuable to God and therefore should be valuable to us. We must see the multitudes as Jesus saw them. That conviction should automatically grow into a real desire to meet their need and look out for their eternal welfare. It involves a clear understanding of the eternal spiritual danger that the lost person faces which ignites a zeal to see them saved. That can only happen when we are moved with the kind of compassion that Jesus had.

A leader who has a passion for souls will always produce a healthy church that will in turn produce more converts. In our age there is a real lack of commitment and conviction about the need to be a soul winner, but it is impossible to grow a church without the element of soul winning. Tom Rainer in *The Church Health Encyclopedia* speaks to the pastor/leader and says "As a leader in your church, you must model evangelism. It is not enough to talk about witnessing. It is not enough to teach witnessing programs to others. If you want to see people share their faith, you must be sharing your faith too."[53]

The fifth building block is *a heart for discipleship.* John 15:8 says *"Herein is my Father glorified, that you bear much fruit; so, shall you be my disciples."*[54] Robert Tenery in The *Operation*

---

53 Tom Rainer & Chuck Lawless, *Church Health Encyclopedia,* The Rainer Group (Louisville, August 2002).

54 John 15:8 KJV.

Transformation Guide wrote, "The responsibility of disciplining Believers, a process that continues throughout our lives, is the responsibility of the Church."[55] There has never been a time in history for a greater more strategic discipleship ministry in the local church than there is today. When any new church is started the number one effort ought to be winning the lost and discipling those who are saved. It seems that it is in vogue to not use the word evangelism but instead only use the word disciple. However, discipleship cannot and will not happen if separated from the idea of soul winning and seeking the lost.

Any restart pastor would be remiss in trying to do a restart without the major element of discipleship training being on the top of the priority list. If the pastor/leader does not see the importance of discipleship, then the church is going to be dwarfed from the beginning. Discipleship must be a priority in the heart of the pastor for the process to be successful.

Engaged in Financial Principles

The restart pastor must have a strong confidence and faith in God that he is going to provide for his family and the ministry. He must make Psalm 23:1 his go to verse when doubt and fear come. The psalmist David said, *"The Lord is my shepherd; I shall not want."*[56]

There will be times when those words will give the planter a much-needed reassurance that God is near and knows his every need. The knowledge that God is ever

---

55 Robert M. Tenery, *Operation Discipleship, Discipleship Guide,* Operation Transformation (Salisbury, 2016) p. 21.

56 Psalm 23:1 KJV.

present, and He knows and cares about personal and family needs will bring great comfort to the entire family. As God meets those needs the end result will be a stronger and renewed faith in God on the part of the family.

The restart pastor must be engaged in *a stewardship way of life.* He must be totally committed to biblical stewardship principles especially in the area of personal tithing and cheerful giving. No pastor can expect the congregants to be tithers or give generously if he does not set the example. This is an area of great need in the traditional older churches because the younger adults attending these churches have never been taught good stewardship habits. The restart pastor must teach, through personal action and Bible exposition, the importance of the tithe if the church he is restarting will ever survive financially. The big question facing the church restart pastor is "Am I willing to be a good steward by my example and by my giving to the mission of the church?" Everyone will be watching to see if you live up to your commitment.

Furthermore, every church restart pastor must learn to live within their means. In other words, they don't spend more than they make. If the pastor is heavily in debt, he cannot focus his attention to the spiritual aspects of the ministry. Jesus said in Luke 16:10, *"He that is faithful in that which is least is faithful also in much: and he that is unjust in the least is unjust also in much."*[57] The pastor must exercise personal Biblical stewardship principles before God will entrust the church finances into his hands.

The restart pastor must be engaged in the management of *church finances and planting funds as a monetary means of ministry.* There are many areas of financial concern for the restart pastor. In fact, in surveys taken many planters rank the

---

57 Luke 16:10 KJV.

financial concern as the number one concern. Money
management in the new church has always been an issue.
Present in a restart are certain financial expenses that are
different from traditional church expenses. For instance, the
restart will have very little money coming in through offerings
and tithes in the beginning. The only other option for having
finances to operate with is to raise funds outside the restart
itself. Fundraising takes time and energy and often there is a
monetary expense to that as well. Because of their difficulty,
financial needs and issues are often shoved aside and ignored.
This is the reason that many restarts and church plants never
succeed.

Another factor in the finances of the ministry is that it is
not the number one topic on the radar of a replant pastor.
Their emphasis is usually placed on winning souls, growing
the church and discipling the converts. The least exciting
thing that they have on their "to-do" list is raising funds for
operational expenses. To complicate things and make
matters worse most restart pastors have never been engaged
in fundraising and it becomes a frightful and burdensome
task to them. Because of all of this the financial matters of a
restart can become a great burden on the pastor.

The restart pastor may need to engage in *the option of bi-
vocational ministry*. This is not nearly as attractive as being
fulltime on the church field for the simple reason that it adds
extra hours and stress on the pastor and his family. However,
it is an option that needs to be left open if needed.
Sometimes pastors see the bi-vocational role as the lesser of
the two options of fulltime or bi-vocational. In some cases,
this option is the most logical, but it is not the preferred way
of restarting a church. To be bi-vocational is a challenge to
say the least but sometimes the reality of not enough finances
drives the decision to be bi-vocational. There are many who
are a big proponent of bi-vocational ministry but strategically
speaking it is certainly not the preferred option. Even though

it will take time the preferred approach is a fully funded restart in order to free the pastor to get to know and minister to the community. It allows him to spend time in the community building relationships and gathering people for the new restart. To me it is a no-brainer…the best option is a fully funded restart.

The restart pastor must be engaged in *continual learning and maintenance of financial management skills.* As has been said before, most restart pastors lack the skills to perform well in difficult financial matters because most have never been involved in budgeting and financial management except in their personal finances. Most have never had to administer a large church budget. A continuing educational process is needed to help the pastor know and understand current economic and financial methods and concepts.

Possess Interpersonal Skills and Methods

The restart pastor must have interpersonal skills that gives the ability to lead properly. B*eing a people person* is a skill that is absolutely necessary for the restart leader. This involves *building strategic relationships* while *understanding the needs of the community.* This skill reveals itself in *leading and mobilizing people.* The end result of these interpersonal skills should be that of cultivated relationships within the community.

These skills are incorporated into a methodology for achieving success as a restart. The method of *team building* is crucial for putting together and *developing a gifted core team* that will assist in the launch and opening of the new church. Part of the method is to develop key leaders by *utilizing their talents* for the *planning* of the future of the restart.

Five Key Ministry Attributes

Basketball players need to be able to jump, dribble and shoot the ball. Automobile mechanics need to understand combustion engines, a knowledge of tools and the ability to trouble shoot. Being a restart pastor calls for a certain set of key ministry attributes and abilities as well. If the restart pastor wants to be successful, these attributes are a must. Discussed previously in this chapter were the many Biblical qualifications and characteristics the restart leader needs but beyond those there are some personal, individual attributes that are irreplaceable as well.

First is the attribute of *visionary leadership*. Proverbs 29:18 says *"Without vision the people perish but blessed is he who keeps the law."*[58] A paraphrase might say it something like this "If people can't see what God is doing, they stumble all over themselves, but when they tend to what He reveals, they are most blessed."

The restart pastor must be a visionary. He must ask himself this question, "What would this restart look like if we were really fulfilling our mission?" What God calls the church to do now is to understand a clear vision for how this mission will be accomplished in the church's culture and geography. This vision creates a description of the future of the church, so it can be actively pursued and become a reality over time.

"Within the local church the task of providing visionary leadership falls squarely on the pastor's shoulders. But the pastor is not alone in this task."[59] The pastor is the initial recipient of a vision from God. It comes from God's heart

---

58 Proverbs 29:18 KJV.

59 Adam Hamilton, *Leading Beyond the Walls* (Nashville, Abingdon Press, 2002) p.132.

to the leader's heart. The visioning process is as follows - God possesses the Vision - He imparts it to the pastor – He shares it with the people – they live it out to the lost! The vision from God is always Kingdom focused. Every church needs a focus and it is the leader's responsibility to zero in on what God wants for that congregation by pursuing the unique vision that God has for the restart.

The visionary pastor is always future oriented, optimistic and positive. They know where God is leading, and they know how God has directed them to get there. They believe that verse previously noted…" where there is no vision the people perish."

Second, is the element of *a clear calling* upon his life. Because the task is great and arduous there is a special calling on any church restart pastor's life. There must be a realization and an acceptance of the tremendous task of restarting a dead church. The Bible speaks of a general calling into ministry in Ephesians 4:11-14. However, because the task is so difficult there is a special call upon the life of a restart pastor. Charles Spurgeon, in his *Lectures to My Students,* asks 4 questions to help a student know whether they are called to ministry or not. Those questions were meant to probe into the heart of the student to make them think through the idea of being called of God into ministry. If I could make a list of probing questions for one contemplating becoming a restart pastor, I think I would ask these 10 questions:

1. Are you totally confident that God's call on your life is to restart a dead church or should you stick to being the pastor of an existing church?
2. Can you relate to other people (lost and unchurched) on a level that shows them that you love them and care for their eternal soul?

3. Are you living a disciplined life of personal worship and personal accountability that is necessary for a restart leader to have?

4. Are you a visionary? Are you walking close enough to God to know His vision for a restart work?

5. What is your motivation for becoming a restart pastor?

6. Are you a consistent witness to non-believers?

7. What has God said to you about becoming a restart pastor?

8. What does your family think about you becoming a restart pastor?

9. Do you have a God given vision from God regarding what a dead church needs to do?

10. Are you ready to go into battle with the opposition to a restart?

Frederick Buechner gives great advice to one who says they are called to ministry, "The place God calls you to is the place where your deep gladness and the world's deep hunger meet."[60] This is excellent advice for the restart pastor. Simply put, if your greatest joy is sharing your faith, then when ministering to people and growing a great church intersects with the great need of a church community, you will be able to experience the joy of being a restart pastor.

Third is the element of *self-start ability*. The restart pastor must be a self-starter. What is a self-starter? The dictionary says, a self-starter is "a person who begins work or undertakes a project on his or her own initiative, without needing to be told or encouraged to do so."[61] Proverbs 26:15 shows the direct opposite of a self-starter. It says, "*The*

---

60 Frederick Buechner, *Wishful Thinking: A Seeker's ABC*, (HarperCollins, Sep 24, 1993) p. 118.

61 Self-Starter, Explore Dictionary.com, www.dictionary.com.

slothful hideth his hand in his bosom; it grieveth him to bring it again to his mouth.'[62] The hand in the bosom just means he doesn't have the heart to work even if it is to provide for food for his own table.

Being a self-starter is a real asset to the restart pastor because they are usually good at exploring new ideas and tackling new and difficult tasks. They are good at setting and attaining personal goals as well as finding solutions to problems that arise. They are usually creative in their approach to their work and they don't mind taking a risk to accomplish a task. They usually take the initiative to do tasks that many others would shun or bypass. Probably the most important trait of the self-starter is they are not afraid of failure. They see failure as an avenue to success. All these traits are tremendously important in the task of restarting a dead church.

The fourth element is *emotional maturity*. Emotional maturity goes hand in hand with spiritual maturity. The two cannot be separated. A person who is emotionally mature has a real sense of self-awareness. They know their strengths and they understand their weaknesses. As a result, they know how to manage their own lives and get the most out their own abilities and strengths.

The emotionally mature leader has no problem with change. In fact, in some instances they thrive on change and in many instances, they instigate change. They have an insatiable desire for interpersonal relationships that help accomplish their life goals. They do not seek gratitude or pats on the back. Their maturity shows in the fact that they derive satisfaction by simply doing the best they can in any given situation. These are healthy traits of an emotionally and spiritually mature leader.

---

62 Proverbs 26:15 KJV.

The fifth element is the possession of *a missional lifestyle*. A clear understanding of the missional lifestyle must be understood by any planter wishing to restart a dead church. Henry Blackaby was one of the first Christians to hint at a missional lifestyle when he encouraged Christians to seek out where God is working and join him in the effort. The emphasis is on the "joining" with God in what he is already doing. The Great Commission in Matthew further teaches the missional lifestyle as it encourages the believer to "go" and work in the world to bring in the harvest of souls. In fact, a clearer rendering of the concept of "go" in the Great Commission is "as you are going" do the work of the Lord. So, the real emphasis in a missional lifestyle should always be the joining God in His work no matter where that takes us or what it costs us.

We understand that all throughout the Bible, God sends leaders. A replant pastor must simply be willing to be sent. He must be willing to adopt a missionary lifestyle as he lives out his life. This whole concept of the church being "missional" is a much better model for being the church rather that the "attractional" model of doing church.

To live a missional lifestyle is to mimic the life of Jesus. Jesus' entire life was missional. He lived out his mission on earth as he accomplished the will of His heavenly Father. He contextualized the gospel as he lived it out in his culture as an example for every culture that follows. It is abundantly clear that missions is no mere program of the church, but rather it is to be the life of the church. Every restart pastor must live through a heart of missions! To sum it all up the Apostle Paul said it like this, "whatsoever ye do, do all to the glory of God."[63]

---

63 1 Cor. 10:31 KJV.

In conclusion, a perfect example of a leader living up to the desperate need before him and becoming the "man for the hour" is the Old Testament character of Nehemiah. The first five verses of Nehemiah 1 reveal the kind of leader he was and the calling to take on an enormous task for the Kingdom. The Bible says in Nehemiah 1:1-5, *"The words of Nehemiah the son of Hachaliah. And it came to pass in the month Chisleu, in the twentieth year, as I was in Shushan the palace, That Hanani, one of my brethren, came, he and certain men of Judah; and I asked them concerning the Jews that had escaped, which were left of the captivity, and concerning Jerusalem. And they said unto me, the remnant that are left of the captivity there in the province are in great affliction and reproach: the wall of Jerusalem also is broken down, and the gates thereof are burned with fire. And it came to pass, when I heard these words, that I sat down and wept, and mourned certain days, and fasted, and prayed before the God of heaven,"* [64]

The man of the hour for building the walls of Jerusalem was Nehemiah. He was broken hearted over the demise of Jerusalem. He had compassion for those who were now back in the city living in the ruins of that great city. He wept over the destruction and sought God for an answer. He was the man of the hour for the rebuilding of the wall and regaining the pride and integrity of that holy city.

The restart pastor is the man of the hour for broken hopeless churches. In these difficult days what these dead churches need are people who will seek God's face about the great need of restarting churches. The church that is dying or already dead needs a man of the hour. It takes a special man...will you be that man?

---

[64] Nehemiah 1:1-5 KJV.

Chapter Three
Developing Critical Mass in a Restart

"Every day their number grew as God added those who were saved."[65]

Back in 1997, I developed a one-day workshop for the Home Mission Board Church Planting Division entitled *Developing Critical Mass in a Restart.* When Richard Harris became the Vice President for Church Planting for what is now known as the North American Mission Board of the Southern Baptist Convention, there were a series of ten articles that were copied from a manual I had developed six months before and had been using around the North Central States and particularly in Michigan. In that manual I talked a lot about church planting but also about church renewal and saving of our dying churches in North America. For the last twenty-two years I have been equipping church planters and what we now call Church Revitalizers in the process of restarting a church. More than three hundred churches have been saved and made great churches again at least in portion by the training they received on getting, finding and maintaining critical mass. Developing critical mass as a church planter is a wonderful thing. Losing critical mass as a pastor is destructive for the church. Redeveloping critical mass for the Church Revitalizer is salvation of a local church. Critical mass is an essential milestone for any church. There are some churches, however, that must reach critical mass as rapidly as possible in order to survive.

---

[65] Eugene H. Peterson, *The Message: The Bible in Contemporary Language* (Colorado Springs, CO: NavPress, 2005), Ac 2:47.

The Formula for Developing Critical Mass66

Everyone wants to see some sort of growth come back to their dying church. Many a church revitalization effort has been hurt due to the leadership within the church, both lay and clergy, waiting too long before they addressed the issue of critical mass. Critical Mass is that size of any church where it has enough members actively working and participating in the weekly work of ministry growth. When a church has waited too long to address the issue of critical mass, it is almost sure the church will die, even if for a moment it keeps it head above the water of closure. Most churches wait until they have passed the point of no return to attempt adjustment. Here is a quick formula for developing and keeping critical mass in one's church:

> 1 % of the church membership is in pastoral leadership.

> Plus 6% of the church membership is passionate about the future of the church.

> Plus 14% of the church's leaders are in positions willingly and are advocating for the future renewal of the church.

> Plus 42% of the church are actively participating and willingly following future directions of the church.

This simple formula equals a growing critical mass for development and the eventual revitalization of the congregation. Does the term critical mass seem foreign to you? It just might be unless you are a Church Revitalizer.

---

66 Go to: http://renovateconference.org/formula-for-developing-critical-mass for this information as well as other resources relating to restarting a church.

Most pastors think about the subject yet are not all that aware of how to develop and maintain critical mass. One pastor told me the term sounded like it was right out of a Star Trek movie. The term has its origin in the field of nuclear physics. The term critical mass is a term used to represent the smallest mass of material that can sustain a nuclear reaction at a constant level. Sunday School leaders have used the term to suggest where a new class size needs to be in order to achieve sustainability. Church Revitalizers have come to understand the term in a similar way. In field of business, it is used to denote a crucial stage in a company's development where the business reaches a self-sustaining viability. For a church in need of revitalization as a restart it means the growth and expansion to a level of participation where the restart church has become self-sustaining, self-sufficient, and self-perpetuating. It refers to the size a dying church must regrow to in order to be viable for the future. There is the point in critical mass where a declining church must not let it fall below or it will certainly cease to exist. Critical mass in church revitalization should never be allowed to fall below fifty adults before immediate action is taken. One of the reasons the replanting strategy is so popular today is because we have failed to teach our churches this critical point and they wait too long before they take action. In some rapidly declining churches this number must be bumped up to seventy-five adults because they have been burdened by more staff then the church can support. Their annual revenue makes it impossible to continue. Critical mass in a restart is an ever-changing target unless you carefully manage the financials, and not a constant one-time only goal. Needless to say, critical mass represents the smallest number (mass) of participants in a restart that can sustain ministries at a constant level. Keeping viability is the critical ingredient.

Have you ever been in a church during some sort of holiday only to find that the church you are visiting is not able to do the regular things of ministry it usually does? That is a church that might be at risk of losing of critical mass. In other words, it can function fairly well when everyone is present, but if a family or two goes on vacation or is away for other things, the church is paralyzed and unable to minister to the community. Church Revitalizers who have the gift of being entrepreneurial are always quite aware of their numbers and whether or not they are dangerously near critical mass. In the field of restarting a church there are sustainable levels to strive towards in order to allow the church to regain its strength and footing for future ministry and expansion. As you pass these thresholds, there are new ministries you can consider and new target groups you can consider. Obviously, achieving critical mass does not happen on a prescribed timeline, and it can vary between churches. If your church is struggling to make it month to month even if you have 50 or more adults actively in service in your church you are about to lose your critical mass. As you grow past these mass numbers, you will have renewed opportunities to try new ministries to reach new niche areas within the community.

Steps to Achieving Critical Mass in a Restart

Initially it is wise to have a discussion with the church leadership regarding not only the mass numbers relating to people, but the financial numbers necessary to sustain the church. By working back from these figures, you can determine what it will take to keep your restart afloat. By having a goal to aim towards, all of the energies in the church can be focused on advancing past these minimals. I am working with a church right now in another state to help them in this area. Through the work of restarting the church, the present pastor has run the finances into the ground and refuses to leave, all while the nice people are too timid to release him and save their church. Here are the basic steps to achieve critical mass:

Work Wisely

Usually, the reason the church has come to the place of considering a restart is because ministries have ceased while no one was keeping an eye on them. Just as your decline did not happen overnight, your climbing above the benchmark of critical mass will not either. Restarting a church takes time and is not a rapid-fire quick fix endeavor. Remember that if you are going to restart your church it will be a minimal investment of one thousand days by both the leadership and the church and every active member. There must be a sense of urgency created in the restart. You cannot sit around and do nothing. Survival terms must be replaced with terms that paint a picture of one thriving.

Know Who You Can Reach

So many declining churches do not know who lives in their ministry areas anymore. If they did, they would have made the necessary changes for survival some time ago. Not knowing one's community and the changes that have taken place is a prescription for pyritization. Knowing who you can reach in the community is one of the most important factors for the success of any restart and towards achieving of critical mass. Keep in mind, so many pastors do not even know who they could be reaching. Far too many churches have been targeting the wrong audience for their outreach efforts only to discover they have lulled their church into decline.

Make a Long-term Commitment to the Process

Until you are all in as a church and its leadership, nothing is going to happen. It is important to stay committed to the end goal of restarting the church. There are no quick fixes and no matter how glamourous planting a new church might sound there are many replants that do not make it. Critical mass will not be achieved instantaneously in any case. Success is only feasible for those who work hard, work smart and stay vigilant to the long-term process.

Seek Balance in Your Outreach

There are only so many of you so do not overload your members with more than they can handle. If you only have four people who can begin to reach out in new directions, do not give them more than two new things to consider. One would be better. In one of my last restarts, I took on only two things the first two years. They were: the ongoing follow up with former members encouraging their return, and the follow up of visitors to the church within forty-eight hours. That was what we could do until we grew some. But understand that was more than enough and it kept me and my deacons busy until others were able to jump in and make an effort. By not allowing us to get overbalanced with too many things and sapping out all of our energies, we were able to bring initial restoration to the church. After that we were able to keep the throttle pressed down and got growing once more. Let me stop a moment and talk about balance. In a declining church that has 50 adults let us consider the numbers. There is a pastor and his wife. That leaves 48 adults to do the work of the church. Most small churches have between five and seven active deacons serving the church. That number now has dropped to 41 adults to do the work of the church. There is probably a church secretary or perhaps an individual doing the bookkeeping for the church. That leaves 39 adults to do the work of the church. The church has a choir director, piano player, and choir. Most small declining churches have about twelve people in the choir so pianist and director make 14 totaled. That leaves 20 remaining adults to do the work of the church. Most declining churches still have a Bible Study hour which consists of a teacher for young adults, one for older adults, one for youth, and one for children. That leaves 16 remaining adults to do the work of the church. There are at least three ushers doing the tasks of serving the congregation during worship. That leaves 13 remaining adults to do the work of the church. There is a nursery and it is staffed with 3-4 adults. That leaves 9 adults to do the work of the church. In the sound room there are two adults who run sound and visuals for worship. That leaves 7 adults to do the work of the church. Seven adults through which you can build new ministries, providing every single adult attender has bought in to do acts of service for the church. Since any new ministry usually takes three or four people to lead and staff it, one can quickly see how easy a declining church can get out of balance by creating too many new ministries during the initial stages of a restart. In one church in my association they created a quarterly outreach blitz Saturday which was designed to bring in new people. It lasted six months before the membership began finding excuses why they could not participate in saving their church. If you find yourself in such a situation, leaving the church to the association is the best thing you could do and allow the director of missions to utilize it either for an office, a church plant, or both.[67]

Spend Wisely

Declining churches get in trouble fast by failing to reduce expenditures quickly. One church I worked with had a pastor, music minister, and a youth minister in a church running seventy-five. They loved each and every one of these staff members. Their refusal to balance the financial ledger actually caused the church to close. None of the staff as I interviewed them was willing to step down and all were of the opinion that they were so well-liked that they would be the last one to be dismissed. When a minister loves his paycheck more than he does the people who provide of that paycheck something is wrong and the church will certainly close

---

[67] If you find yourself in this situation, be sure to read the chapter in this book on *Leaving a Legacy*.

because of every one's refusal to take action. There are times when a church will invite me in and allow me to set up a steering committee which will run the church and make all of the necessary decisions for the next three years. In one church the pastor, who was ten years past retirement, said he hoped that the church was still around until he reached his eightieth birthday. When well-meaning laity cannot take action, it is best to hand the property over to the association and allow them to manage the facilities. One of the indicators that your restart is reaching critical mass is when there begins to be a positive cash flow where formerly there was a negative one.

Developing Measurable Goals for the Initial 120 Days

The restart will always be adapting and re-evaluating its goals during the thousand-day journey. Begin by developing the first set of goals for the initial 120 days. There is a song titled, *Fly Me to the Moon*, and every time I hear it, it makes me think about restarting churches. It is a great song. What it reminds me to do in a restart revitalization effort is to shoot for the moon. If I miss, I will still land among the stars. Aim big in a restart but develop one's goals for about 120 days initially and then keep the process of one or two steps forward until you have walked your way all the way through the revitalization of your church. Aim at something bold and big and press towards the mark. To ensure that critical mass is achieved, the church and Church Revitalizer must have initial measurable goals. Do not move forward in the goal setting until the goals are met. Avoiding reality and establishing a new set of goals before the initial goals are met is unwise.

Elevate Your Early Adopters

Not everyone is going to be gung-ho at the outset, so be sure to elevate those risk takers who right out of the starting gate have jumped all in. There will be middle adopters and late ones as well. Honor those who were in the fight to save the church right from the start. In one of my restarts, I had men who were all in and supported the effort to restart the church. There were some who took flight and eventually returned, but I always honored and still honor those men to this day who passionately were all in for the cause of Christ to save that church. They believed that the church was worth saving. Do you remember the story in Numbers where Joshua and Caleb urged the Israelites to enter the land God was giving to them?

> *When Moses told all of this to the People of Israel, they mourned long and hard. But early the next morning they started out for the high hill country, saying, "We're here; we're ready—let's go up and attack the land that GOD promised us. We sinned, but now we're ready." But Moses said, "Why are you crossing GOD's command yet again? This won't work. Don't attack. GOD isn't with you in this—you'll be beaten badly by your enemies. The Amalekites and Canaanites are ready for you and they'll kill you. Because you have left off obediently following GOD, GOD is not going to be with you in this." But they went anyway; recklessly and arrogantly they climbed to the high hill country. But the Chest of the Covenant and Moses didn't budge from the camp. The Amalekites and the Canaanites who lived in the hill country came out of the hills and attacked and beat them, a rout all the way down to Hormah.68*

A caution I give to you is what we read in the Book of Numbers. Be careful who you listen to. Joshua and Caleb were the early adopters. In a restart, it is easy for the ten in the crowd to lead a rebellion. In the text above the rebellious

---

68 Eugene H. Peterson, *The Message: The Bible in Contemporary Language* (Colorado Springs, CO: NavPress, 2005), Nu 14:39–45.

even wanted to stone Moses because he wanted to lead them into the land the Lord had promised to them. The other ten were doing what they wanted rather than what God wanted. If you study the text further at the end suddenly they jump all in like they were never not wanting to cross over to the promised land. The day after their great failure, the Jews were supposed to start on their long march through the wilderness, but the nation refused to obey. Warren Wiersbe says that their, "unbelief, a spirit of complaining, and a rebellious attitude are terrible masters that cause no end of trouble in the lives of those who cultivate them."[69] The account ends with a reversal of the fortunes for Israel due to their rejection of God. Dennis Cole, my seminary professor, declares to attempt to advance into the land of blessing without the Lord's blessing is to set a course for failure.[70] These types are everywhere, wondering why God will not bless them nor be with them in their declining church. When you presume that you can act disobediently and the Lord will still allow you to restart a church there is a lesson to be learned. In the text in Numbers, the people realized their mistake too late. Sometimes a church fails to repent of its sins and repentance comes too late. The word *Hormah* in the passage means devoted to destruction. That is what the ten spies were doing and many a declining church which refuses to accept God's offer of a new beginning through a restart. When God says go, you best go now and not later. I have seen in my ministry that the Lord opens a door for me to cross over but He does not give me a second chance usually if I do not take immediate action.

---

[69] Warren W. Wiersbe, *Be Counted*, "Be" Commentary Series (Colorado Springs, CO: Chariot Victor Pub., 1999), 61.

[70] R. Dennis Cole, *Numbers*, vol. 3B, The New American Commentary (Nashville: Broadman & Holman Publishers, 2000), 239.

Wrapping it up!

Do you want to see your church get back in the game? Ministry should be fun. A church restart is one of those things a rapidly declining church can do to see it get back to doing meaningful ministry. Do not wait like so many of the churches I have initially worked with when considering a restart. If you as the leader and the church as a whole wait too long it can be the most devastating thing to everyone. There is no reason to give up a church and sell the land to developers. If you are not up to the task, allow your director of missions to come along side of you and add value by working to develop a team which could lead your church through the process. You will be so glad you did.

Chapter 4
Conditions that Lead to a Restart

Anyone who won't shoulder his own cross and follow behind me can't be my disciple. "Is there anyone here who, planning to build a new house, doesn't first sit down and figure the cost so you'll know if you can complete it? If you only get the foundation laid and then run out of money, you're going to look pretty foolish. Everyone passing by will poke fun at you: 'He started something he couldn't finish.' "Or can you imagine a king going into battle against another king without first deciding whether it is possible with his ten thousand troops to face the twenty thousand troops of the other? And if he decides he can't, won't he send an emissary and work out a truce? "Simply put, if you're not willing to take what is dearest to you, whether plans or people, and kiss it good-bye, you can't be my disciple.71

It is an established fact that many churches in America are in a death spiral and the result will be that thousands will close their doors if there is no intervention. In fact, we are told that between 4,000 and 4,500 close their doors in any given year, give or take a few. Many churches are merely trying to survive on a journey to certain death. For some, that death may be sooner that the congregation thinks. These churches need assistance. They need an awakening to their need of a restart.

To make things worse, statisticians say that there seems to be a migration away from churches of an estimated 3,500 people a day. The question is: Can this be reversed? Can we stop this deadly spiral? The answer lies in the hearts and hands of those who are members of those dying churches.

In early 2017 I was asked to lead a revitalization project in a church in the city where I live. At one time the church

---

71 Eugene H. Peterson, The Message: The Bible in Contemporary Language (Colorado Springs, CO: NavPress, 2005), Luke 14:27–33.

had been a thriving church with 450 in attendance, but they had declined to an average of 15. Through the years several things happened that changed the total make-up of the area where the church is located. It didn't take long to realize that there was no mere revitalization process that could bring new life to this ailing congregation. It was doomed to die! We began to talk to the few that remained about dying with dignity and allowing its legacy to remain by restarting the church. They agreed and while I write this chapter the restart is moving forward. During my time with this church and others in which God has allowed me to minister, I have found many of the same conditions that prevail in every case.

Why would any church continue a march toward death without any effort to change course? Actually, there is a more pressing question: What conditions can be found in these churches that would cause them to die? Allow me to share fourteen conditions that were present in the dying church that I mentioned and in others where I have worked as a Church Revitalizer.

The Presence of Deadly Denial

The biggest obstruction to any form of church revitalization is the unwillingness of a church and/or the pastor to admit that a problem exists. Churches and pastors simply refuse to admit that they are ailing and in need of outside help. Many of the churches that are prime candidates for restart have declined by as much as 90% and yet they refuse to admit there is a problem. In many of the cases the testimony of the church has been sullied by a church split, open infighting and internal conflict. As a result, there is little or no witness to the community in which the church is located. This often results in the church turning inward, resulting in the community turning its back on the church and ignoring its existence. Most, if not all, of these churches have not seen a convert in several years; yet they continue to wonder why things are as they are. Thom Rainer sounded the alarm that each church would be wise to heed. He said, "Denial is deadly. Denial means the problems are not addressed. Denial means more and more churches will be closing their doors."[72] Rainer continues to say that, if the decline is ignored, the problem will only get bigger and the chances of salvaging the church will be less.

The church that is unwilling to admit that it needs help is usually the church that has ignored God's leadership in the past. When a church admits it needs help early in the decline, it is much easier to accept a solution. The sad reality is that most churches are clinging to the past and reminisces about the "good old days" when everything was going great in the church. They are convinced, within themselves, that everything is ok. As a result, they are so proud of the past that they cannot face the present to save the future of the church.

Most churches that arrive at this juncture are usually disobedient and self-willed. Steady decline in such churches comes because of disobedience, mediocrity and apathy. As one blogger put it, "they are just too proud to admit that they are sick."

Stubbornness is a major element in the unwillingness to admit there is a problem. It's much like one older matriarch said about her church when a change that would bring new life to the church was discussed. She said, "This is my church and there will be no changes until I die. After that you can do anything you want to do." What a tragic statement for an

---

72 Rainer, Thom. "Ten Dangers of Denial in A Declining Church," Lifeway Christian Resources, March 5, 2014, https://thomrainer.com/2014/03/ten-dangers-of-denial-in-a-declining-church/

elderly person to make. That statement did, however, define the future of that church.

Jesus, addressing the church at Laodicea in Revelation 3:17-18 says it best, *"Because thou sayest, I am rich, and increased with goods, and have need of nothing; and knowest not that thou art wretched, and miserable, and poor, and blind, and naked: I counsel thee to buy of me gold tried in the fire, that thou mayest be rich; and white raiment, that thou mayest be clothed, and that the shame of thy nakedness do not appear; and anoint thine eyes with eye salve, that thou mayest see."*[73] The Laodicean church was convinced that they were fine until Jesus made it clear to them that they were sick and needed help.

Often the church that refuses to admit need is lax in standing for a pure doctrine that will convict of sin and bring sinners to a place of repentance. Most of the time the leadership in this kind of church has settled into a niche of selfish leadership that has a strangle hold on the church and if that leadership continues the church will die. There usually does not exist a real sense of community because one or two people are making poor decisions for which everyone else will pay the price.

The church in need of a restart must learn that humility is a virtue and that admitting the need for help is the beginning step toward wholeness again.

Change in Community Demographics

The demographics of American communities are ever-changing. The church is caught in these changes and must change with the demographics if they are to remain a viable force for righteousness in society. One of the most obvious conditions that causes a church to decline to the point that a

---

73 Rev. 3:17-18 KJV.

restart is necessary is the inability or the refusal to adapt to the changes in demographics around the church community.

As communities get older the population gets older. As schools change the makeup of the community changes. In fact, the makeup of any given community can change so drastically in 10 years that it looks very little like it did the decade before. The reality is that as a community changes the needs, ideas and attitudes of the community will change as well. The challenge for the church is to adapt to meeting those needs with the Gospel of Jesus Christ.

The stark reality is, however, that in most instances the congregation chooses to ignore the changes and the church drifts into a death spiral that is difficult to stop. Many of the members of congregations that find themselves in a changing community want to live in the past when things were comfortable and familiar. As a result, many will refuse to change to meet the needs of the changing community demographics.

This is a difficult situation for any church because personalities, often different cultures, races and certainly different age groups are involved. In such a setting the church cannot remain static. The church must look like its community if it meets the needs of that community. A different culture may require a different approach to ministry. Please note that we are talking about approach to ministry, not the message of the ministry. In a changing demographic the community may have many and varied belief systems but that must never dictate the message of the church. You can never adjust the message to satisfy any group, culture, ethnicity or race of people. Herein lies the difficulty of a church to minister in a changing demographic. In most instances for the church, the problem lies in the fact that they simply refuse to adapt. In some instances, there is a reluctance to approach the changing demographics because the church does not know how. In some instances, the church may simply be fearful of the situation and the fear leads to a reluctance to approach the problem. It is, however, a very difficult situation for the traditional, established church congregation to deal with but if they do not adapt…the church will surely die!

The pastor plays a key role in how the church approaches the problem of changing demographics. Bill Henard says in his book *Can these Bones Live?* "…a pastor needs to be aware of, not just the demographic shifts in the area, but also the attitudes the church maintains because of these changes."[74] Changes in the community almost always lead to a decline in the church but if the pastor is astute, adjustments can easily be made to meet the needs of that changing community.

Infectious Lazy Leadership

Laziness is infectious! A lazy pastor will always produce lazy followers. The adage "birds of a feather flock together" is blatantly true in the church. Lazy pastors lead lazy people. Therein lies the condition that often leads a church to death and the need for a restart.

Leadership is the most critical issue in a church restart. John Maxwell says, "everything rises and falls on leadership." Leadership is the catalyst that brings effectiveness to the restart process. Leadership is charged with the task of moving the church into a revitalized life of effectiveness. It is leadership that influences people to change bad habits the church has drifted into over years of disobedience to God. At the same time, it takes great leadership to persevere when the opposition to revitalization comes.

---

74 Bill Henard, *Can These Bones Live: A Practical Guide to Church Revitalization* (Nashville, B&H Publishing, 2015), 129.

Acts 20:28 says, *"Take heed therefore unto yourselves, and to all the flock, over the which the Holy Ghost hath made you overseers, to feed the church of God, which he hath purchased with his own blood."*[75] It is the pastor leader who is responsible to the Lord for how he leads the people of God. If he is lazy the church could surely die.

Lazy leadership will always kill the *mission* of the church. To be truthful, it is *unfaithful stewardship* of the calling that God gives a leader. Laziness in a leader, especially a pastor, will often mean to *squander opportunities* that the church may have in reaching a community. The lazy pastor is one who usually *disconnects* from his congregation and by his laziness refuses to care for them as the Word of God demands. The lazy pastor is seldom, if ever, accused of over work. In fact, many are known for their "don't care" attitude. Many lazy pastors depend on their personal charisma to carry them thru the role as a pastor but below the surface there remains shallow and inefficient concern for the work that God has called them to.

Laziness is a sin! It is sinful because it neglects the gifts and opportunities that God gives to the leader. Proverbs 6:6-11 says it well… *"Go to the ant, thou sluggard; consider her ways, and be wise: which having no guide, overseer, or ruler, provideth her meat in the summer, and gathereth her food in the harvest. How long wilt thou sleep, O sluggard? when wilt thou arise out of thy sleep? Yet a little sleep, a little slumber, a little folding of the hands to sleep: So shall thy poverty come as one that travelleth, and thy want as an armed man."*[76] Then in Proverbs 18:9 the Bible says, *"He also that is slothful in his work is brother to him that is a great waster."*[77] And finally, look at Proverbs 24:30-34, *"I went by the field of the*

---

75 Acts 20:28 KJV.

76 Proverbs 6:6-11 KJV.

77 Proverbs 18:9 KJV.

slothful, and by the vineyard of the man void of understanding; and, lo, it was all grown over with thorns, and nettles had covered the face thereof, and the stone wall thereof was broken down. Then I saw, and considered it well: I looked upon it, and received instruction. Yet a little sleep, a little slumber, a little folding of the hands to sleep: So, shall thy poverty come as one that travelleth; and thy want as an armed man."[78]

You should notice how the writer of Proverbs repeats a very important statement in the Proverbs 6 and Proverbs 24 passage. He says in both, *"Yet a little sleep, a little slumber, a little folding of the hands to sleep: So, shall thy poverty come as one that travelleth, and thy want as an armed man."* In other words, laziness will end in *destruction.* The lazy leader brings reproach to the Lord Jesus and His church. The church is personal to Jesus. He died for it. He gave himself for it. It is His bride. So, for the pastor to be lazy in his leadership of the church is an affront to the Lord Jesus and His church.

Disconnect from the Holy Spirit

One of the most tragically neglected necessities of the church is the presence and power of the Holy Spirit. It is important to say that a "real" presence and manifestation of the presence and power of the Holy Spirit is missing from the average church. This reflects itself in an absence of the presence of God in worship when the church gathers. In such cases the worship service becomes man's effort at approaching God and seeking God while lacking the presence and power of the Holy Spirit in its efforts. In such instances people gather with no purpose. Sermons are preached with no power. Therefore, there is no power to convict of sin or a call to repentance to the people of God.

The Holy Spirit is the most important ingredient in Church health! The church that can minister in this 21st century world must be a Holy Spirit powered church! The

---

78 Proverbs 24:30-34 KJV.

church can function as the Lord intended only if it is powered by the Holy Spirit. It is in the midst of this atmosphere, when the world is careening toward chaos, that church leaders are wondering why their churches are plateauing or declining. The Church, by God's design, must be Holy Spirit powered to succeed in doing the will of God. The Spirit must accompany purpose. Without the power of the Spirit, purpose only becomes wishful thinking.

The Holy Spirit gives power to the paper and ink of Holy Scripture. The Holy Spirit guides us in the proper understanding of the Scripture. Without the Holy Spirit, we cannot understand the deep truths of the Word of God. The Spirit is our comforter and our guide, our Paraclete (παρακλητος)!

It is the empowering of the Spirit of God that makes the difference in the life of the man of God. David recognized the necessity of Holy Spirit power in his life. (Psalm 51:11) It was the prophet Joel who gave the word of the Lord concerning a day in the future when the Lord said, "...*that I will pour out My Spirit on all flesh; ...*" (Joel 2: 28).[79]

The Holy Spirit can be grieved. This happens because the Holy Spirit is sensitive to the needs and the behavior of man. When we revert to our old habits it grieves Him. When the church ignores Him, it leads to spiritual death.

Furthermore, the Holy Spirit can be quenched. The church must live according to the leadership of the Holy Spirit and when it fails to do so the Spirit is quenched and the work of the church ceases. In either of these situations the church could end in a death spiral that would lead the church to a restart that would instill the presence and power of the Holy Spirit back into the leadership role of the church.

---

79 Joel 2:28 KJV.

First Samuel 4 shows that Israel knew the power of God's presence and how they prospered and were strengthened when they faithfully followed the Lord. When Israel made the choice to turn from God, then the presence of God was no longer among them. The story of how the "glory departed" from Israel is a stark reminder that the glory of God can also depart from the church of the living God. The passage tells of the Israelite army being plundered by the Philistine army, so the Israelite army decided to bring the Ark of the Covenant onto the battlefield. Everything was going well until the Philistine army gained the upper hand and defeated the Israelites and took captive the Ark. As a result, the two sons of Eli, Hophni and Phinehas, were slain. A messenger was sent to Eli to tell him of the tragedy and the defeat. As the messenger gave the grim news, Eli fell backwards in his chair, broke his neck and died. The glory had departed. In I Samuel 4: 20-22 we have the record of Eli's daughter-in-law, the wife of Phinehas who was expecting a child. When she heard the bad news that her husband and father-in-law were dead, she went into labor and died **in** child birth. The Scripture says, *"And about the time of her death the women who stood by her said to her, 'Do not fear, for you have borne a son.' But, she did not answer, nor did she regard it. Then she named the child Ichabod, saying 'The glory has departed from Israel!' because the ark of God had been captured and because of her father-in-law and her husband being dead, and she said, 'The glory has departed from Israel for the ark of God has been captured.'"* Notice she named her son "Ichabod," which means: "The glory has departed." Because of the disobedience of Israel, they were defeated and "The glory departed from Israel."[80]

Another Biblical example can be found in Revelation 3: 14-22. Notice when Jesus spoke to the church at Laodicea, the members of the church thought everything was well, but Jesus told them they were "wretched, and miserable, and

---

80 I Samuel 4:20-22 KJV.

poor, and blind, and naked." In fact, the Spirit of God had left the church and they did not even know it. There is a statement in that passage that is often overlooked. Jesus said, "Behold I stand at the door and knock. If anyone hears My voice and opens the door, I will come in to him and dine with him, and he with Me." If Jesus was knocking…He was knocking to get in. So, He must have been outside.

It is clear from the scripture that when a church disconnects from the presence and power of the Holy Spirit it surely writes its own death warrant. Many of these churches die a slow and embarrassing death. But there is a possibility of life after death for these churches with a restart process.

Nitpicking Power Brokers

The truth is that there is no area of life where power brokers are not present. They are in communities, business, social organizations, politics, and even in the church. Often these power brokers will kill the organization they serve.

The problem of power mongering in the church is seen when people cease in seeking the glory of God and begin to look for and depend on getting recognition and pats on the back by men. This causes people to seek positions and titles that will make them feel more powerful and as a result become a power monger. This is a grave danger in the local church. Every pastor can tell horror stories about their encounter with a power broker in the church. The problem is so big that many churches are literally killed by the never-ending carping criticisms of the power mongers.

It is safe to say that it is possible that these trouble makers have never been saved or at least they are backslidden spiritually. Where there is a power broker there is usually a void of the presence and power of the Holy Spirit. Thom Rainer says about power brokers, "These church members often are the informal but true decision makers of the church. Some of them have great influence. Some of them are big financial givers to the church. Some of them are both."[81]

There are not only power brokers in the church but there are power "structures" in the church as well. They are usually controlled by a very influential power broker. These people always operate off of a love for power and control. Their efforts can be devastating to the local church.

A good example of power mongering is found in Acts 8:18-24 which says, *"And when Simon saw that through laying on of the apostles' hands the Holy Ghost was given, he offered them money, saying, 'give me also this power, that on whomsoever I lay hands, he may receive the Holy Ghost.' But Peter said unto him, thy money perish with thee, because thou hast thought that the gift of God may be purchased with money. Thou hast neither part nor lot in this matter: for thy heart is not right in the sight of God. Repent therefore of this thy wickedness, and pray God, if perhaps the thought of thine heart may be forgiven thee. For I perceive that thou art in the gall of bitterness, and in the bond of iniquity. Then answered Simon, and said, pray ye to the Lord for me, that none of these things which ye have spoken come upon me."[82]* When power mongers get active, the devil is active. We know that the devil hates the church and everything it stands for, so he will seek to destroy it by any means possible and often it is done through self-appointed power brokers in the church itself.

There are several different categories of power brokers in the church and each can be a tool of Satan. Let's examine them.

---

81 Thom Rainer, "Ten Fears of Church Leaders," *Lifeway Christian Resources Blog,* April 5, 2014, accessed July 13, 2018, https://thomrainer.com.

82 Acts 8:18-24 KJV.

First, is the *"know it all"* broker. They always have a better idea and everyone else is expected to accept that idea and be happy with it. They project the idea that everyone else is incapable of knowing the will of God and understanding what God is seeking to do in the church. Sometimes these brokers have a very deceived following of people in the church because of their ability to influence others. They are much like E. F. Hutton, "when they speak everyone listens." Often it is this broker that possesses a position of power and if one ever disagrees with them that person will become their "enemy" and they seek to discredit and or dismiss them. They are very difficult to deal with.

Second, there is the *"wannabe"* broker. They really have no power with a large group of people, but they really strive toward a position of authority. These people are not to be taken lightly because it only takes a few persistent people to cause a real problem that could kill the church. Usually their power comes from their role or elected position in the church. They will, however, usually acquiesce to a stronger power broker.

Third, is the *"displaced"* broker. These power mongers are usually in a place of no authority on their job or in their business and when they get just a little power it "goes to their head" and they become very difficult to deal with. Any power given to them in the local church is an opportunity to be the boss and show everyone their misguided power and authority.

Fourth, is the *"undercover"* broker. They are seldom in the forefront of any controversy because they have their followers to do their dirty work. This is probably the most difficult power broker to detect because they exercise their power behind the scenes as they give instructions to their subservient followers. These power mongers are very dangerous to the wellbeing of any church because having a hidden identity seems to give more courage to the broker and they tend to do more damaging things to pastors and congregations.

Finally, there is the *"manipulative"* broker. These brokers know how to politic to get their way and to cause trouble. They know how to work through other people while they are very open about their role in the problem or trouble. They endear people to themselves so that when criticism comes their way, their followers will rally alongside them and defend them to the end.

Almost all these power brokers gather cliques around themselves. Some are more powerful than others. All are very detrimental to the future and well-being of the local church. Many churches die and find themselves helpless because of the constant work of one or more power brokers in the congregation.

Dwindling Dollars

Churches are closing their doors every day because of dwindling finances. Statistics show that in less than one quarter into a new church year the average church budget is already running behind. Good financial health in the local church is always seen in at least four areas. First, is the church's good financial care of its pastor and staff. Second, is the paying, without difficulty, of its everyday operational costs. Third, is the church giving regularly to missions at home and abroad. Fourth, is the ability of the church to maintain its existing facilities and keep them presentable to the public.

Sad to say, that many churches are not able to succeed in the four areas mentioned above. The problem has been developing for a long time in the church world. Over the past many years giving to the church has decreased steadily. This has resulted in many churches cutting their budgets, cutting staff positions and even cutting pastor's salaries and benefits. This problem is not just found in the church. In fact, giving to benevolent and nonprofit entities has fallen short for several years as well. Churches are having a rude awakening when they run out of money and must close their doors. That is when a restart is necessary.

There are a number of churches that are in financial straits as this book is being written. Many are on that downhill slippery slope that leads to death and closing their doors or, at least, they have an ineffective ministry because of a lack of funds. The reason for this decline of income for churches is seen in at least four areas.

First, in many of the older established churches most members are older and are on a *"fixed income."* As churches age the more prevalent this problem becomes. Those on a fixed income are seldom able to give more than a tithe if they give that much. This takes a large chunk of money out of the church's coffers and if there is no other source of income it could be fatal to the future of the church.

Second, is a *"lack of understanding of Biblical tithing."* If a church is made up of senior adults who are on a fixed income then the middle aged to young adults giving, in most cases, will be inadequate to meet the financial needs of the church. The reason is simple; most young adults and many middle-aged adults have never been taught the importance of Biblical tithing to the work of the Lord. Giving is not a priority to many in this present generation because they prefer to spend their money on things that bring quick gratification and satisfaction. We must be reminded of the words of Jesus when He said, "where your treasure is, there will your heart will be also" (Matt. 6:21). They think that it is not spiritually required of them, so they use their money in many other endeavors. Furthermore, when a church is dying or dead, few people will be motivated to invest their finances in it.

This leaves the church with a large financial deficit. It is simple: few people are supporting the church with their tithes and offerings.

Third, is the *"mishandling of funds."* It is essential that money given to the church be handled properly. Mishandling of funds in this context is not necessarily embezzlement or that sort of thing, but it is, however, making sure that the money is being handled properly and securely. Many churches find themselves in a bind by spending more than they take in while others, when they get in a bind, begin to deplete any savings that they might have. One such example is in central North Carolina. The church membership, over the past 15 years, had fallen from 450 down to 18. The church did not take in much in tithes and offerings because almost everyone left in the church was on a fixed income. At the same time the church was paying a bi-vocational pastor, a pianist and a bookkeeper. The salaries, however, were being paid out of their savings of $32,000. The church survived 2 years this way, and now it is in the midst of a restart process. This church should have not been paying salaries. Instead it should have made an early commitment to a restart. As a result, the church died.

Fourth, some churches *"over extend"* and they get into financial straits and die a slow death. How the church handles the money given is an important element in the health of the church. Often a church will get overextended by building buildings much larger than they need thinking that if they build it people will come. We know that is a fallacy. Furthermore, some churches get overextended by having too many staff members for the size of the congregation and in some cases salaries that are much higher than the church can afford. Churches are accountable to God for the way they handle the money. Dennis Bickers said it best in his book *The Healthy Small Church,* "A church will never be healthier than its finances."

Refusing to Change

I don't know of anyone who likes to change unless they initiated the change. It does not matter how old or how young, how educated or uneducated or whether you are a man, woman, boy or girl. Put simply...no one likes change!

Bill Henard in his book, *Can These Bones Live?* states, "Initiating change represents one of the most difficult tasks, if not the most difficult task, that pastors face. Whether one desires to instill an evangelistic DNA into a plateaued congregation or just wants to initiate new ministries or programs, change proves difficult, even impossible."[83] One of the favorite last sayings in the average church is "we ain't never done it that way before." These are the words of a dying church.

Some years ago, during a church revitalization project in a small country church a revitalizer was sharing about some things that desperately needed to change in the life of the small congregation. After the revitalizer finished sharing, an elderly person came to him and said, "I'm 87 years old and been in this church all of my life and you are not changing anything here until I die. Then I don't care what you do with this church." You might be saying "Wow, what an attitude!" The fact is though, you can multiply that attitude many, many times over in churches across this land. Because of this "no change", unspoken policy in the local church, 4000 churches per year close their doors. No doubt change is painful, but it is necessary to stay alive.

Some churches will change but they are very slow at the task. Many of our churches are years behind societal norms. As a result, the church becomes more and more irrelevant to the community. If the church is to survive, change is

---

83 Bill Henard, *Can These Bones Live; A Practical Guide to Church Revitalization* (Nashville: B&H Publishing, 2015), 209.

necessary. There is no choice. It is, in most cases, change or die!

Why would a church member or a church resist change if it would bring new hope and new life to the congregation? Research reveals several reasons;

- *Unwillingness to break ties with the past.*
- *It threatens the established traditions of the church and church members.*
- *It threatens the leader's positions of authority.*
- *It takes a congregation into unknown territory.*
- *They see change as an enemy…against anything and everything the church ever professed to be.*
- *They get offended at what they need to give up rather than encouraged about what they will gain.*
- *The older members simply don't see the need for the change even though the church is dying.*
- *Some believe that the changes will not make a difference in the future of the church.*

Acts 15 is a perfect example of the church dealing with change. This example is much like what many churches are facing today. This entire chapter deals with the Jerusalem Council when the discussion turned to accepting Gentiles into the ranks of the church. Up until this point the Jewish Christian had dominated the church but now the gentile Christians were threatening their position so Paul and Barnabus went to Jerusalem to speak to the issue. Part of the dispute had to do with circumcision because certain Jews said the gentile Christians should be circumcised. Paul, however, made it clear that circumcision was not necessary because the Gentiles trusted Christ by faith just like the Jewish Christian did. This represents the first big change the early church had to deal with. They met the need for change head on and the church grew by leaps and bounds.

The dislike for change has always been present in the church. The truth is; however, we cannot avoid change. Everything in our lives changes daily. When we get out of bed in the morning, we wake up having experienced change during the night. When we retire for the evening, we retire a changed person from the morning when we arose. Our natural world is ever-changing. We are ever-changing. Change is real. So, if the church is going to survive it will have to change, or it will become so weak that it is useless, or it will simply die a very slow death.

Jeff Woods said, "While quantitative research shows that 61 percent of all worshipper's report that they are ready for their congregation to try something new, qualitative research reveals that many members will accept the new thing only if it is in their own self-interest or not too different from what they already have."[84]

The key to accepting change is to realize that God will carry the church through. He knows the need and He will bring success. It is His church and He will bless it.

The Tragedy of No God-Given Vision

A God-given *vision* is a clear, challenging picture of the future of a church's ministry that is fueled by the conviction that it can be accomplished with God's provision. Without a clear God-given vision, the church has no future because it has no direction. Dan Southerland said, "We must keep dreaming and keep visioning to keep our churches, ministries, and personal lives from perishing."[85] The truth is that most

---

84 Jeff Woods, "New Tasks for the New Congregation: Reflections on Congregational Studies," *Resources for American Christianity,* 2003, accessed July 1, 2018, at <http//resourcingchristianity.org.

85 Dan Southerland, *Transitioning* (Grand Rapids, Zondervan Publishing House, 2002), 24.

pastors have no clue about a vision from God for their church and in turn the church has no clue either. When a church has no vision, it exists in a vacuum of failure.

The importance of a vision for the local church cannot be underestimated. A church with no vision is a church that is doomed to failure. A church ministry's vision begins with and is the primary responsibility of the pastor. If the pastor is visionless concerning spiritual matters the church will flounder and loose its effectiveness. "Few things are more important to effective leadership than vision. Good leaders foresee something out there, vague as it might appear from the distance, that others don't see. Godly leaders who are followers of Christ must first have a vision of who God is and the future he holds for them. They must also have a sense of what God has called them to do."[86] Leadership must never be afraid to believe God and attempt the things that God leads them to do. The first task of any pastor is to set the vision, the God given vision for the church.

The process of visioning is as important as the vision itself. Just any old vision will not do. It cannot be the preacher's concocted vision. It cannot be some perceived vision of the people that stems from some personal desire or agenda. A true vision has its origination in the heart of God Himself. If it is not God's vision for the church it will doom the church to failure. Here is the process: GOD possesses the Vision. HE Imparts it to the PASTOR. The Pastor shares it with the PEOPLE. Finally, the PEOPLE live it out in a LOST world.

If the church *lives in a vacuum of no vision* the congregation has no clear direction for ministry. It has no planned approach to meeting the needs of a lost community. The leadership will not function properly because they have no purpose or clear plan of action. A vision always promotes

---

86 Kenneth Boa, "Vision," Leadership Qualities, (November 4, 2005): accessed July 15, 2018, https://bible.org/seriespage/13-vision.

passion and risk-taking. It provides the energy to accomplish the ministry task. In fact, a clear vision will promote and facilitate giving on the part of the congregation because they see the purpose and direction of the church and want to be a part of its ministry.

Lyle Schaller says that "Without a vision of a new tomorrow, we are all inclined to attempt to do yesterday all over again."[87] Many churches continue to do the same things over and over, even when what they do is not fruitful. Some churches have settled in to a pattern of activity that goes back decades while no vision for the future exists. This is a deadly approach to ministry and accounts for why 90% of Evangelical churches in America are plateauing or declining. Without a vision the church will die a slow unfruitful death.

One final thought about the vacuum of vision is that a God given, clear vision has a unifying element. A church that is going in the same direction with the same purpose will be united for the task. A church that has no vision, direction, or purpose is bound for conflict and disunity. In fact, many church splits are a direct result of visionless pastors who lead visionless churches!

Failing Facilities

The question each church should ask itself is "What do people think when they pass our church?" Facilities can create a hindrance to the church's spiritual health. The message your building sends to the community around it is very important. What do visitors and guests think when they attend the church? Failing facilities turns people off and causes people to look elsewhere for a place to worship. No one would allow their home to get in the physical condition of some churches. "The church building always seems to be

---

87 Lyle E. Schaller, *Innovations in Ministry: Models for the 21st Century* (Nashville: Abingdon Press, 1994), 96.

the downfall or albatross for churches. The repairs or maintenance of the building becomes too big of a burden to bear for small congregations and either depletes the savings or endowment fund or goes ignored and the building falls in further disrepair."[88]

Often the reason for a failing facility is a lack of funds. As stated previously, when a church ages out and everyone is on a fixed income; it becomes quite difficult to keep buildings in worthy repair. Costly repairs can be disastrous to the struggling church. Well-kept buildings may not drive church growth, but it is clear that failing facilities will certainly hinder growth.

The "law of first impressions" is real on Sunday morning when people visit the church. What they see initially in their visit will usually leave a lasting impression and may well be the determining factor as to whether they will return or not.

The truth is that every church building sends a message. That message may be quite welcoming, or it may be offensive in nature. It is offensive because it is 25 years behind times and it has become disconnected from the culture and community. Usually the last people to see the need for repairs or facelifts will be the congregation. They are accustomed to seeing what they see each week. They simply are not on the outside looking in like a guest would be. The church needs to ask the question, how are our facilities looking? Most often, when a church facility falls into disrepair and lacks proper maintenance, it reflects the spiritual health of the congregation itself.

---

88 Theresa Cho, "10 Problems of a Dying Church and How to Fix Them," *Sojourners* (July 2011); accessed July 17, 2018, https://sojo.net/articles/10-problems-dying-church-and-how-fix-them.

One final word about failing facilities…everything the church does communicates a message to the community. Is your church communicating the right message?

Inward Survival Mode

The word "focus" in the dictionary means "a central point, as of attraction, attention, or activity." The key idea here is where attention is placed in a situation. "Inward" focus means the church pays more attention to the inner wants and desires and needs of the existing congregation. "Outward" focus means the church is giving attention to the world around it with the greater intention of sharing the Gospel.

Without exception every church that dies or is dying has turned exclusively inward in its approach to ministry. This is one of the major danger signs that a church is failing. Every church will have a degree of inward focus but the church that is sick will have no outward focus. Often pastors are pushed into an exclusively inward focus because of unreasonable demands of the existing congregation. Churches sometimes turn to an inward focus because of inner conflict and disunity brought about by power struggles and pride.

Most Church Revitalizers agree that an inward shift in ministry is almost always fatal. Inward focus turns all efforts of ministry to the congregation with the exclusion of the real task of the church of reaching a lost world. Inward focus has no evangelistic thrust and no community ministry. Worship, finances, fellowship and activities are all geared to the existing congregation. As a result, there is no attempt to minister to the community the church resides in. Usually, the church lives in the past almost, revering it. The church loses all perspective as to why it exists and for God's plan for its ministry because there is no God-given vision or purpose.

When all of this takes place, the church ceases to be a Great Commission Church!

There are numerous warning signs that a church has turned inward and most of them reflect an attitude of self-centeredness and selfishness. Some of the signs are as follows:

- *Focus on programs rather than people.*
- *A budget that only meets the needs of the existing congregation.*
- *More and more opposition to any kind of change.*
- *Everyone thinks that the church owes them something rather than having a servant's heart.*
- *More and more demands on the pastoral staff to meet the needs of the existing congregation.*
- *No desire to reach the lost or grow the church.*

These are by no means all the signs, but they are indicative of many churches that have turned inward in its focus.

Probably the most tragic result of an inward focused church is that it has lost its sensitivity to the needs of the lost masses around the church. It loses its sense of mission and purpose. As a result, the church community is ignored, and people remain lost without a witness! The fact is that any church that is not reaching new people with the Gospel is already in the downward spiral toward death.

Many churches that have turned inward have reverted to a survival mode. They have become weak in leadership. Weak in finances. Weak in manpower. They only exist to survive week by week. These churches are never going to pull out of the spiral except by restart.

Desertion from Evangelism

Another major condition that leads a church to a restart is a lack of intentional evangelism. When a church enters the downward spiral toward death one of the conditions is always an abandonment of evangelistic efforts. A growing church is called to an evangelistic lifestyle. Acts 1:8 says *"But ye **shall** receive power, after that the Holy Ghost is come upon you: and ye **shall** be witnesses unto me both in Jerusalem, and in all Judaea, and in Samaria, and unto the uttermost part of the earth."*[89] The key word here is SHALL. It does not say "I hope you will be" or "I'd like you to be" or even "If you'd desire to be." No, it says you SHALL be. The church has been given the enormous task of winning the lost to Jesus Christ. When a church ceases to be evangelistic…it ceases to be a New Testament church. In fact, it becomes good for nothing.

There are debates going on today in religious circles, on blogs and internet posts about the validity of evangelism in the local church. Topics like "Is it the church's place to evangelize?" and "What role does the church play in evangelizing the world?" These questions reveal a real lack of Biblical understanding that in the end will kill a church. Any church that ceases to be evangelistic is certain to fail and die a slow agonizing death.

Statistics show that many of the churches that are supposedly growing are growing only by transfer of membership. Most are not reaching people with the Gospel. There are new churches popping up everywhere that boast of great growth and success because of the large number attending their services when in fact they are growing at the expense of other churches in the area. In reality, transfer growth in the church is no growth at all.

---

89 Acts 1:8 KJV.

Evangelism is the only method of growing a great church because it is the New Testament method of church growth. The problem with little or no evangelism in the church is revealed in several failures of the church and its leaders. In most cases, when the church is not evangelistic, there has been little effort on the part of pastor and other leaders to model an evangelistic lifestyle to the congregation. This results in a congregation that sees no need for evangelism. Another failure is not teaching and preaching about the need for evangelism from the pulpits of our churches. It seems that preaching about evangelism is not in vogue in the church today. It's not important enough to preach and teach about anymore. Churches are not attractive to lost people anymore. They do not present themselves as welcoming to lost people and for the most part they shun lost people. When the people lose their passion for souls, the church begins to die. All through the book of Acts, during the birth of the church, it was stated numerous times, "and souls were added to the church daily." Listen, when people are not being saved regularly in the church the church is on a death spiral. It may take years to die but it will die if it doesn't change.

Here is the truth about the matter. If the pastor does not preach, teach and model evangelism…it will never be a matter of importance to the congregation. Churches that have no evangelism or evangelistic zeal are the churches that are dying and in need of a restart.

Bad Theology

Glenn Daman talks about what makes an effective church, "More often, there is little said regarding the theology and teaching of the church. Nevertheless, the church, without a solid theological and biblical base no longer has a basis for ministry. A church can survive and be reasonably successful without a clear understanding of its vision, but it cannot survive shoddy and incorrect theology."[90] Daman goes on to say that when a church has no clear Biblical theology as a basis the church becomes a mere social organization. Herein lies the problem with many churches currently. Bad theology will kill a church. It will zap the spiritual strength out of a congregation.

Some would ask the question, "Then what is the basis for good theology?" This discussion is not new in religious circles. Good and bad theology have been debated for centuries. The clear line drawn in the sand between good and bad theology is found in one's belief about the reliability and inspiration of Scripture. Without a high view of Scripture there will always be the possibility of bad theology creeping into the church. Many churches find themselves in difficult times because they have abandoned the Bible as their authority. The wisdom of the Word of God has been replaced by Mans wisdom and knowledge leaving the church void of any real spiritual depth.

For a church to grow and prosper spiritually there must be clear Biblical preaching. This is critical to the wellbeing of any congregation. It is sad to say that often, when a church wavers in its theology, the problem originated in the pulpit. When pastors do not proclaim the truth of the Bible it puts the wellbeing and future of that church in jeopardy. A church that finds itself living with bad theology must begin to rebuild its foundation of Biblical truth through Biblical preaching and teaching.

The value of good theology should never be underestimated when it comes to the health and spiritual wellbeing of the local church. Titus 2:1 says it thus, "But speak thou the things which become sound doctrine." A closer look at the verbiage in this verse shows a clearer

---

90 Glenn Daman, *Shepherding the Small Church* (Grand Rapids: Kregel Publications, 2002), 66.

meaning of the phrase, "sound doctrine". It could be, "healthy teaching." What an admonition for our time.

Problems arise in a congregation that can lead to spiritual death when bad theology is present. The intent of the Word of God is to, as Hebrews 4:12 puts it, be useful in rebuking and correcting the hearts, thoughts and actions of humanity. Bad theology cannot do that. So, mankind continues to live based on human wisdom; not on God's divine wisdom. Here are a few reasons that it is important for a church to possess good theology:

- *It presses individuals to live a Godly life.*
- *It enhances the real ministry of the local church.*
- *It is a requirement for the true church and the committed Christian.*
- *It points out to the Christian the presence of sin and gives answers to deal with that sin.*
- *We cannot build a great church on bad theology.*
- *Only the truth of God's Word (good theology) will suffice to meet sinful man's spiritual needs.*
- *Good theology will always foster church growth.*

The final point to be made about good theology in the church is that it allows for no compromise. In this age, compromise is expected. Those who will not compromise are marked as bigots and are ostracized by a compromising world. Good theology leaves no room for compromise. The reality is that many churches that are in the throes of death have compromised their church health because of bad theology.

Church Splits/Disunity

There has always been conflict between people, nations and yes…even in the church of God. Acts 15:39-40 records one such conflict between Paul and Barnabas. The conflict was over the fact that Barnabas wanted to take John Mark on the journey with them and Paul did not want to take him because John Mark had deserted them in Pamphylia. It says, "And the contention was so sharp between them, that they departed asunder one from the other: and so Barnabas took Mark, and sailed unto Cyprus; And Paul chose Silas, and departed, being recommended by the brethren unto the grace of God." Paul and Barnabas decided to go their separate ways. Conflict has always been in the church from the very beginning. It is how the church handles the conflict that determines the life or death of the church.

Church conflict is caused by various situations. Sometimes it comes from outside forces or situations and at other times it comes at the hand of inside forces. Disagreement and quarrels stemming from pride are the most common causes. People just naturally want their way, and many are willing to cause all kinds of trouble until they get what they want. Often, in smaller "family chapel" type churches, the conflict and disunity come at the feuding of two or more dominant families trying to wield power. More often than not this is the cause of many churches' horrible death.

Fear of the unknown that comes from an attempt to change things in the church can also cause disunity. There is a church in North Carolina that experienced this kind of conflict, so they decided to have a split and form two churches. The one church that left the existing church wanted to take the name of the former church with them and of course this caused a major conflict so the church that left simply tacked the number 2 to the end of their church's name. The community was left with two churches that were and are till this day quite unhealthy. I will call them (not their real name) Unity Baptist Church #1 and Unity Baptist Church #2. What an affront to the church and the Kingdom of God.

When a church has repeated conflict, people begin to get discouraged and they leave not wanting to be a part of bitterness and unkindness. Not only do many leave the church but the church gains a reputation in the community as a "fighting church" and no one will visit or want to be a part of it. The most irreparable thing that can happen is for conflict to taint the life of the church in the community. It is hard to regain a good reputation once it is lost!

If any church is to survive it must learn to deal with conflict when it comes. Godly remedies must be sought and put into practice or the church will sink into a death spiral that it can't pull out of. The church that is in a constant state of disunity and conflict has no hope other than inevitable death. These are the churches that will be dying in the next 5-8 years and will need to experience a restart.

Apathetic Church Members

An anonymous writer once said, "The nice thing about apathy is you don't have to exert yourself to show you're sincere about it." Most dictionaries describe apathy as a lack of emotion, feeling, interest or regard. The church that is apathetic is living in a state of spiritual indifference. There is nothing good about apathy. Apathy kills everything it touches. A good definition of apathy is "coming to a place where you don't care, and you really don't care that you don't care!" It really translates into spiritual indifference. This is the condition of many churches today and it is deadly.

When a church stops caring it will surely die. Apathy reveals itself in seeing the church and worship as insignificant and for the most part useless. Apathy always looks away from the spiritual needs of others and refuses to see the worth of a living soul. It's bad enough that the need for salvation of lost souls is ignored but it even brings about an unconcern for the Christians and their needs in the church.

Following closely behind is a real disregard for missions at home and abroad.

A Biblical example of an apathetic church is seen in Laodicea. Revelation 3:15-17 says, *"And unto the angel of the church of the Laodiceans write; These things saith the Amen, the faithful and true witness, the beginning of the creation of God; I know thy works, that thou art neither cold nor hot: I would thou wert cold or hot. So then because thou art lukewarm, and neither cold nor hot, I will spue thee out of my mouth. Because thou sayest, I am rich, and increased with goods, and have need of nothing; and knowest not that thou art wretched, and miserable, and poor, and blind, and naked:"* What a picture of apathy. Being neither cold nor hot is a horrible state for a church to be in.

Spiritual apathy and spiritual indifference can affect churches of all sizes and structure. Whether it is caused by conflict, bad leadership, bad theology or any other foe, it is deadly. For the church to be healthy it must deal with apathy. That's not an easy task because apathy is based on human emotions and for apathy to be dealt with the human emotion must be dealt with. The church that has grown apathetic should reflect back to better days, not trying to relive those days but remembering that God can and will do it again if He is trusted. The apathetic church must come to a place of repentance and confession. Apathy is a sin and like all sins it must be confessed, repented of and dealt with before the church can experience the fullness of joy once again. As the church repents, the strength of the church will be renewed, and new life can once again reveal itself in the congregation. If the church remains apathetic it will die, and the death will be slow and agonizing to the congregation.

Conclusion

It is important to note that this is not an exhaustive list of conditions in which churches find themselves when a restart is needed. The list is, however, the most common problems that lead a church to a restart. The problem is that many pastors and churches ignore these conditions and refuse to consider that the church's death is imminent.

When cancer in the human body is found early it can mean life or death. The proper medication and treatment can be administered after the diagnosis has been made. Treatment is administered and hope for future healing can be a reality. The church is like that cancerous body. Early detection and diagnosis can and often does mean new life.

Why a pastor or a congregation would ever refuse a diagnosis and let the church die a slow and hopeless death is a mystery, but it is happening every day as church after church closes its doors to never open them again.

Chapter Five
Do You Have the Right Stuff?
Churches Which are Viable Candidates for a Restart

But for right now, friends, I'm completely frustrated by your unspiritual dealings with each other and with God. You're acting like infants in relation to Christ, capable of nothing much more than nursing at the breast. Well, then, I'll nurse you since you don't seem capable of anything more. As long as you grab for what makes you feel good or makes you look important, are you really much different than a babe at the breast, content only when everything's going your way?[91]

Usually a declining church waits until it is far too late to turn it around by conventional means so that the only thing which is often left is for the church to consider a restart. There are dwindling churches which are small, and yet before it reaches a crisis mode they take the necessary actions to begin bringing about renewal. Some will renew by getting a new pastor who knows how to revitalize a church and has experience in doing so. There are churches that will merge with a stronger congregation and survive through a church merger. A few churches sitting on a financial war chest can simply pack up and move across town to a place with younger families and a growing population. What do you do though when a church and its members simply wear out and are unable to do anything to bring about a revitalized church? If you act promptly there is a great chance for the church through a restart to have new life. Some church revitalization restarts originate from the decline of others due to failure to remain on the cutting edge of community transitions. Sometimes our memories of how things use to be hinders us from seeing what we could become. I know that death is painful, Jesus Christ can bring something new out of the sorrow. But if you have read all of this and you are saying we

---

[91] Eugene H. Peterson, *The Message: The Bible in Contemporary Language* (Colorado Springs, CO: NavPress, 2005), 1 Corinthians 3:1–3.

have not done any of this and have waited until it is too late, then the good news is that you are a great candidate for a restart. The restart church revitalization model is being used all across North America. Any group working in the area of church revitalization should have a restart strategy if it is going to be a wise steward. One critical point from the start is a complete change of leadership and direction, as this is a must in order for this model to be successful. It is hard to admit sometimes but the concept of letting the declining or dying church die is huge if you are going to restart it and make it a growing new work. For good healthy change, there needs to be a spiritual death for that church. There is mixed opinion in the area of whether a church revitalization restart should close up for a time or continue on. I believe a case could be made for closing if not for even a short time. Some, to be fair, say that a rebirth of vision is all that is needed. That may be too optimistic. In my experience too unrealistic as well.

Ken Priddy shares relating to restarting a church:

"I came to realize that this attempt to restart what had been a dying church would need all of the pioneer spirit, entrepreneurial skill and even methodology of church planting, but it would need more. It would require shepherding the families that were the congregation of the former church. It would require working through policies and procedures that had been in place for decades. It would require instilling vision in people who had lost vision and it would require moving people who had been reactive and passive to become proactive and aggressive. Church planting is starting from scratch. This effort would require starting from less than scratch."92

---

92 Priddy, Kenneth Earl. *Restarting the Dying Church* Doctor of Ministry Dissertation, Reformed Theological Seminary, May 2001. Pg. 6.

Do You and Your Church Have the Right Stuff for a Restart?

Does your church have the right stuff for a restart? Do you as the Church Revitalizer have the right stuff to lead a restart effort? The reason far too many church replants take place today is because our denominations have done a meager job in developing and training restart pastors. It is left up to church revitalization organizations that are the boots on the ground groups because they have the necessary skill sets to teach and train while the others are trying to blow in from a fifty-thousand-foot level to rally churches to give their facilities to a church planting organization. Why not take the necessary time to walk with these churches and give them three years of your life to help bring about a restart?

I love the 1983 American epic historical film *The Right Stuff*. This adaptation of the non-fiction 1997 novel by Tom Wolfe chronicles the first 15 years of America's space program. By focusing on the lives of the Mercury astronauts, including John Glenn (Ed Harris) and Alan Shepard (Scott Glenn), the film recounts the dangers and frustrations experienced by those involved with NASA's earliest achievements. It also depicts their family lives and the personal crises they endured during an era of great political turmoil and technological innovation. I am fascinated how, for the astronauts, everything ramps up so quickly the last thirty-one seconds before launch. As the 120-ton space shuttle sits surrounded by almost 4 million pounds of rocket fuel, exhaling noxious fumes, visibly impatient to defy gravity, its on-board computers take command. Four identical machines, running identical software, pull information from thousands of sensors, make hundreds of milli-second decisions, vote on every decision, check with each other 250 times a second. A fifth computer, with different software, stands by to take control should the other four malfunctions. At T-minus 6.6 seconds, if the pressures, pumps, and temperatures are nominal, the computers give the order to light the shuttle main engines - each of the three engines firing off precisely 160 milliseconds apart, tons of super-cooled liquid fuel pouring into combustion chambers, the ship rocking on its launch pad, held to the ground only by bolts. As the main engines come to one million pounds of thrust, their exhausts tighten into beautiful blue diamonds of flame. Then and only then at T-minus zero seconds, if the computers are satisfied that the engines are running true, they give the order to light the solid rocket boosters. In less than one second, they achieve 6.6 million pounds of thrust. And at that exact same moment, the computers give the order for the explosive bolts to blow, and 4.5 million pounds of spacecraft lifts majestically off its launch pad.

What is the right stuff that Church Revitalizers need to restart a church? I have compiled what I believe to be the right set of behaviors to be a successful restart pastor. While I understand I might have missed one or two from your perspective, and while not a definitive list, these nine are the most significant ones you must possess.

Must Have a Vision to Restart the Church

A Church Revitalizer must have a deep yearning to restart the church and an undeniable vision for what it will be. Such a visionary leader is necessary for the restart. They have a vibrant vision for where they want to take the church, and they are able to communicate that vision and future direction in a captivating way that makes new and former church member to want to follow. Without a strong vision for the former church becoming the new church a restart is less likely to come into fruition. This behavior is so important that without it you should not venture into a restart. The church members from the former church will not join you and the new participants will not stick with you if you do not know where you are going.

The Church Revitalizer is Inquisitive

They are endlessly inquisitive. New ideas and actions are part of the restart strategy and the revitalizer is always thinking about how to advance the once dead church as it restarts and grows into a fully functioning church. Because of their inquisitiveness they are always gaining insights from others and seeking to make these insights work towards the best restart possible. They are not all that interested in cheerleaders as they are in thinkers seeking practices which will regrow the church. The thought and opinions of those who desire to be part of the restart effort are important to the Church Revitalizer. Such inquisitiveness leads a once dead church out of the doldrums and moves it towards it indented purpose of revitalization.

They are Unwavering Dogged Towards Achieving Their Objectives

They are unwavering dogged towards achieving their objectives. They are determined to achieve their goals. They will go around, underneath, over the top, or just bust straight through obstacles, but they will not be stopped. This determination is why they can restart a church when others are not able to do so. Their sermons are strong and their faith is even stronger.

The Restart Pastor is a Risk Taker

Risk taking is an essential ingredient in ministry for the Kingdom of God. Our Lord Jesus was a risk taker. Many of our much-remembered Bible heroes were risk takers. Abraham took a great risk when he was willing to sacrifice Isaac. Noah, at the bidding of God, built the Ark. Elijah took a risk against Ahab and Jezebel's false prophets. David took a risk no one else in the army was willing to take as he stood against Goliath. The paradox is that in the realm of organized religion, and even within many local churches, risk-taking is non-existent. In fact, it is often frowned upon. Most Christians in America have never taken a risk as most stay within recognizable confines their whole lifetime. Risk taking at times needs to be bold and calculated. Other times require the freedom to go with your instincts. A restart pastor must have a higher-than-average tolerance for risk.

Remember when Jesus challenged Peter to get out of the boat? *"Come!" He said. And climbing out of the boat, Peter started walking on the water and came toward Jesus."93* The Church Revitalizer needs to lead the church towards a new future. During his journey he will learn much about the need to take risks during this time for the cause of Christ. Eventually the church will stabilize. But stability can also make it hard to take risks and move onward.

One of our pastors has stated that as the leader of the Renovate Group, my passion and willingness to take risks would ultimately be what moves us into the future. I felt humbled to have him be so poignant. So here I am and perhaps you as well as a natural risk taker. In environments where conformity and uniformity are stressed so highly that those among us who dare to take risk can easily become prey. Yet that is exactly what the local church and this association needs to be today! Yes, there will

---

93 Matthew 14:29.

be times when one will be mistreated, misunderstood, mislabeled, and misrepresented. There will be times when you are allowing the natural seasons of ministry to catch up where you might be labeled by the non-risk taker as a settler. Yet ministerial risk takers are needed now perhaps more than ever. Risk takers are always looking ahead just over the horizon for that which might touch more people for the Lord Jesus. While settlers remain comfortable with the now, pioneers stretch churches and individuals towards something new and exciting. Our forefathers of this great association were pioneers and God needs for us to be ones as well. I challenge you to remain a strong support of your local association! We can do more things together than we can do on our own.

There are many differences between pioneers and settlers. Settlers wait until the pioneers have blazed the trails and fought the battles. The voice crying, "Is it safe out there?" is the settler. The voice calling back, "Sure, it is safe now" is the pioneer. God is shaking up this world in which we live. Uncertainty and fear are in the air. If God challenges you in the future to do something unusual, be willing to take the risk. Be true to who you are in Christ Jesus and do not compromise your integrity. Non-risk takers will strip your integrity away and if you let them, they will never let you be who God wants you to be. As a pastor and church leader I pray you will become one of those who are willing to take risks in order to advance the Kingdom of God. Risk taking will be required to transition our churches to meet the changing challenges of tomorrow. None of us know those challenges, but they are coming rapidly. I encourage you that when the time comes to rise up, do it, do not fear it, be willing, and take risks as necessary. Do not force God to have to go around you to find someone who is willing to the take risks for Him that He had positioned you to take. After all, is there really even a real risk involved when stepping out in faith to fulfill the will of God? No, there is no risk. The risk is when you do not step out on faith and you refuse to do something God has asked you to do. It could be because of: little faith, much fear, being too firmly set in one's ways, or allowing non-risk takers to influence you. Some Christ followers are faith driven, while others are just restless souls. No doubt movement brings things to the surface; however, restlessness is more a product of flesh than faith. A British Preacher said, *"A man would do nothing, if he waited until he could do it so well that no one would find fault with what he has done."* And, "Progress always involves taking risk; you cannot steal second base and keep your foot on first." There are those who are willing to dare to fail greatly which will ever achieve greatly. The pessimist whines about the wind. The optimist expects it to change. But it is the leader who adjusts the sails. There are those who appear to move without fear or trepidation at any number of tasks and they make the hardest task seem so simple. They make the impossible appear easy and the complicated seem elementary.

When we look at them, we admire the restart risk-takers. For without them our declining churches would be done, finished, over. Without them our lives would be even more difficult than we think it is. The restart pastor challenges those around him. They expand the boundaries of what is and what can be done for the cause of Christ! They shatter our perceptions and our pre-conceived opinions. Thank God for the restart pastors who are risk-takers and bring a fresh-air to the old, while bringing a brand-new vision to old dreams, which then become new dreams. We admire their strength. We admire their tenacity. We admire their courage. We admire them. Take some chances as a church and a Church Revitalizer in the name of the Lord Jesus Christ. God is faithful all the time.

The Restart Leader has a Clear Mandate

Church Revitalizers who lead out in restarting a church have a clear mandate from the Lord regarding the mission of the church. They have prayed about how to restart the church, have heard from the Lord, and they are willing to be all in for the work necessary to achieve the goal of restarting the church. Additionally, these restart leaders surround themselves with people who are likewise committed to the mission and mandate. They have a deep understanding of the wave that is necessary to turn around the church and are always seeking to move the participants forward towards health and vitality. These restart leaders are the first to spot something that will disrupt the ministry for the better and be in a position to take advantage of it. They are the ones at every church revitalization training event and have read the latest book that can help their church restart.

The Restart Leader Thinks Creatively

As the one who will lead the restart, there is a high demand for creativity since the lack of it was a portion of why the church has rapidly declined and is in need of a restart. Restart leaders must be the creative ones. There is no one else who initially can take that over for you. Trying to bring life back to a dead church takes a high degree of faith and creativity. Creating something new is part of a restart philosophy. If it is not you are in trouble. Restarting a church is not for followers, it is for leaders of church renewal. These creative restart pastors know their strengths and how to leverage them, but they also know their weaknesses and how to work around them.

The Restart Leader Recognizes the Big Picture

The Church Revitalizer must see the big things and recognize how he can utilize them for his advantage as a restart pastor. They understand and appreciate both the macro and the micro, and they can see how all the pieces fit. Before they start putting the pieces of the puzzle together, they look at the picture on the box. While working for the North American Mission Board in the Church Planting Group, my boss and vice president, Richard Harris had Dan Cathy in to speak to our group. He told a story that I have never forgotten. Dan shared that when Truett Cathy opened his first *Chick-fil-A* in Atlanta's Greenbriar Mall more than 35 years ago now, he saw something that no one else noticed: the consumer's insatiable appetite to shop and eat. Although his initial location at the Greenbriar Mall was not the best, the experience of being there formed the cornerstone of many food court operations in malls coast to coast. Cathy's ability to see the big picture truly paid off.

The Restart Pastor Creates a Positive Learning Environment

Restart pastors are always leading, learning, and guiding those who are on the journey with him. They are life learners and not afraid to listen to other people. Outstanding preachers, leaders and revitalizers are superb listeners and observers. Listen and you will learn. Listen and you are more likely to generate loyalty and commitment.

The Restart Leader Forges a Positive Attitude

Most successful restart pastors are optimists. Depression in the work of church revitalization is a danger. Leaders consumed with depression are not the best candidates for a restart. The optimistic Church Revitalizer will use their positive attitude to weather the rough spots. This is no easy task, especially with all the planning, fund raising and other innumerable elements involved in restarting a church. To stay upbeat and forward thinking is a must. Depressed leaders draw together a group of depressed individuals. Optimistic restart pastors will draw individuals which believe in the cause and will not take flight once something hard comes their way. Strengthen an optimistic attitude by reading, associating with positive people and keeping tabs on your own spiritual energy. As the restart leader, begin networking with other Church Revitalizers to re-energize ideas and goals. Cultivating the right stuff is no easy task. Once done, however, it is easy to see its impact on the church restart, inside and out.

The Church Revitalizer working towards a restart must recognize and understand their individual strengths and weaknesses. Learning to play to strengths and compensate for weaknesses can go a long way in cultivating the positive attitude and leadership skills necessary for success. If you are going to succeed, you will have to be able to identify what you do well and what you do not do so well. Do not panic if you discover that you have weaknesses, since we all have them. The key to success as a restart leader is not so much in having every behavior skill (although that would help) as it is in finding ways to compensate for the weaknesses. Normally, we like doing things we are good at and we do not like doing things we are not good at.

Churches Which are Viable Candidates for a Restart

We have considered the restart leader and the right stuff that is necessary for them to possess. Now we want to discuss what a church that is a viable candidate for a restart looks like. Not every church is a good candidate for a church revitalization restart. Rural areas that are losing population, areas of ethnic change, and declining neighborhoods are difficult. The area around a restart church needs to have a definable target group of sufficient size which may be effectively reached by the type of ministry that local association or state convention has to offer. Here are some essentials which make a church a viable candidate for a restart:

Members Who are Willing to Still Sacrifice

If a church membership is unwilling to make sacrifices for the cause of Christ, the chances for revitalization are non-existent. Memberships must be willingness to sacrifice. You must be willing to accept the fact that, as a small declining church ministers will need to make sacrifices, programs will need to make sacrifices, the preferences of the laity will need to be sacrificed all for the good of the church. There will be times when your paycheck as the pastor will be late. Leaders are often the last ones paid in declining churches. The light bill is paid and any other pressing payment, but often in these churches the treasurer will ask embarrassingly if the minister would mind not depositing their check for a few days. You must also be willing to sacrifice much of what once was your free time as the leader. The membership also must make sacrifices for the chance that the church will be restarted. They will need to become friendlier towards outsiders for instance. The things they like that are not a draw to the community must be sacrificed and discontinued. Their comfort must be sacrificed.

Make Sure There Is Growth Potential in the Facility's Location

You have heard it said that the three most important things for planting a church is Location! Location! Location! The location can make a huge difference for the revitalization of a declining church. As stated above, not every church is a good candidate for a restart. Rural areas that are losing population, areas of ethnic change, and declining neighborhoods are difficult. The area around a restart church needs to have a definable target group of sufficient size which may be effectively reached by the type of ministry that denomination has to offer. A restart has a greater chance for survival when there is ample population base around it to draw new people to a new vision for a new restart. Does your facility still have room for more people? In revitalization it is always best if you have more space than you need and can regrow into filling your facilities. A poor location will only hurt your revitalization efforts. Location of the church is sound advice but the reality of it all is that most declining churches have no idea what this really means. Things to consider in a restart relating to location are: the centrality within a city or lack of it; accessibility to the church by major traffic routes; church locations that that leave them locked into an area with only one way in and one way out; and a location that has space around the facility for future commercial development.

These Churches are Not in Debt

Churches that are in rapid decline have a better chance to be restarted if they are not handcuffed with large debts. In my area of Orlando, we had a church on the east side of Orlando that was in need of a restart. I had been working with them for about two years preparing them and training them for the restarting of their church. We were less than six months away from launching the restart when we discovered that the pastor and one aggressive lay leader had actually taken a mortgage out on their property for $300,000. While the pastor was excited for the resources they now had, I knew that they would run through the monies in about two years and then be in trouble. After eighteen months the pastor felt led to move on to another church, leaving the declining church to discover that he had spent all but twenty thousand dollars of the monies and they were broke. The church came back to me and said we are ready to be a restart church now. I had the uncomfortable task of telling them that they were no longer a viable candidate for a restart. Great debt cripples a churches ability to be revitalized. Think about this question: Is it right for a rapidly declining church to go into debt? I do not believe so. Nowhere in the Scriptures does the Lord give consent for a church to go into debt. While it does not seem wise for a declining church to be in debt, many hurt any future chances for revival by procuring a loan that the declining membership can pay for. In nearly every instance where debt is mentioned in the Bible, it is in a negative light.94 Think about the opportunity to realize the Lord's blessings and sustainability for a

---

94 C.f. Deuteronomy 15:6; Deuteronomy 28:12; and Proverbs 17:18.

restart if you do not lock your church into loans that are detrimental.95 Many a revitalization effort has been destroyed by secular thinking that if they borrowed a large sum of money it would allow them the ability to reach more people. In turn they would be able to help pay off the debt. That rarely happens in church revitalization and renewal Studies have consistently shown that most churches that go into debt spend more on their interest payments than they do on evangelism or mission work. In revitalization there is enough tension around being created by trying to turn around a corpse. Laity are further stressed by adding to the effort a loan payment and interest each and every month. If the restart does not grow right away, which seldom they do, financial challenges are right out front. When a declining church goes into debt, it is essentially trying to serve two masters: God and money.96 The world walks by what it can see while the church should walk by its faith in the risen Lord. So many churches needing to be restarted have been set back by their inability to pay off an unwise debt incurred by individuals seeking the easy way out. If you are unsure, you can lead a revitalization effort then give the property to the local association and allow them the chance to utilize the facilities for training of laity and development of new churches as an outreach center. We have a church that was given to us as an association by a loving church body that had declined past recovery. We have three churches meeting there now and the total number for a Sunday totals above 180 individuals. That is incredible as the legacy of the former church lives on by its willingness to deed the facilities over to the association for the work of the Lord.

---

95 C.f. 2 Corinthians 9:8-13.

96 C.f. Matthew 6:24.

They are Not Afraid of Trying New Things

Is your church in the ministry of yes or the ministry of no? When I arrived to where I serve now, I immediately noticed that all of the staff were more interested in saying no than they were to saying yes. Churches can get in the mundane habit of always saying no towards new ideas. Become a "yes" revitalization leader. When confronted with new experiences, challenges, and ideas, avoid making excuses and start doing. You will find that the benefits almost always outweigh the risks. Life is too short and ministry too precious to get stuck in a bland routine. If you are afraid of trying new things you will not be able to save your church. You as the leader of a revitalization effort should always be open to trying new things. The reason for this is you and your church never really know until you try if the idea will help your church grow. The Church Revitalizer should not be afraid to try new things when new things are presented to you. The leader of revitalization and the church embracing revitalization should actually have a state of YOLO attitude. Do you have it? Do you even know what it means? The leader and the church must realize that **Y**ou **O**nly **L**abor **O**nce in church revitalization. You will not be given multiple opportunities so make the best of the hard work you are called to accomplish. Do not let "no" and "I can't" define your existence as a church and leader. Embrace new things with positivity, because you never know where a scary-seeming task might lead you. It could be somewhere awesome! There is really only room to grow and advance, and considering you only get one shot at this, you might as well make the most of it. May I suggest why you should not grow weary trying new things for the restarting and renewal of your church. Here are my best ones for the restart church:

Declining Churches Who Do Not Try New Things Live with Regrets

Many churches in decline have been given by the Lord an opportunity to be revitalized only to walk away at the critical moment. Months or years later the membership and its leadership look back wishing they had said yes not no to God's plan for revitalizing their church. It breaks my heart as a revitalization leader when I see a church dying quickly while another church nearby took the opportunity to be blessed by the Lord and tried the exact same thing and are coming out of the decline and beginning to get healthy and vital once more. The declining church that was too afraid to say yes now lives with regrets, sorrows, and disappointments.

Declining Churches That Embrace Change Develop the Necessary Confidence

When a restart church embraces the required change necessary, they develop a renewed confidence that the Lord has returned to their House of the Lord. There is something really rewarding about trying something new. It enables you to realize the hand of the Lord is upon you and that gives you the confidence to press on. The fear of failure is replaced by a godly confidence that something divine is happening within the fellowship. Small victories blossom into substantial victories. The feeling of being empty is replaced by a feeling of empowerment.

Declining Churches That Try New Things Forge a New Future

In restarting a church, as I have worked with about three hundred or more churches in the restart strategy, I have discovered that those who try new things that might be a little outside of their comfort zone are better able to forge a new future for the church. These new experiences and efforts make you known in a community. For many declining churches that is something you had never experienced previously. Families begin to see the gifts and talents in your church and how you are utilizing them to reach a community for Christ. Suddenly an unappealing church becomes an appealing church. The flood gates of new opportunities begin to flow your way. All if you are willing to stop resting on the old and get into the new. Happiness begins to be seen in church and in the lives of its participants.

Declining Churches That Try New Things Inspire Creativity

Rapidly declining churches that embrace the "no" complex are often filled with formerly creative individuals who have and the joy juice sucked out of them. This could have been due to a militant pastor that was threatened by the creatives in the church. It could have been by abusive lay leaders who feared their position of influence would be threatened. Breaking out of the creativity sapping mode will help the restart effort. Creatives can assist your church in making a comeback They will demonstrate that the key to their success is a commitment to trying new things.

Trying something new regularly requires nerve. Trying something new opens up the opportunity for your church to experience new avenues for ministry. Trying something new keeps the membership from becoming bored. Trying something new forces your church to develop. Growth seems to require that we take the initial action, whether it is adopting a new attitude or a new way of thinking, or literally taking new action. A spirit of perpetual challenge keeps you humble and open to new ideas that very well may be better than the ones your church currently holds dear.

These Churches Have Forward Thinking People

Successful restart churches have leaders and followers that can think future and forward progression over living in the past of the status quo. Remember in the Book of Joshua when David came to the Israelite camp and found all of the warriors scared because of the giant Goliath? He was the only one willing to look past the giant and see their future. What is it that your church and leadership see? Do you see the giants or do you see God? Who do you follow? Do you follow the mob or do you follow Gods leader? Where does your church want to go? Backing to the wilderness or into the promised land. Where are you looking? Do you look past what is in front of you, especially when daily duties take up so much time and vitality? Churches and church leaders that focus on the future are set apart from those who are stuck looking over their shoulder at the past. Many pastors are only able to look ahead about seven days. They are always lagging behind and playing catch up. A minimum of looking forward ninety days is helpful. The Church Revitalizer should set aside some time each week to look out into the distance and imagine what special ministry may be out there for their revitalizing church. Developing a future focus is an initial step for a restart effort. Stop hunkering down on what is currently the state of affairs. Survival is a staggering dilemma. Short term can eat away our ability to think out front of problems and issues. Begin thinking forward and take the full picture into account. Forward thinking leaders and church members provide the indispensable oxygen to keep the fires of a restart going. Develop the discipline to spend more time learning about the future. No church restart effort can afford short term, few-days thinking. That is often what got them to the current state of stagnation. A forward focused revitalizer will be able to infuse his congregation with a brighter future over a long Debbie Downer look at the past. Remind your church where the Lord is telling you He wants it to go and then show the church how together as a church you are going to get there. Talk to other Church Revitalizers and pick their brains. Learn what is working and not working in the field of church revitalization and renewal. Forward thinking church members contribute to the creation of a healthy restart. Think forward and be courageous. Get your people out of the ruts of the past and into the race of the future. Eliminate as much of the emotional baggage of defeat that has crippled the church previously. See the future the Lord desires for your restart. Revisit your vision frequently so not to become locked motionless in methodologies that stalemate the church. Think outside of the box. Get up and keep moving. If you stumble, get up again. If you falter, get up again. If you lose your focus, get up again and find it fresh and renewed. If one idea proves unfruitful, get up and find a new one. Just get up!

Wrapping it Up!

Churches that have the right stuff are able to separate from old outdated methodologies and embrace new fruitful ones. It might be the best thing for your restart to establish a steering committee that is made up of people outside of the current church leadership. Such a transition committee can make all of the critical decisions while the church is brought back to life. When working in a restart, I always work to empower the transition team for at least three years, which will give the church the greatest chance for survival and renewal. Do not just fix the mistakes, fix whatever permitted the mistake in the first place. Remember, a restart will really need a Church Revitalizer with the energy to lead boldly for the next one thousand days. J. David Jackson, a long-time friend and fellow church planter and revitalizer, says in his book *PlantLIFE: Principles and Practices in Church Planting* that in the restart approach, the congregation usually agrees to stop public services in their church building for at least three to six months, meeting only for home Bible studies and prayer, before relaunching public ministries. He declares that five conditions should be met:

1. The original church body must be willing to die, dissolving its bylaws and legal status.
2. The restart must have new leadership, both pastoral and lay; often a church planter becomes the restart pastor.
3. The new church relaunches with a new name to give it a new identity and reputation.
4. It relocates, at least temporarily, to a new site for its meetings.
5. It must develop new statements of mission, vision, and core values to guide its future.
6. It must normally refocus on a different ministry group. Based on a renewed understanding of the demographics and dynamics of the community, the

new church reaches out to a different slice of the local population.97

I was taught many years ago by Dr. Ralph Wilson that a complete change of leadership and direction are musts for this model to be successful, and the new leader must have abundant energy and faith. Today Dr. Wilson says: "Restarting a church takes mountains of energy and the faith in God's power necessary to ward off discouragement, along with energy and faith should come fresh vision. Dying churches can celebrate their past victories and then mentally move on to a vision focused on outreach and growth."98 Rapidly declining churches need to be rescued. They have a future which can be glorious if they choose restarting over replanting. In reality, both strategies can work. The rapidly declining church must ask themselves the question: Do they want to keep on and leave a legacy, or give the church away to a church planter and walk away? Both of these choices carry with it opportunities and challenges. Helping a church that is in decline ought to be a task that vibrant healthy churches embrace. Helping in a restart is a great way to do the missionary work of revitalization. He Lord Jesus desired to help declining churches. Paul the great missionary desired to help declining churches, it could be the igniter to the next great awakening if we as church leaders desire to help restore the witness of a declining church and give it a new opportunity to advance the gospel in a community that needs their light. Not every struggling or failing church is a viable candidate for a restart. If it is decided that a restart is not a viable option, the church should be led to transition to a church closure with the property deeded over to the local

---

97 J. David Jackson, *PlantLIFE: Principles and Practices in Church Planting* (Missional Press, 2008).

98 Dr. Ralph F. Wilson, "Restarting a Dead Church," http://www.joyfulheart.com/plant/restart.htm.

association for the purpose of launching new works or as an outreach center out of which future ministries could operate.

Chapter 6
Warning Signs of a Disastrous Decline

I see what you've done, your hard, hard work, your refusal to quit. I know you can't stomach evil, that you weed out apostolic pretenders. I know your persistence, your courage in my cause, that you never wear out. "But you walked away from your first love—why? What's going on with you, anyway? Do you have any idea how far you've fallen? A Lucifer fall! "Turn back! Recover your dear early love. No time to waste, for I'm well on my way to removing your light from the golden circle.[99]

On Sunday, July 25, 1999, the Guardian, a British media company, reported on the plane crash that took the life of John Kennedy, Jr, his wife and her sister. The cause of the crash was reported to be pilot error. It seems that he was not proficient in instrument flying at the time of the crash. Aviation experts suggest that he lost visual contact with the horizon because of haze and clouds and experienced "spatial disorientation" that eventually led to the plane going into a "graveyard spiral", or as some aviators call it, the "death spiral." The tragic end was the death of Kennedy, his wife and her sister.

In an interview with George Joyce, a corporate pilot, he pointed out what seemed to be a correlation between the "graveyard spiral" of an airplane and the "death spiral" of a church. This "spiral" concept depicts a clear picture of what is taking place in the church community. While the concept is taken from aviation's "graveyard spiral" or "death spiral", it paints a picture of what can happen to a church as well. Joyce mentioned what is called "spatial disorientation." The FAA describes it as "the inability of a person to determine his true body position, motion, and altitude relative to the earth or his

---

[99] Eugene H. Peterson, *The Message: The Bible in Contemporary Language* (Colorado Springs, CO: NavPress, 2005), Re 2:2–5.

surroundings."[100] Joyce says that a "graveyard spiral" usually happens at night when the pilot mistakenly thinks the plane's wings are level when they're banked left or right. If the pilot cannot discern how the plane is banking the plane could end in a spiral toward earth. If not corrected the plane will crash because the pilot can't see the horizon. The pilot feels the descent but not the turn. According to pilots that have lived to tell their account of the graveyard spiral, the only way they prevented a crash was by trusting the planes instruments and Joyce says the main instrument is the "Attitude Indicator." Notice it is "attitude" and not "altitude." This indicator shows the pilot the placement of the nose and wings of the plane, the two most important "attitudes" that determine the lift and flight of the plane.[101] Joyce further stated there are two things that are vital for air flight. First, you must know your instruments and secondly, you cannot fly by feeling. These facts are true as well for the church that desires to be successful for the Kingdom.

Some church researchers have now coined the phrase "death spiral" to refer to the disastrous decline many churches are experiencing. Statistics tells us approximately 90% of all evangelical churches are in plateau or decline or as researches put it…in a "death spiral." Estimates are that between 4,000 and 7,000 churches close their doors every year. Researcher Thom Rainer gives a more startling estimate of between 8,000 and 10,000 closing this year alone. America's churches need an immediate wakeup call!

---

100 "Spatial Disorientation," Federal Aviation Administration, accessed August 1, 2018, https://www.faa.gov/pilots/safety/pilotsafetybrochures/media/SpatialD.pdf.

101 Joyce, George. Interview by James Sells. Phone Interview. Salisbury, NC, August 13, 2018.

Church attendance statistics have been debated for some time. Some researchers place the average attendance of evangelical, mainline and Catholic churches at about 40%. David Olson refutes those figures. He has researched and tracked the attendance of 200,000 churches and his figures show that less than 20% of Americans attend church regularly. This is a stark difference from the 39% the Gallup poll reported and the 37% that the Pew Research Center reported. Every poll taken has shown a steady decline in the attendance of Southern Baptist churches over the last 30 years.

Many churches in America are in this "death spiral" and will not survive unless immediate action is taken. Thom Rainer reports "Declining smaller churches decline much more rapidly than larger churches. Once the declining church goes below 100 in attendance, its days are likely numbered. Here is the sad summary statement of this portion of the research: Once a church declines below 100 in worship attendance, it is likely to die within just a few years. The life expectancy for many of these churches is ten years or less."[102]

When a church enters this downward direction, it is very difficult to bring it back to life. Most often the church has taken its eyes off the horizon just as there are signs to a pilot that things are not right with the plane, there are also some clear signs that a church is in a downward spiral. How the church responds to these signs will determine whether the church will live or die. In a later chapter we will discuss the church lifecycle and how the position on the cycle a church finds itself in will dictate how successful a revitalization process will be.

---

102 Rainer, Thom. "Growing Healthy Churches. Together." *Is There a Church Death Spiral?* July 3, 2017. Accessed August 2, 2018. https://thomrainer.com/2017/07/church-death-spiral/.

Expanding the Lessons Learned from a Pilot

First, *knowledge* of air flight and aviation is an absolute essential. Pilots can get into trouble when they ignore the signs that the instruments and the plane are giving them. The pilot must always understand what is happening to the plane while in flight. They must be able to recognize trouble when it comes. Likewise, the church gets into trouble when the congregation and its leaders don't care to know what is happening to the church. As a Church Revitalizer, I have learned that the hardest obstacle to overcome when trying to help a church is to convince the pastor and the church to face the "present reality" about their church. They love to keep their heads buried in the sand and hope the problems will go away. This will be discussed later in this chapter. For the most part, church members either don't recognize the danger signs or they do, and don't really care. Often, they will ignore certain death because of their selfish desire to control.

Second, the pilot must *obey the instruments and not feelings.* As stated earlier, there is an instrument called the "Attitude Indicator" for the pilot to use. It reveals where the plane is in relation to the horizon. It tells the direction and posture of the plane. If the "attitude" of the plane is right most everything else will be right as well.

Likewise, in the church, attitude is everything. It is true that some churches need and deserve an attitude adjustment. Anywhere humans are present there are attitudes. Some attitudes are good, and some are bad. The number one bad attitude that is present in the church today is cynicism. The Cambridge Dictionary defines a cynic as one who is:

> "not trusting or respecting the goodness of other people and their actions,

but believing that people are interested only in themselves."[103]

C. M. Joyner writes in Relevant Magazine, "Cynicism doesn't always present itself in the sweeping, broad negativity we see on TV. In the day-to-day life of the church, it looks more like quick, unwarranted, 'constructive' criticism. I'm not talking about the critical thinking required for success as an adult. I'm referring to the way we constantly evaluate and critique people and what they do:"[104] Cynics are racking havoc in our churches. Quarreling, backbiting, division and disunity all come because of cynical attitudes from cynical troublemakers.

A close examination of declining churches reveals some specific signs that need to be accepted and dealt with if the church is to survive a plunge to certain death. Let's examine some of the warning signs that are present in the declining church. It should be noted that this is not an exhaustive list but sets forth some of the most important signs.

Spiritual Signs

The most important signs that are almost always present in a declining church are spiritual in nature. These signs are the most important because they usually determine the spiritual walk of the church and reveals a lack of real spiritual maturity and commitment.

---

103 Cambridge Dictionary, "cynicism," accessed August 13, 2018, https://dictionary.cambridge.org/us/dictionary/english/cynical.

104 C. M. Joyner. "Relevant." *The Most Damaging Attitude in Our Churches: Why subtle cynicism doesn't look like Jesus.* June 21, 2018. Accessed August 13, 2018. https://relevantmagazine.com/god/church/most-damaging-attitude-our-churches.

The first spiritual sign is the *minimization of the importance of missions*. I intentionally use the word "missions" and not "missional." The concept of being "missional" does not place importance on global mission work that focusses on reaching the lost masses in the world through evangelism. Instead it dilutes the concept of missions down to meeting physical needs much more that meeting spiritual needs. The Great Commission is "soul-centered." When the church makes little of missions it makes little of its calling from God. Missions is the Great Commission's command which feeds life into the local church and without it the church will die. Missions shows the churches real concern for reaching a lost world. Furthermore, the church that does not have a mission mindset has disregarded the Great Commandment to "love our neighbor as ourselves."

Mission minded, more traditional churches seem to camp on sending the message of the gospel to a lost world. It is clear that missional churches tend to spend their time focusing on service to people rather than presenting the Gospel to those who have never heard. The church that loses its sense of missions will surely be a church that ends in disaster. A church reveals its commitment to, or its lack thereof, by what is placed in their budget to do world evangelization through its missions giving. When a church ceases to give to world missions it is treading on thin ice.

The second spiritual sign is a *lack of obedience to the will and plan of God*. A pastor in his first few weeks of his first pastorate shared this story. He shared that while in the first church council planning meeting, preparing for the next year's ministry, each head of each ministry in the church gave a long list of what "they" wanted to do and accomplish in the next calendar year of the church. As they went around the room the young pastor became more and more concerned because he never heard anyone say that the Lord had revealed to them His plan for the coming year. At the close of the meeting one of the leaders looked at the young pastor and said, "Pastor will you pray and ask God to join us and help us accomplish all of what we have discussed?" The young pastor thought for a moment and responded…" No, I can't do that!" The leader said, "what do you mean you can't do that?" The pastor asked, "Are these things (as he pointed at the list) what God wants for this church or is it what you want?" Of course, that did not go over very well with the leaders in the room, but he made his point. It is of utmost importance that we find and do the will of God in the church. The sad fact is that most churches don't even ask and the ones who do sometimes refuse to be obedient to God's plan. I like what Henry Blackaby said in *Experiencing God,* "Find out where God is working and join him."[105] Most churches that are in a disastrous decline have stopped obeying God to do their own selfish will.

A third spiritual sign is *little evangelistic fruit.* Statisticians tell us that a healthy church will reach one lost person for every 20 active members in the church. However, most churches are nowhere near that statistic. In fact, most churches that make up the 90% of plateaued or declining churches have "no" conversions. Of all the spiritual signs of a disastrous decline, this is by far the most debilitating and disappointing. There seems to be no urgency on the part of the church to win the lost. This attitude is in part because, as has been stated previously, the church has turned inward. The "me" generation is only concerned with having their own personal needs met while they neglect the real spiritual needs of the lost around them. Furthermore, many churches are simply so apathetic toward spiritual things that they just do not care about the lost. Having said this, there is also a

---

105 Henry T. Blackaby and Claude V. King, *Experiencing God: Knowing and Doing the Will of God* (Nashville. Tennessee: B&H Publishing, 65.

theological view that is becoming more prevalent in our churches that does not encourage evangelism. After all, if God is going to save who He will no matter what…then why evangelize?

A fourth spiritual sign is found in Revelation 2:4 where Jesus tells the church at Ephesus *"You have left your first love."* The church that is teetering on death's door has most likely left its first love. Christ knows His church inside and out. Everything that happens in it He sees and knows. The church cannot fool Him. A close examination of the church at Ephesus will reveal that they were existing amid a pagan society. However, that was no excuse for their problem. The church was being persecuted by the culture it was ministering to because of the existence of the temple of Diana, a fertility goddess, as paganism was dominant in the area. For their existence in this pagan setting, Jesus commends them for not tolerating wickedness within the church and their removal of false teachers from their work. A closer look at the church reveals that their doctrine was right. The church was ministering in the community and seeking to meet needs. Jesus was describing a church that, from the outside looking in, looked like a model church. But then Jesus turns the conversation toward the problem.

Verse 4 says there is one thing wrong… *"You have forsaken your first love."* What is "first love?" What does this statement mean to the church today? First love in this context means a deep burning desire to please God was not present in the church any longer. Let's be clear. The condemnation was not that they had forsaken the "who" of that love (Jesus), but they had lost a real desire to please Him and serve Him as they had once served in the past. Their love had grown cold and indifferent. They no longer served out of that dynamic love but out of habit and obligation. It seems that the generation of younger members had lost the fervency of serving Jesus that their parents once had. They were simply going through the motions of service, not out of love but obligation. That simply means that the devotion they once had was gone. The joy of serving Jesus was no longer real in their life. There was no real fire in their hearts which resulted from a close walk with the "King of King's." Simply put, Jesus was no longer the priority in the church. Ironic isn't it? The one who died for the church is no longer very important to the church. What a chilling thought but oh so true! As a result, churches die a slow agonizing death because of their desertion of the faith.

Lethargic Signs

It is almost inexorably true that when a church has left its first love, we find a church that is plateaued or declining, and we also find lethargy on the part of the people. The worship services have become perfunctory. It is often the case that church leadership has become lax in their preparation and the responsibilities that they have accepted are often unattended. Tragically enough, the church stops doing the things that brought growth to begin with. In the parable of the Great Supper, it was the command of Jesus that men should, *"Go out into the highways and hedges, and compel them to come in, that my house may be filled."106* Churches that grow take Jesus seriously at this point. That is what organized visitation programs are all about. A growing lively church will also train workers in the ministry of making disciples or winning the lost. It is not something that one wants and then forgets, but it should be an ongoing ministry of the church. Several years ago, many churches began Bus Ministries. They began bringing children to church whose parents were not in church, but many of those parents became Christians and active members, supporting the church. Today, many of those children who came to church on buses are in the ministry and have graduated from college and seminary.

---

106 Luke 14: 23.

Effective churches also have a posture of evangelism in their organizations such as the Sunday school. At one time, more than 90% of the converts in a church came by way of the Sunday school. This bespeaks of a Sunday school with well-trained leadership and well-prepared teachers who regularly talk to their classes about the Plan of Salvation. Recently, an Interim Pastor was approached by a member of the congregation who was thrilled that the Interim Pastor gave an invitation. He told the Interim that he had not seen an invitation in that church for several years. This kind of thing is what happens in a church that has forgotten the Great Commission of our Lord when He said, *"Go ye therefore, and teach all nations, (make disciples) baptizing them in the name of the Father, and of the Son, and of the Holy Ghost..."*107 Similarly, Jesus repeated that command in Acts 1:8 at His Ascension when He said, *"... Ye shall receive power after the Holy Ghost has come upon you: and ye shall be witnesses unto me both in Jerusalem, and in all Judea, and in Samaria, and unto the uttermost part of the earth."*

When a church has lost its first love, it will not be careful in carrying out these commands of Jesus but the church that is empowered by the Holy Spirit will always be successful. It is a profound truth of the New Testament that the Holy Spirit will be received by anyone who is willing to ask for Him (Luke 11: 13). There is really no need for any church to be powerless because Jesus give us the assurance that if we will sincerely seek the Holy Spirit, He will empower us!

Attendance Signs

There are some signs that are impossible to miss when looking at the attendance in a declining church. The rate of those leaving the church is increasing every year. The reasons vary from dissatisfaction with the present church and its

---

107 Matthew 28: 19.

operations to simply leaving the church and never going to another. Many church theorists say that very high numbers are leaving the church because of shallow teaching and preaching. For many who stay around, their commitment is not found to be as it had been in the past.

The first attendance sign is *the obvious abandoning of the sinking ship by the staff and leaders.* Church members are dropping out and the absentees on Sunday mornings seem to be increasing. Staff members and lay leadership are jumping ship as churches find themselves in a death spiral. Stats show that over 1,500 pastors left the ministry every month last year and that over 1,300 pastors were terminated by the local church each month, many without cause. Many churches have a real problem keeping staff for various reasons. These churches are in real trouble. Every church has staff turnover but when it becomes the norm after a couple of years it becomes an internal problem that must be addressed.

Statistics also show that the average church will have 40-60% of their membership inactive or irregular in their attendance. The number of unaffiliated people is growing every day. One of the largest groups today have been labeled as the "none's" or the "none of the above" group referring to their relation to the church and faith. Many young people make up the "none" category and they say that church for the most part is boring and has no relevance to their lives. Stats show that only 28% of young adults between the ages of 23-37 attend church regularly. There are very few new young members in churches today because the church has a very difficult time meeting their needs both emotionally and spiritually. There are many reasons why people are abandoning the church, but a few reasons stand out above the rest. Some who are leaving the church, have had very bad experiences with the church. Some have grown tired of the division that seems to prevail in most dying churches. Still others are responding to the lack of concern that many church members show toward a world that needs a savior. Even further, some leave because they feel they do not have the freedom to be a part of a ministry that is significant and fruitful.

A portion of the "none's" are millennials. Stats show that 59% are leaving the church even after they grew up in Christian homes and under the influence of the local church. The reason is much like that of the "none's." They do not believe that the church is relevant to them any longer and it is not meeting their needs. Pew Research reports that "Perhaps the most striking trend in American religion in recent years has been the growing percentage of adults who do not identify with a religious group. And the clear majority of these religious "none's" (78%) say they were raised as a member of a particular religion before shedding their religious identity in adulthood." The research goes on to reveal that "half of the 'none's' left their childhood faith because of a lack of belief. One in five cite dislike of organized religion."[108]

The action of these groups raises an important question that needs to be addressed. The question is "Do these groups understand the theology behind the local church, or is it because they are so self-centered that everything has to revolve around meeting their needs?" This is an important question because the very existence of these groups and their attitude speaks horribly loud about how they were raised to view the church. It projects a consumeristic attitude that "I'm here and you have to meet my need no matter what else you do and if you don't, I'll go elsewhere to find a place that will meet my need." It is sad that the church is faced with such a

---

108 "Why America's none's left religion behind," Pew Research, August 24, 2016, accessed August 22, 2018, http://www.pewresearch.org/fact-tank/2016/08/24/why-americas-nones-left-religion-behind/.

dilemma. A consumeristic attitude toward church and worship is killing our churches.

Everyone agrees that attendance is down, and people are searching, as a consumer, for that church which will satisfy them. There is also an agreement that change is needed. The big question is, "What kind of change?"

The second obvious attendance sign is the extremely *noticeable aging out of the congregation.* To put it bluntly some churches are a few years of funerals away from closing the doors of the church. C. Peter Wagner says in his book *The Healthy Church,* "…in my opinion the number of churches built on programs designed specifically for senior citizens urgently needs to be multiplied in many parts of the United States today. Demographic studies have been telling us for some time that the quantity of people of retirement age is increasing in a dramatic manner. Plans need to be implemented now…to cope with these changing conditions."[109] It is no secret that the population of our churches are growing older by the minute. In an article in Insights into Religion it says "Unless current social trends change, Mainline Protestant churches will face an even bigger drop-off in coming years. Anyone who has sat in a back pew peering over rows of gray heads can attest: American churches are aging." The article further states "In 24 percent of evangelical churches, one-quarter of members are 65 or older." David Roozen points out in the same article that "graying congregations are beset with challenges. The older the church's membership, the more likely that church is to have falling numbers, weaker finances, anemic youth programming and a sense of spiritual fatigue."[110]

---

109 C. Peter Wagner, *The Healthy Church* (Ventura, California: Regal Books, 1996), 48.

110 "Aging Congregations May Be Churches' Biggest Concern," Insights into Religion, accessed August 12, 2018,

While these are eye opening facts the age of a congregation has little to do with the spiritual health of the church. It is true that the church that refuses to reach out and appeal to younger families will die a slow death, but this can be rectified. The key to restoring declining church because of the aging out of its members is to take seriously the Great Commission as wells as the Great Commandment. There is no good reason that older Christians and younger Christians should not get along in the family of God.

The third attendance sign is an *absence of visitors*. Many pastors wonder why guests don't stick around. Declining churches battle this reality week after week. There is nothing more devastating to a church than a lack of visitors. Even more frustrating is when a visitor does attend but never return because of the unpreparedness of the church for visitors. How a church responds to visitors will of course determine whether they return. Some years ago, a pastor and his family decided to take a weekend vacation and visited a small rural church where a friend had been a member. The pastor and his family arrived between the morning Sunday school and the worship service. They sat down, taking a whole pew, and waited for the service to begin. As people were making their way out of the educational part of the building and coming into the worship area two elderly men walked slowly toward the pew where the pastor and his family were sitting. They stopped at the end of the pew and one said to the other..." well these people have taken our seats. I guess we will have to find another place to sit. They turned and walked away. There was no welcome...no glad to see you with us...nothing. At the close of the service no one greeted them, and they left without even a greeting from the pastor. That scenario can be repeated over and over in churches

http://www.religioninsights.org/aging-congregations-may-be-church%E2%80%99s-biggest-worry.

across America and we wonder why visitors don't return. People will not return to a place where they are made to feel unwanted, unwelcomed and uncomfortable.

Congregational Signs

There are many different signs that become obvious to the church member and or the person looking for a church home. Often these signs are not as clear to the church as they are to the outside world. These are the underlying signs that can cause real damage to the future of any church.

The first congregational sign is an increase in *internal conflict*. Internal church conflict is the spear head that kills many churches. Here are some startling statistics from the Duke University's National Congregations Study 2006-2007. David A. Roozen concluded in the study these facts:

- 25% of churches experienced conflict in the last two years that resulted in people leaving the church.
- 1,500 pastors leave the church every month because of conflict, burnout or moral failure. Only 1 in 20 pastors serve as pastors until retirement.
- Every year more than 19,000 congregations experience major conflict.
- During the last 5 years 75% of churches in America have experienced conflict; 25% of which indicate the conflict was severe enough to permanently impact church life.[111]

People have conflicts with each other. It is not the fact that there is conflict in the church that destroys the church,

---

111 David A. Roozen, Church Mediators, "Surprising Statistics," Duke University's National Congregations Study 2006-2007; American Congregations 2008, Cooperative Congregational Studies. http://www.churchmediators.org/pages/page.asp?page_id=353899.

but the way the conflict is handled. The problem of conflict is not new. It is as old as the church itself. People are people everywhere you go, and they have conflicts with each other. However, the one place that people, especially guests, should not have to endure conflict is in the local church. People who are looking for a church to call home are not going to settle for a conflict riddled congregation. They simply move on. In the past, many established members would overlook the pettiness and disunity in their church to remain in the church, but more and more congregational members are saying enough is enough and they leave to find a place of peace. People who attend church regularly simply want a harmonious place to worship and serve.

Conflict in the church is disastrous for the congregation and often the pastor and staff. The trauma of conflict often leaves and indelible mark on the congregation, the pastor and the community where the church serves. Most of the time when conflict comes it targets the pastor because he is the most vulnerable. This is especially important to understand when a small church is involved in conflict. Many times, the conflict results in the pastor losing influence with the people and the community. Sometimes he and his family become isolated from the congregation and they end the ministry there by leaving under pressure. Many churches that are declining and headed toward certain death have a bad habit of putting the pastor in these bad no-win situations. This will affect the church when they start seeking another pastor. It is true that a church's reputation "precedes them." If the pastor stays on the field, he and his family often become discouraged and unresponsive to the needs even of the people who support him.

Conflict is also disastrous to the local church because it can destroy the church's testimony in the community if conflict remains unresolved. Any small community will be aware of the conflict that is present in the local church. Many churches have such a bad reputation in the community that people joke about never wanting to be a part of that "quarrelling crowd." Thus, the church's reputation is destroyed, and no one wants to attend the church.

When the church lives in constant conflict that is never resolved it will end in closing its doors. The pastor will leave out of frustration and the good, non-quarrelling members will leave to find peace. The church will die because of internal, unresolved conflict!

The second congregational sign that the church is in a disastrous decline is the *tolerance of sinful lifestyles*. Billy Graham said in a sermon he preached in the 1950's, "One of the pet words of this age is 'tolerance.' It is a good word, but we have tried to stretch it over too great an area of life. We have applied it too often where it does not belong. The word 'tolerant' means liberal, broad-minded, willing to put up with beliefs opposed to one's convictions, and the allowance of something not wholly approved. Tolerance, in one sense, implies the compromise of one's convictions, a yielding of ground upon important issues. Hence, over-tolerance in moral issues has made us soft, flabby and devoid of conviction."[112]

Even though this article appeared in a 1950's edition of *Christianity Today* the principle has been amplified 10-fold for the local church today. Many churches have fallen victim to the sin of tolerance and they pay the price of death as a result. Tolerance has taken on a whole new meaning in the last decade. It used to mean that we were to put up with sinful lifestyles or the like but now the meaning is that we not only put up with them, but we must accept them as a norm and

---

112 Billy Graham. "The Sin of Tolerance," Christianity Today, February 2, 1959.

allow them if we are to have a prominent place in the church and society.

A perfect example of the church tolerating sin is the church at Thyatira in Revelation 2: 18-23. The text says, *"And unto the angel of the church in Thyatira write; These things saith the Son of God, who hath his eyes like unto a flame of fire, and his feet are like fine brass; I know thy works, and charity, and service, and faith, and thy patience, and thy works; and the last to be more than the first. Notwithstanding I have a few things against thee, because thou sufferest that woman Jezebel, which calleth herself a prophetess, to teach and to seduce my servants to commit fornication, and to eat things sacrificed unto idols. And I gave her space to repent of her fornication; and she repented not. Behold, I will cast her into a bed, and them that commit adultery with her into great tribulation, except they repent of their deeds. And I will kill her children with death; and all the churches shall know that I am he which searcheth the reins and hearts: and I will give unto every one of you according to your works."*[113]

What was the sin of Thyatira? The scripture says the church had tolerated Jezebel who was a prophetess that seduced many into fornication both physically and spiritually and she had encouraged the eating of food offered to idols. She was leading Christians astray and God was going to hold her accountable for her actions. The only solution was to deal with the sin. Matthew 18 presents a clear outline for dealing with sin in the fellowship, but few churches will ever utilize its instruction. Matthew 18 directs the church to deal with sin in the church confrontationally. God expects the church that Jesus died for to not tolerate sin in the fellowship.

It is interesting to note that the sin and sinner on the outside of the church was not attacking the church; rather it was sin on the inside that was working to defeat the church and cause her to stumble and fall.

---

113 Revelation 2:18-23, KJV.

The third congregational sign that the church is in a disastrous decline is the *presence of weak, lifeless worship*. Weak worship reveals itself in a lack of joy and excitement in the worship service. People who attend to sincerely worship can sense when the worship service is vibrant, lukewarm or dead. Guests will seldom return when worship is weak and sick. When the worship service is weak and lackluster people who truly want to be a part of a dynamic church setting will leave and look for a place where worship is healthy and vibrant. Many churches today have forgotten the main purpose of the church or in the least have twisted that purpose to meet the individual need. The type of worship in most churches reveal a self-centered, consumeristic attitude that seeks only to get something rather than give anything. This is evidenced by the so called "worship wars" that many churches must battle through. The simple fact is that worship is not for my benefit. Worship is for God's benefit. We come together to worship, to give honor and to give praise to God. When we make it about us as a consumer, we distort the Biblical reasoning behind worship. The reality is when we insist on a certain kind of music, worship style or service it is from a very self-centered position. God can be worshipped with any style of music. To insist it must be contemporary, or traditional or liturgical speaks of personal preference not God's preference.

Jesus said, *"But the hour cometh, and now is, when the true worshippers shall worship the Father in spirit and in truth: for the Father seeketh such to worship him. God is a Spirit: and they that worship him must worship him in spirit and in truth."*[114] It is plain and simple...God desires our worship. He is blessed by our worship. It is our responsibility wrought out of His love for us that we should worship Him. As we worship Him we reveal our gratitude and thanks and love to Him for what He

---

114 John 4:23-24 KJV.

did for us in Jesus' sacrifice on the cross. We are to worship Him in "spirit and in truth." The Bible tells us that "God is a Spirit" and when we worship our spirit should connect with Him in such a way that true worship occurs. This cannot happen when I come to Him with a selfish or self-centered attitude based on what I can get out of the experience.

Amos 8:1 gives another aspect of weak worship. It is a lack of preaching the Word of God. It says *"Behold, the days come, saith the Lord God, that I will send a famine in the land, not a famine of bread, nor a thirst for water, but of hearing the words of the Lord."*[115] Commentators note that the reason for seldom hearing the Word of God was a result of God's divine judgement upon them. Many people leave the church because sound doctrine is not being preached from the pulpit, nor taught in the classroom. Many sermons are preached with little or no Bible text. Sermons built around stories, sports events, personal experiences and even jokes seem to be the norm in some churches. No wonder people are abandoning these ships.

People leave the church when worship is weak, or people centered because it does not call the worshipper to a higher level of experience with God. Worship loses its desirability when it becomes "me-centered." Weak worship does not bring the worshipper face to face with God. When worship becomes "horizontal" (what I can get out of it) rather than "vertical," (what God gets out of it) it becomes a practice without power and true worshippers will not stay around very long when this is the reality. Any worshipper with a heart that is thirsty for the things of God will not hang around in a church with weak and dry worship. The true love and relationship a congregation has for God will show itself in a strong, exuberant, exciting worship experience. Churches that are in a disastrous decline never have strong worship.

---

115 Amos 1:11 KJV.

Positional Signs

The first positional sign that a church is in a disastrous decline is *a self-absorbed congregation*. The attitude of being one big happy family and it's me, mine and ours not theirs is killing churches!

Churches with this mindset are usually in a disastrous decline and in a constant struggle to keep their doors open. The deciding factor for the future of any church is; does the church exist to serve people just like those attending or does it exist to serve people who are not like the church attenders or people who may be considered outcast and needy.

Most churches make decisions, form budgets and plan programs based on the loudest voices from their congregation. Decisions of great importance are based on the specific wants and desires of those who are already in the congregation. Usually the controlling group of any church makes the decision as to what direction the church will take, and those decisions are all focused inward in their approach and impact.

The church that is self-absorbed has always turned inward in its approach to ministry. We discussed this previously, but it is of importance when discussing the self-absorbed congregation. Every decision made always focuses on the needs and wants of the existing congregation. The budget never reflects the need to reach outside of the existing congregation. Programs are never geared to reach those on the outside.

The second and most damaging positional sign is the presence and embracing of *untouchable sacred cows*. The Dictionary.com defines sacred cow as an individual, organization, institution, etc., considered to be exempt from criticism or questioning. In essence, a "sacred cow" becomes an idol.

Exodus 32 clearly describes idolatry at its worst. The passage records the fact that, while Moses was on the mountain, Aaron and the people decided, out of a sinful heart, that they would melt down all the gold they could gather and create a golden calf and the children of Israel were to bow down to it as their God.116 No pun intended; the golden calf might have been the first "sacred cow" recorded.

An article in *Facts and Trends* puts it clearly when it states, "Likely, there is not a pastor or church leader who has not had to shepherd around a sacred cow, be it sleeping, grazing, or tottering on its last legs. Church folks and religious institutions are notorious for putting some things—be they physical items, programs, or locations—beyond the realm of serious inquiry or discussion."[117]

The sacred cows in the local church take on a much more diverse identity. In the modern-day church almost anything could become a sacred cow. Sometimes the church makes idols of tangible articles like furniture in the church, buildings and name tags, or paintings behind the baptistery. People of the past and present like matriarchs and patriarchs can become sacred cows. A certain translation or type of Bible can become a sacred cow. Programs, committees and positions in the church can become idols. Anything that the

---

116 C.f. Exodus 32:4.

117 "Important Insights about Sacred Cows Gleaned from the Golden Calf," Facts & Trends, November 9, 2017, accessed August 23, 2018, https://factsandtrends.net/2017/11/09/important-insights-sacred-cows-gleaned-golden-calf/.

congregation deems more important than God or things of God can and most likely will become sacred cows. Churches are dying slow deaths because of the untouchable idols we call sacred cows.

The third positional sign is an *unwillingness to face "present reality"* that may be choking the very life out of the church. There are two questions that will help any church face the present reality about their church.

The first question is… "What is the spiritual condition (Present Reality) of your church?" There are 8 engagement questions that should be answered as well:

- Has your church focus turned inward?
- Does your church have clarity about its future?
- Does your church have a clear, God given vision for ministry?
- Is your church impacting lostness in your community?
- Is your church disconnected from its "real" community?
- Is your church focused on programs rather than people?
- Is your church accepting of all people?
- Does your church make prayer a priority?

The answer to these questions will give you a clear picture of the present reality in your church.

"Present reality" is also gauged by a clear examination of how the church is doing in the areas of six-character traits of a healthy church. Those traits are:

- Evangelism

- Discipleship
- Ministry
- Prayer
- Fellowship
- Worship

There is a second question that must be asked and that is: "If nothing changes what will your church look like in 3-5 years?" This is an eye-opening question. Most churches that are honest and believe the truth will see a bleak future because of the answers to the previous eight questions.

The one sure thing that must happen is the church must face the future. It can do that in one of two ways: It can ignore the truth that has been found and allow the church to waste away and die or it can hear and understand the problems and set out to fix them. Most churches wait too long to face reality and end in death anyway. The church must face "present reality" with a sense of urgency; if it does not the church will end in a death spiral. Sad but true, many church pastors and leaders have the Ostrich Syndrome. They bury their heads in the sand and refuse to accept the truth. This kind of church will not think about or face unpleasant facts about the churches condition. The church must face facts, it cannot continue to "bury its head in the sand."

The fourth and final positional sign is *"the looking back syndrome."* This is looking back more than looking forward. It is a focus on the past rather than charting a course for the future. As a Church Revitalizer, most of the conversations I have with churches revert to the past because that is where the church is living. Churches that are dying are living in the past and trying to relive the good ole' days. Those may take the form of a previous pastor, baptism or attendance records, programs or events that seemed at the time to be fruitful.

However, the good ole' days are gone and the failures and successes of those days are gone.

Philippians 3:12-14 is the perfect passage that deals with living in the past. It says *"Not as though I had already attained, either were already perfect: but I follow after, if that I may apprehend that for which also I am apprehended of Christ Jesus. Brethren, I count not myself to have apprehended: but this one thing I do, forgetting those things which are behind, and reaching forth unto those things which are before, I press toward the mark for the prize of the high calling of God in Christ Jesus."* Paul says the Christian and the church must focus on the future and forget the past. One self-made philosopher said it this way "You can't get ahead with your head stuck in the past. You live forward by understanding it backward."

This is not to say that there are some things in the past that are not important. However, the church cannot live there and if they do they will fail to accomplish the will of God for the future. The past is worth remembering but not reliving.

When the church becomes nostalgic it glories in the past and the past then becomes dangerous for the church. Mark Batterson said in an article in Relevant Magazine, "One of our biggest spiritual problems is this: we want God to do something new while we keep doing the same old thing. We want God to change our circumstances without us having to change at all." He goes on to say, "We get stuck, and sometimes mad at God, because we keep doing the same thing while expecting different results! Routines are an important part of growth, but when the routine becomes routine, change it before you turn into a veggie. What got you to where you are might be holding you back from where God wants you to go next."[118] When a church lives in the past it

---

118 Mark Batterson, "Living in the Past is Killing Your Future," Relevant Magazine, March 24, 2014.

will simply live in futility, never accomplishing the present will of God. Living in the past the church is not nearly as open to change as it should be. Living in the past causes the church to continue the same obsolete methods of decades ago but are useless in the present situation. Living in the past keeps us from pursuing the future Will of God for the church and that can be deadly to the church. "The answer is simple: You won't find God in the past. His name is not *I Was*. His name is *I Am*. If we obsess over what God did last, we'll miss what He wants to do next. God's at work right here, right now. God's always doing something brand spanking new."[119]

The question is, What about your church? Are your church members constantly talking about past glory days? Is the future of your church hindered because the congregation is living in the past? Does the leadership of the church have a clear, God-given vision for the church's future? If not, the church will have a bleak future!

Conclusion

All of these signs are disastrous. None of these signs are good, but the key is to recognize them and respond quickly. If any of these signs are present in your church it may mean the church is in a "death spiral." If the church is in a disastrous decline the direction must be changed or the church will end in certain death. It is important to remember that if the church shows signs of decline it is because the church has taken its eyes off Jesus and the plans God has for His church. Churches decline and die because they seek after what they want, and desire rather than what God wants. When a church finds itself in this "death spiral" it would be wise to remember that the church is His and not ours. The church should be given back to Him and removed from the

---

119 Batterson Ibid.

hands of those who may be choking the life out of it. There must be an "attitude adjustment" in the leadership and congregation to get the church back one track. It is His Church and we are His people. The church must refocus on the higher purpose of pleasing God and doing His will. The church must return to the presence and power of the Holy Spirit with absolute confidence that He will guide the church into the future!

Chapter Seven
The C.L.U.E. for Saying Something New in a Restart

"After some time had passed, Paul said to Barnabas, "Let's go back and visit the brothers in every town where we have preached the message of the Lord and see how they're doing" Acts 15:36.

When you finally get it in a restart, you have come to a place as a Church Revitalizer where both you and your people realize you have few options left, often because you waited too long, and you are now frantically seeking the Lord's help and those who have the revitalization experience to come along side of you and your church. Frantic fears wondering what you can do have been replaced with a viable working plan and now it is time to move forward to save your church. The remaining membership has ceased to be in the proverbial boxing match each week with one another and have joined forces. The blaming of each other has passed. The challenge of holding on has taken over. Now you are ready as a church to be a restart. The Church Revitalizer must lead his church members to stop blinking back the tears of remorse as to what they have become in such a decline and begin to see the Lord's opportunities through new eyes. There is a clue for saying something new in a restart and if done correctly, this will be your moment of awakening and renewal. The hope for something new while doing nothing has been replaced by both laity and clergy making plans and taking steps to bring the church into a state of renewal. Far too many dying churches have an "I hope so" mentality. They are praying for the spiritual marines to come over the horizon and save their church. It is God's will that the church and all of its remaining membership saves the church. A restart effort to save your church is not based upon a mystical fairy tale ending. If you and your church want to live happily ever after, it must begin with the revitalizer leading the laity to develop new systems and opportunities to reach into the community in which you are located. The restarting church must champion itself because no one else will. Through the restart journey the Lord will give you confidence that He indeed has everything planned for your survival. A church in which the Lord is working must learn to rest confidently in the hands of God, while learning how to stand boldly on its own and taking care of the present remaining member while making a way and the room for new members. Many a dying church which placed their hopes on a church planter to save them eventually discovered that he did not and that their self-reliance on the remaining committed was what really saved their church.

Starting Over When You Have Over Started

Have you ever had to start over again when you were doing an assignment in school? I remember during the early stages of computers as I was learning how to utilize one and had not learned the importance of practicing the importance of securing my data. I quickly learned that my lap top needed to be like Jesus and that meant being willing to save everything. The number of times I lost my sermon notes on a Tuesday for Sunday's sermon all because I did not hit save when I was done. The sense of loss was gut wrenching. Sometimes it may have been a little embarrassing to have had to start over. Churches often over start when a new leader arrives on the scene to revitalize and move the church forward. Church Revitalizers can at times over start because they are so much in a rush to get something going before the tiny amount of resources available runs out. In the effort to stabilize a rapidly declining church, they push too hard and go too fast. Both of these scenarios display a disordered dysfunctional methodology that will often cause the renewing church to stall, drift or become stuck and in need of regrouping, revisioning, and refocusing. Mark Twain said, "The secret of getting ahead is getting started, the secret of getting started is breaking your complex overwhelming tasks into small manageable tasks, and then starting on the first one."[120] If you have been a Church Revitalizer very long, admittedly there have been and will continue to be days when you would really like to start over. Have you ever gone to a wedding and forgot the wedding gift on the kitchen table? I have. Have you ever gone to the grocery store and realized once you got there you left your shopping list at home? Once I was headed out to a rather large meeting I was part of and discovered about two hours into my trip, that I had left all of my hanging clothes still in my closest and we as a family had to turn around and head back to Atlanta so I could pick up my clothes. My wife and children were not very happy with me that day. Have you ever had such a day that you just wished you could start it over? There are times when a new project, or a new event in one's life can be something wonderful. Other times however starting over can be the most difficult thing in life. Mary Anne Radmacher has stated that, "Courage doesn't always roar, sometimes courage is the quiet voice at the end of the day saying, "I will try again tomorrow."[121] That is a fitting moto for the restart leader.

Discovering the C.L.U.E. for a Restart

There are discoveries taking place all around the discipline of church revitalization and renewal. Churches are being rejuvenated all over North America. While that is encouraging there are so many which are not willing to make and take the actions promptly enough to comeback. Discoveries in these churches are not welcomed and avoided at all costs. Think about it for a moment: What would your

---

120 https://quoteinvestigator.com/2018/02/03/start/. There was also reference to:
http://www.gurteen.com/gurteen/gurteen.nsf/id/X001D5AC2/.

121
https://www.goodreads.com/author/quotes/149829.Mary_Anne_Radma
cher.

personal ministry be like if it were not for the incredible discoveries you have made in ministry during your journey. My granddaughter Olivia, just discovered the joy of walking and now she is giggling and smiling in her new discovery of mobility. Discovery in church revitalization is so important. I believe that invention and discovery in a restart is as vital to a church's survival as is food to our survival. One of the chief reasons churches rapidly decline is because they are no longer engaged in discovery. Innovation has been replaced with stagnation. A Church Revitalizer utilizes discovery as an act of creating something new that will re-embrace a community and prospects. While I say something new, there are times when revamping something old works also. New formats, strategies, events, and vision are all part of reengaging a community from which the restart church pulled away. Discovery and innovation in a restart are vital. There is a clue for saying something new in a restart:

C *atch their attention*

In a restart it is important to connect to the community and its people. A positive outreach strategy will provide for more effective friendship and neighborhood evangelism. Touching the unchurched is the most important priority when planning a hard-hitting restart plan. The church must look for ways to touch the hearts of the unchurched in large numbers. What does a community know about your church? Develop at least one thing you can be known for in your area. Some churches have outstanding crisis pregnancy ministries. Another a wonderful music program. Others are known for their unending commitment to reach people with the gospel of Jesus Christ. Being known in your community helps with the saturation and evangelization of your ministry area. For real communication to be completed, some type of focus on a felt need is imperative.

L *ook for where the Lord is working in your community and embrace the opportunities*

God wants to multiply His life a thousand-fold, and He wants to do it through you. A restart must embrace the opportunities it is given to readdress the needs of their community. God never gives up on a community so part of your strategy would include finding where the Lord is already doing something and see how your church could help out.

U *nderstand that you cannot repeat the past ministries that declined your church*

This is such an important issue and yet many church members think if they just work harder, the things they are doing would bring about change for the betterment of the church. It is just not so. If the ministries that you currently have deployed as part of your ministry strategy are declining your church, then just trying to do them better is not going to work. Here will need to be a sense of discovery that as a declining church regresses much of that has to do with the ministry choices you are offering your target area. If you are still following a model that is more than one hundred years old it is no wonder that the methodologies are declining your church. The message is still the same that Jesus saves. Yet if you are not open to try new ideas in the ways you are doing ministry, repeating what you are currently doing is not a solution.

E *mbrace new people and new methodologies*

Any church seeking to reach its community for Christ must analyze the community to best reach the unchurched individuals. Be clear when stating who you are and what you do. Seek to know who makes up your community. If you have a community of Millennials, stop trying to reach them with a senior adult focus in your ministries. Do not underestimate your audience. If your church has a negative image, it must first be overcome before any real progress can be made in reaching a new audience. Provide a well thought out platform that will address all the creative, spiritual, and social needs of the church.

Implement your strategy slowly. Test it, refine it, and keep following through by consistent evaluation and monitoring of the plan. It is sad when we realize that today we are strangers in our own cities and towns. We do not know and cannot see how things work. What kind of image does your church present to the community? Are there any hidden statements that hinder your witness for Jesus Christ? The churches that will make the greatest headway into the twenty years will be those who allow their membership to take risks. Far too often, the church has tied the hands of the truly creative within the confines of your church. There is a natural tendency to fight change, and it will take courage to truly develop creative approaches to ministry. The church that overcomes decline through a restart will only be those willing to take greater risks will keep pace and minister to our changing society! Churches willing to take risks, will see a ripe and fruitful group of believers to develop. Churches today compete with more messages bombarding the listening audience than they did twenty years ago! Amazingly, the average person encounters over 1,400 messages a day.

Practical Advice for the Church Restarter

Church Revitalizers working in a restart effort always ask me for some nuggets I have learned along the way on restarting a church. I often start by asking: Are you restarting it or replanting it? These concepts are certainly cousins but they are not siblings. One is a bring into existence strategy while the other is a resurrection strategy. One is filling its proverbial lungs for the very first time while the other is gasping for another breath. The latter is resuscitating the ministry where the former is raising up a ministry. So here is some of the practical advice I share with every restarter seeking to bring life to a church gasping for air:

Restarting a Church is a Walk Not a Run

A church planter is always sprinting to get the church up and going while a restarter is better served if they will move more slowly. Church planters want to prove to the denominational office that they are worthy of funding so aggressiveness is usually part of their game plan. It is wise to take a walk with the members in a church that want to see their church revitalized through a restart. Praying and asking the Lord to renew the church is a portion of that slow walk. Dreaming together of what a restarted church might do differently is also part of that slow walk. Developing new groups is part of the slow walk and that takes time.

Look for the Ten Up and the Ten Down in Your Relationships

Many people never stop to realize that their best chances of relationships are with those individuals who are ten years older and ten years younger than you. Everything in between is a fair chance of you and your people making a connection. The restarter should spend time with the people still in the church who are older. Far too often they spend it with the younger people and miss out on the blessings. Youth ministers turned pastors are usually challenged with this concept because they spent most of their lives in ministry reaching out to a younger generation and forgetting about the older generations. It is a substantial alteration in one's ministry to make such a turn. Start spending equal amounts of time with the fifty through seventy-year old's that remain in your fellowship. They will joyfully continue to support the work of the church that is reaching the younger generations if you stop treating them like they have no voice or influence. Their faithful commitment of financial resources ought to demonstrate that they want you to reach the younger generations but they do not want to be left out of ministry. There is much to be learned from these groups. The wisdom they possess has been acquired over the years of faithfulness. In fact, there is a great chance that these elderly church members have been walking with Jesus longer than you have been on this earth. Their views can help you if you let them have a voice.

Be Pleasant and Smile More in the Pulpit

Far too many Church Revitalizers are so serious that it turns others off. While church revitalization is a serious endeavor, it does not have to be an unpleasant one. Lighten up a little. Stop acting like you are ill all the time. Display the grace of the Lord to your congregation no matter if it is only a few members to begin with in the restart. Because you have time weekly with your attenders, stop being so stoic and start being a little more jubilant. Put some fun back in the church restart effort. Enjoy those that the Lord has given to you to begin your restart. In a short while, as the Lord begins to turn around the church there will be more new people coming so spend this time investing in these wonderful people. Do not be so serious all the time. Ministry is hard work and restarting a church is as well. But it does not have to be so serious all the time. Choose joy over solemnness. Jesus ought to bring a smile to your face and a little jump in your step. People like smiling, humorous, and friendly pastors.

Avoid Isolating Yourself as the Restarter

I have a friend who is a Church Revitalizer who is always depressed. Having spent time with him at various events, what I immediately began to notice is that he chooses to isolate himself from the very people he is trying to assist with renewal. His very job was to connect and yet he sought to disconnect more often than not. Because he was a church planter for most of his ministry it might be a byproduct of the loneliness of leading a new work into existence. His isolation could be a danger for him as a revitalization leader. Relationships will either make you or break you so put the time in to becoming more relational. Church restarters should take intentional steps to develop relational connections with not only the restart team members but the entire church as well. Stop displaying signals that you are unapproachable and begin exhibiting an open life policy of connection. Confirm for them so that they discern that you care more about them and their families than you do about the church restart. The rest will take care of itself.

Share the Victories Church-wide

I am amazed at how often the church staff and pastor celebrate victories yet forget to share them with the entire church. In a restart when something good happens, share it with everyone. I learned that as a church planter when I was in my twenties. In a restart it tells the congregation that the Lord is doing something good once again in their church. Church planters focus on continually getting better in various ministries while Church Revitalizers focus on keep drawing members to the core so they can work together to revitalize the church. Celebrate the little things and the big things early and often. When God blesses even a micro blessing, then celebrate. That will lead to macro blessings as we respond to the Lord's leading. My friend John Bailey worked with me at a missions agency ten years ago and often things were quite hard. John would run out and get ice cream for the staff and then ask the rest of us as team leaders to share in the expense. The staff always appreciated it and it did lighten the burden. Do not be afraid to celebrate even if it is just buying a little ice cream. Celebration displays that what you are doing in the restart while difficult is indeed worth it. These impromptu parties are a good thing. It brings hope.

Remember Who Is Your Most Important Asset in the Restart

John Maxwell taught me more than thirty years ago as a church leader that my most important asset in a church are those who volunteer continually and faithfully. People are the absolute most valuable asset at your restart. Those who remain in the church while they may not be the coolest person on the face of the earth, they are the faithful. Church planters often select cool over the committed. Those who have remained with the restart have made great sacrifices to be there and have been continually generous with their investment of time, energy and money to see a vision for the restart church realized. Affirm these members. Appreciate them repetitively. Pray for them unceasingly. Recognize them regularly.

Start with Jesus, Proceed with Jesus, and End with Jesus!

Church revitalization is all about the Lord's leading. He is there as you consider revitalizing the church. He guides you through the peaks and the valleys. There will be great highs as you see the Lord provide. Sometimes there will be lows but that is part of revitalization and renewal. He is with you even as you celebrate the renewal of your church. Church revitalization is a risk-taking endeavor but with the Lod's guidance you are never alone. God's faithfulness gives you the stamina to see the restart through to completion. The Church Revitalizer reminds the congregation that the effort is viable because the Lord Jesus is worth our sacrifice.

Train Your Leaders Because No One Else Will

The restart pastor will need to gently train the membership in relevant techniques for revitalization. Do not expect that they have been trained previously. I went to a national training put on by a large denomination only to find out that they were not training revitalizers, they were merely trying to give a pep talk to them. They spent five days talking around revitalization but never equipped those in attendance. There were a lot of touching stories but they were lean on the training. It was as if either they did not know enough about the subject of revitalization or they were more interested in being seen as a movement maker. Never leave it to someone else for the training of your leaders. That is the Church Revitalizers responsibility.

Revitalize Your Church and Stop Looking at the Church Down the Road

God calls a Church Revitalizer to revitalize a church not to keep looking at the other guy down the road revitalizing the church. Get up each day and work on your church. Stop thinking about how much ahead or behind you are on the revitalization continuum as compare to another Church Revitalizer. That never helps either church. The Lord has a plan for your specific church so follow His plan and not someone else's.

So, there are my nuggets for the moment. While they are not a final list, they are sage advice for the restart leader.

The Hazards and Pitfalls of Running Too Fast in a Restart

In Webster's New World Dictionary, a "pitfall" is defined as (1) a lightly covered pit used as a trap for animals and (2) an unsuspected difficulty, danger or error that one may fall into.122 Church revitalization is chock-full of pitfalls. It is best to be aware of them as you begin the adventure of restarting a church. If you have already relaunched and suddenly find yourself needing to start over because you have over started in your renewal effort, ask God to clearly show you what needs to be eliminated and what needs to be elevated. Our God is sovereign as we rely upon him, he can help us out of the pitfalls and revive the church and get it moving forward again. Let's look at nine hazards or pitfalls that are often present when a church over starts and needs to restart:

---

122 http://www.yourdictionary.com/pitfalls#wiktionary.

Hazard #1 – There is no real manifestation that the Lord is in this endeavor to restart.

With church planting in decline in North America today, it is easy to fall in love the romantic notion of revitalizing a church. The pitfall is the idea that you can revitalize a church without discerning from the Holy One whether church revitalization is the call of the Lord for your life. I received a call today from a man in Orlando who had just participated in splitting a church here in central Florida. He asked if we had a church he could "help" that was struggling. This individual has already hurt three churches in the area and he thought I would be willing to allow him the chance to hurt one of our churches. Nothing that he touches demonstrates the real manifestation of the Lord so I caution churches who think he is a savior. He is anything but. Revitalizing a church may appear a romantic notion but it is extremely hard work and not to be entered into lightly. It takes a particular type of individual to successfully revitalize a church. Today's restarter must be highly relational, an extreme entrepreneur, and driven to bring something out of the ashes of rapid decline. The scripture is clear: *"Unless the Lord builds the house, its builders labor in vain."*[123]

Hazard #2 – The Church Revitalizer has an unrealistic expectation of the type of church in which they can revitalize.

Not every one of us has the same gifts for church revitalization. I have people call me and ask me if I would recommend them to a particular church as a revitalization leader. I am often surprised because they have such an unrealistic expectation of their skill sets. Today, what is really missing in most Church Revitalizers, is the ability to be an

---

[123] Psalm 127:1.

effective gatherer and personal evangelist. They have unrealistic expectations of what they can do and how those gifts can lead to a fruitful church revitalization effort. Wishful thinking is presumptuous at best, despite some who have a great desire to enter the field of revitalization. The Lord does not owe you numerical growth. Unrealistic expectations have hurt many a potential revitalizer and the church he is leading. Allow the Lord to place you where your gifts are the exact thing that is needed.

Hazard #3 – The one who is leading the revitalization effort is not a revitalizer but more of a maintenance pastor.

When a pastor of an established church does not have the characteristics of a successful Church Revitalizer and yet he attempts to restart a church, he often falls into a pit.124 The impulse of the pastor may be that the established church is too repressive. There are some called to ministry who are called to be founding pastors of one church and stay there forever. Others are more catalytic and they have the gifts necessary to restart, revitalize, or renewal multiple churches. If you are not sure whether you are really a church restart leader, then answer these few questions:

> Are you a visionary person that can get others to follow your new ideas?
> Do you take initiative and lead courageously?
> Do you relate well to the unchurched?
> Is your spouse on board with this vision to become a Church Revitalizer?
> Would you say that you both have the ability to persevere?

---

124 For more on this topic go to: RenovateConference.org/downloads and search for the presentation *"Skill Sets Deemed Necessary for a Church Revitalizer."*

How flexible and adaptable are you?
How resilient are you?
Do you have a gift for gathering a lot of people?
Do you work hard or are you lazy?

These questions allow you to begin to face the realities of your ability and skill sets to successfully revitalize a church through a restart.

Hazard #4 –Premature restart of the church before it is fully ready.

Probably the most common killer of any restart effort is the desire to restart the church revitalization effort to soon. Without out a doubt, far too many restarts are defeated by early and premature take-off.125 There are consequences to the church and the restarter if you decide to prematurely take-off. When the church reintroduces itself to the public before it is ready, it can stall the church for a long time. I have had many a restarter who wants to close the church one Sunday and reopen it the following Sunday. That is never wise. You only get one chance to say something different and it can't be achieved in one hundred and sixty-eight hours between Sundays. I have a church in my community where the pastor wanted to do a restart and he chose to make the change in seven days. They have a cooler name today. The have the system of governance that the pastor desired. They have new organizations that previously were impossible to introduce in the church. Yet, they are so much smaller than they were previously. The church restarter made the change too quickly and the flight of present members became former members. Today they are about a third of the former attendance

---

125 For additional help in this area go to: RenovateConference.org/downloads and download the presentation: *Eleven Consequences of a Premature Launch* by Tom Cheyney.

numbers.126 Some might have left certainly, but others did leave because the new direction was forced upon them and they were not given enough time to embrace the new idea. I acknowledge that you have to get started, but if done too quickly, it will further decline your church and keep it from achieving the desired goal of being revitalized.

Hazard #5 – Inadequate preparation and attention by the restart leader.

What makes a church planter so different than a pastor? Often while a church planter is a great visionary, able to sell participants on a future which has never been tried and is unsecured, what they usually lack are the skills to make appropriate planning to achieve the dream and the ability to administrate the realities of the dream once things begin to be accomplished. On the other hand, many a pastor has the ability to dot every "i" and cross every "t" in the area of planning and administering but lacks the ability to successfully develop a dream and see it to the end. Church planters are usually big picture thinkers and explode due to the minutia, whereas pastors are able to manage the routine yet lack the ability to sell the new vision for renewal in the church. Where one lags in getting stuff done the other lags in selling the vision. The restart leader must realize that they will need to sell and resell the vision for a restart over and over for the congregation to catch the vision. Assimilation will need to be focused on the new and re-assimilate those who are able to be reclaimed for the restarting church.127 Many a

---

126 For more on this topic go to: RenovateConference.org/downloads and search for the presentation *"Numbers that Matter in Church Revitalization and Renewal"* by Tom Cheyney.

127 For more on this topic go to: RenovateConference.org/downloads and search for the presentation *"How to Reclaim Inactive Church Member Utilizing the R.E.C.L.A.I.M. Strategy"* by Tom Cheyney.

restart leader hopes they can rebuild a large group quickly simply because they are gifted expositors. That is seldom the case so having a focus on leading those you have will help keep the core while you go after even more. Having a plan and a focus is a must in this area.

Hazard #6 – Insufficient funding streams developed prior to restarting the revitalization effort.

It takes funds to restart a church and keep it going throughout the three years necessary to see a turnaround. Lack of enough sustaining resources preceding the church revitalization effort will hurt your chances to succeed. If your church is considering a restart, you must have the support of the membership towards the efforts of the restarter. Money is not thrown at church revitalization efforts like it is at church planting efforts. That is a shame. Think what our churches in America would look like if Protestantism had not placed its sole chances for success in church planting. If even fifty years ago we had denominations willing to see the challenges facing existing churches, we would not have the eighty to eighty five percent of our churches plateauing or in decline. If we had developed a system to help place Church Revitalizers in declining churches before they were all but dead, what a difference we would have made. Today much of our denominational revitalization efforts are a band aid at best with limited resourcing. Church restarters coming to restart a church always over-estimate the financial requirements they will need to raise for the church. Many a revitalization journey has been stalled or ceased due to a lack of adequate resources to turn around the church. Revitalization efforts can be paralyzed by the failure to acknowledge the monies needed to keep going. Can the church afford to even have the church restarter come to lead them? That is critical because many think the restart pastor will love the Lord so much that they will not need to be paid a livable salary to sustain one's family while they are working towards renewal. If the church cannot afford a Church restarter, the renewal effort is going to suffer a great loss in the near future.

Hazard #7 – There is unconfessed and unrepented sin within the leadership ranks.

Churches are not owed a successful restart. If there is a high degree of sin running around the church in leadership, it will keep the Lord's hand from blessing your church. These sins must be dealt with. You are vulnerable as the Church Revitalizer so watch out. Jesus said that when the shepherd is struck, the sheep scatter. Influential lay leaders who fall into sin and do not immediately repent of such sins can actually cause the church to fail. The membership is shaken and Satan seeks to destroy the restarters efforts.

Hazard #8 – Inadequate, deficient, and lacking outreach by the restarter and the church revitalization leadership team.

I believe one of the reasons a church actually begins to plateau or rapidly decline is because of a waning commitment to outreach and evangelism. It begins with the pastor and then eventually filters down to the laity leadership and concludes with the church membership all lacking any desire to reach the lost. When a declining church places evangelism and outreach as a low priority the church is in trouble. Because it takes a minimal investment of one thousand days in a revitalization journey, the restart church ought to be epitomized by outreach of all types and in all areas around your target area. In scripture we see that at Pentecost, the Lord used an incredible outreach effort to draw people in the city together to hear about Jesus and become a community of Christ followers. It is amazing how quickly the church can lose focus on outreach and evangelism. It is the Lord who compels individuals and families to His church. One of the initial goals of revitalization is for the restarter and the lay revitalization leadership to tell as many people in their target area of the church about the restart project going on at the church. Many restarts continue to fail because they ignore outreach and evangelism.

Hazard #9 – A Church Revitalizer who rejects accountability or guidance.

Even the most successful pastors need a coach at times in their ministries. In like manner there are times when a Church Revitalizer would be wise to accept guidance. In one of my restart efforts when I arrived at the church many of the membership suggested that I avoid two men in the church because they disliked pastors. In reality the opposite was true so I accepted as much guidance and accountability as these two men would offer. They loved the church and only wanted the best for that church. I knew that others had bought into the former pastor's unwillingness to be held accountable by anyone let alone these two great leaders. You cannot be a loner as a restarter. If you are you will fail. As an experienced Church Revitalizer, I realized that even successful ones needed accountability and guidance at times. Untried and previously unsuccessful restarters are vulnerable to disaster without guidance.

The Ruts from Running Too Far Too Fast in a Restart Without Assimilation

Ruts in one's road of ministry are often hard to navigate. Such ruts will cause severe damage to the church renewal effort and the church restarter. Here are a few common ruts that come from running too far too fast in a restart without proper assimilation:

1. Imitation of other successful Church Revitalizers over allowing God to create a unique you!

God has called you to restart His church and not copy someone else's version of a restart. While duplication of another techniques is often a way to learn, copying another church's ministry and expecting the same outcome is unwise. Ask the Lord what He desires in a restart and then rest on His unlimited sufficiency in your restart effort. In church planting there are so many church planters who want to copy their favorite church planter. Even these planters offer a franchise approach to copying their church's ministry. What amazes me though is that none of the churches copying the original has been blessed in such degree as the one in which God planted. The same is true in church revitalization and renewal.

2. There is an adage that one's strengths can also be one's weakness.

When you are strong in specific areas of ministry caution must be taken not to allow your strengths to become a means to leave God out of the restart equation. When we have those Sampson-like impulses to do our own thing it keeps us from hearing what the Lord desires for the church. It is the Lord who builds the church and who revitalizes it as well. Remember what the Lord Jesus said, *Without Me, you can do nothing.*

3. Remind yourself just whose church you are revitalizing.

It is critical to understand that even while you are the out-front revitalization leader, you are to follow the example of the John the Baptist when he declared, *"He must become greater; I must become less."*128 If you are not careful your individual goals and dreams will point out to others that your objectives are more important than God's interruptions. Church consists of believers coming together in the same physical space in the name of Jesus Christ. To gather together in the name of Jesus means gathering together to publicly worship Jesus, serve Jesus, and help others love Jesus. We need to be reminded whose church we are revitalizing. Church Revitalizers often drop out because they become overwhelmed with the responsibilities of leading the restart. They act like they are the proverbial chipmunk who is running inside the cage on the spinning wheel. They are running hard but are getting nowhere except more worn out. The church is a living organism, with Jesus Christ as the living Head.

4. If you confuse passion with strategic planning you are only a day dreamer and not a revitalizer.

Planning as a Church Revitalizer wins out more often than a passion as a Church Revitalizer. If we confuse our passion as strategic planning, we are merely a day dreamer and not a Church Revitalizer. Strategic planning mobilizes the restart. Passion might motivate them to stay at the task but full and complete buy-in is achieved through mobilization. Both are important to the restart. When you have

---

128 John 3:30 NIV.

motivation, but lack the ability to mobilize others you are left with a daydream. When you have mobilization but lack the ability to motivate others you are left with a nightmare. But if you have the ability to motivate and to mobilize others you will see your passion become a reality and your dream fulfilled.

5. When you lead as one over lead as many

The church restarter must bring others with him on the journey. When you lead as one over leading as many it is impossible for the renewal effort to survive. Leading alone without bringing others aboard as part of the leadership team is a short course for failure as a revitalizer. Thinking team is far better than thinking individual talent. Coming together is the beginning. Keeping together is progress. Working together is success. Restarters must learn to think team over leading alone.

6. Church restarters display desperation due to failure to develop others for the task of revitalization.

If a Church Revitalizer fails to train and develop volunteers for the task of revitalization, his inability will begin to show the crack in his armor and he will begin to display a sense of desperation. That is the "I'm winging it mentality." Far too many leaders in churches needing to be revitalized are afraid to admit that they need help in this area and they do not make the time to train others. This is demoralizing to the church and even more so to the pastor once he realizes he is over his head and lacks the ability to train others for the task of revitalization. Never get so anxious for leaders that you neglect the developmental process. Watch out for those who come along side of you but show signs of drifting once the hard work of renewal begins. I was in a church today that was being revitalized and discovered that a layman had raised in prowess only to discover he was a prowler. Once he did not get his way he took about one hundred people from the revitalized church. Prowlers will leave you at first light often when the going gets tough. Watch out for people who always want to be out front. Be careful with those who seek to lead but repel from accountability.

7. Choosing to be steady when it is transformation that is needed.

Stuck churches in decline are usually steadily dying. The trademark of a declining church is slow and steady. While revitalization efforts are usually paced more slowly, they are not on the perpetual loop of doing nothing. In a restart transformation is an ingrained value of the church restarter. Caution should be shared that you do not act as an erratic restart leader. Church Revitalizers who are under developed as a leader are often erratic. Many restart efforts fail because the church restarter was erratic and changed just for the sake of change and not for the need of the church. The church needs to be transformed so do something each day towards renewing the church.

Peak Performance Principles for Church Restarters

I would like to share with you five peak performance principles for church restarters. It was C.S. Lewis who said:

"You are never too old to set another goal or to dream a new dream."[129]
Here we go:

Principle #1 - It Is Never Too Late to Start Over Again!

Some people say, "Oh, things will never change in my situation", but in God's time it is never too late to start over. The Apostle Paul learned this from his own experience. He had persecuted the Christians. He was into rules, legalism, and rigidity and in the ninth chapter of the book of Acts we are told that he had a vision of God that changed him forever into a follower of Jesus Christ and he started over! Let me be quick to say that you may not need to do a total revitalization effort. God may want you to start over right where we are! God may be calling you to start over in the church you are leading. Listen Church Revitalizer, this may be the time when you need to start over right where you are! Take small steps. Make a list. Then do three of those on the list today. Not tomorrow. Make a start and take a step it will motivate you to take the journey.

Principle #2 - When we start over we never really start completely over!

God seems to build into our lives all of the hurts, all of the issues, all the pain of the past, all of that is part of who we are now, everything we've ever done, all of the times when we've blown it and weaves all we are and all that we have been into who we are today. So, you see, when we start over, we don't start completely over. God takes all our experiences and uses them I believe to make us stronger. As a Church Revitalizer do not be ashamed to admit that you have made mistakes. I responded to a question in a large church revitalization conference I was speaking at a few years ago when a young restart pastor asked: "how did you come to be

---

129 https://www.passiton.com/inspirational-quotes/6686-you-are-never-too-old-to-set-another-goal-or-to.

a successful Church Revitalizer?" I responded, "Three simple words, *made good decisions!*" The revitalizer continued and asked, "How did you learn to make good decisions?" I responded, "one word, experience." Well, where do you get experience, two words, *bad decisions!* We never start completely over because God takes everything we have ever learned and creates us into a new person through it all. Have you ever realized that most of us do not get wisdom in our early twenties? You do not get wisdom at 25 or 30. To get wisdom you have to start over again and again and you often go through the school of hard knocks, to get wisdom you have to strike out two, three or four times.

Principle #3 – Do not seek perfection. Seek movement.

Far too many of us are perfectionists in the ministry. Do not allow yourself to get stuck on perfection as a Church Revitalizer. Stop overthinking an idea or feeling like it needs to be perfect before you get started can be a big roadblock to actually getting started at all. In my experience, ideas and concepts evolve over time, and unless you get started you will not be able to go through that process. They do not need to be perfect at the beginning in order to be great in the end, so let go of the idea of needing the idea to be perfect, take the pressure off yourself and just make a start. You will be glad you did.

Principle #4 – Keep at the effort and do not stop.

Distractions can hurt the Church Revitalizer. Keep going with the effort of revitalization. Once you have started, you will probably want to celebrate, so do just that. But once you have done that, it's time to keep going. Something I find can often happen is that you might have the motivation to start something, and take the first few steps, but then falter on the next ones, and let the idea drift. So, here is the lesson: once you have started, continue on. Keep listing small steps, putting them on your list for each day, and doing them. Do not allow yourself to get distracted in idea modeling. Get an idea and work on it first and foremost. You do not need more than one to start. When that one is accomplished ask the Lord for another one. Stick with the one you have started, commit to the time it will take and, as they say, finish what you started.

Principle #5 - In God's providence if we our offer hearts and minds to our Almighty God, then when we start over there are always wonderful surprises awaiting us.

In 1899 a man named Charles Duell was the Secretary for *The Department of Patents*, and he urged President McKinley to close the Department of Patents in 1899. McKinley said, "Why should I do that?" And, Charles Duell said, and I quote, "because everything that can be invented has been invented. It's a true story. The Lord has some wonderful surprises waiting for the church restarter. We need to remain prayerful. We need to allow the Lord to work. We might even feel like we are locked in prison like the apostle Paul. Did you hear what happened to the Apostle Paul when he was in prison?

The whole Praetorian Guard was talking about his imprisonment! The Praetorian Guard was the division of guards that guarded the emperor – 10,000 of them. They were the crème of the crop. When they had served between 12 and 16 years they finally became Roman Citizens. Isn't it interesting that one of the Praetorian guards was chained to Paul's wrist? He was under house arrest, he was not in prison as we might think of it and this guard is chained to guard all the time and as people came to the house and visited Paul and talk with Paul, and Paul prayed with them the guard had to listen to it all. And the guard member changed every few hours and if you had wanted a strategy to change the Roman

Empire you couldn't have come up with a better strategy. He was converting them one by one!

God is full of wonderful surprises. Sometimes you think you are at a dead end, but have faith, God is not finished! Success in the field of revitalization can consist of going from one seeming failure to another apparent failure without loss of enthusiasm. You learn in renewal that the axiom is true, the only thing you must truly fear is fear itself. Church restarter, you must learn to step right into and through your fears because you know that whatever happens you can handle it with the Lord. To give in to fear is to give away the right to live life on Gods terms. You learn to fight for your life and not to squander it living under a cloud of impending doom.

Chapter 8
Diagnosing the Dying Church

Take this most seriously: A yes on earth is yes in heaven; a no on earth is no in heaven. What you say to one another is eternal. I mean this. When two of you get together on anything at all on earth and make a prayer of it, my Father in heaven goes into action. And when two or three of you are together because of me, you can be sure that I'll be there.[130]

Speaking in an Evangelism Conference several years ago the late Dr. Vance Havner, Evangelist from North Carolina, a small man who never weighed over 120 pounds, jokingly said "I'm the healthiest sick-looking person you've ever seen in your life!" He went on to say that an individual's health cannot always be judged by an outward appearance. That's why doctors call for all kinds of diagnostic tests to be done to check a person's physical status. The fact is, it's not easy to tell the state of a person's health by looking at them. Some abnormal conditions are harder to diagnose than others. So it is with the church.

The over-riding question is, "What does a sick church look like?" This is an important question because dying churches are becoming epidemic. As is true with human life, it is imperative that a correct diagnosis must be made before the sick church can recover. We must know what made the church sick to begin with if we intend to bring healing. In an article published by the International Mission Board of the Southern Baptist Convention, the author stated that, "Not every church is in good health. Some are gravely ill. Some are downright toxic. All are certainly in process, but toward what, exactly, is that process meant to move them? How can a sick church heal without first knowing in what direction health

---

[130] Eugene H. Peterson, *The Message: The Bible in Contemporary Language* (Colorado Springs, CO: NavPress, 2005), Mt 18:18–20.

lies? What, after all, is a healthy church?"131 We must understand how these questions are to be answered if we are to help sick churches into good health again. The size, income, facilities, or location are not necessarily relevant.

Tony Evans believes that we must understand the basic nature of a church when he says, "Christ's Body, the Church, is not an organization, but an organism. We can create a robot and have organization. The parts connect to each other so that it works but the problem with the robot is that it has no life. It is organizationally connected, but it is not a living being. A human body, in contrast, has organization that makes it function, but it also is an organism."132 In the human body, one is not even aware of the operation of his digestive system but if that digestive system becomes sick, one is not aware of anything else. The church, the Body of Christ, operates in much the same fashion. Now, let us consider some treatments for the sick church.

Assessing for the Big Picture

The initial assessment includes all that has been discussed in previous chapters, but this section will be more specific. This part of the diagnosis deals mainly with the church's past. This procedure is an examination to identify the church's areas of weakness and its strengths to be able to conclude about spiritual condition and illness. What the assessment should look for are those things the church has done right and those things the church has done wrong. There are at least 10 areas to be examined.

---

131 *12 Characteristics of a Healthy Church*, IMB, August 31, 2016, accessed September 11,2018,
https://www.imb.org/2016/08/31/2016o83112-characteristics-healthy-church/'.

132 "The Body of Christ", The Urban Alternative Blog, accessed September 11, 2018, https://tony evans.org/the-body-of-christ/.

First, the area that should be assessed should be the past and present *focus of the church*. In a previous chapter the difference between and inward and an outward focus was discussed. The question that needs to be answered during the assessment is, "what is the main focus of the church?" Tracy Keenan in the article titled "Finding the Focal Point" says, "Church health is a matter of focus: a focus on Christ, not the church. Our focus determines whether we have a survival mentality or a service mentality."133

That which the church spends most of its time on is a sure sign of where their focus lies. There is no focus as important to the church as its focus on Jesus Christ, His will and obedience to His will. Any other focus will end in disaster for the church. To emphasize what has been said in a previous chapter…the church that has turned inward in its approach to ministry is on its way to death.

Second, the area to be assessed has to do with past and present *understanding of its purpose*. Does the church understand the true purpose of a New Testament church and specifically its personal purpose in a particular setting? This is a key to success. Many churches have forgotten what the Bible teaches about the work of the local church. In many instances the congregation has diverted the Biblical purpose to fit their own personal desires and likes or dislikes. The main purpose is the propagation of the Gospel (Good News) to the community it resides in and ultimately to the world. Without an understanding of the church's Biblical purpose it becomes only a civic/secular organization that will have no transforming effect on those it touches.

---

133 Tracy Keenan, "What Does a Healthy Church Look Like? (Part 1) *Christianity Today,* July 1997, https://www.christianitytoday.com/pastors/channel/utilities/print.html?type=article&id=2860.

Third, the past and present *condition and quality of leadership* should be assessed. Darrin Patrick says, "Most churches do not grow beyond the spiritual health of their leadership." Patrick goes on to say, "A pastor must always be fearless before his critics and fearful before his God. Let us tremble at the thought of neglecting the sheep. Remember that when Christ judges us, he will judge us with a special degree of strictness."[134] The quality of leadership has been discussed in a previous chapter. Any diagnostic process must include an examination of the leadership in the church. Has the leadership in your church shown a high level of honesty and integrity? Does your leadership inspire the congregation to accomplish great things for God or have they become "lone rangers?" Are they passionate about their ministry, the Gospel and leadership? Are they good communicators? Are they decisive and capable of making good decisions? Are they creative in their approach to ministry? Do they encourage others to get involved and do ministry in the body? These are all pertinent questions to ask when assessing present and past leadership.

Fourth, the past and present *influence/reputation* in the community must be assessed. Many churches suffer from a tainted reputation in the community. For that reason, when a church restart is initiated, the name of the church must be changed to have a new beginning in the community. Infighting and church splits destroy the good name and integrity of a local congregation and that reputation is very difficult to salvage. To prescribe a solution to the dying church, there must be a determination of how damaged the church is by its past.

A good example of this is a congregation of around 600 in the Savannah, Georgia area. The church had been thriving

---

134 Darrin Patrick, *Church Planter: The Man, The Message, The Mission*, (Wheaton: Crossway, 2010) 25, 81.

and growing rapidly until conflict came. The conflict threatened the work of the pastor. He weathered the problem for a while, but some members left because of the conflict. After a few months another conflict arose and as a result the pastor left under pressure. This was followed by the migration away from the church by over 200 members. The church began to struggle with finding a pastor because of its bad reputation for infighting. People in the community began to talk about the disunity which resulted in no one visiting the church. After they called a new pastor and he was there for 9 months another conflict broke out after he and the chairman of deacons got into a physical altercation and everyone but 25 of the faithful left. Finally, when a church revitalization group stepped in to help, the reputation of the church had been ruined. The name of the church was changed. Six months later the church opened to 175 new faces. The church recovered from near disaster, but it was not the same church. The community saw a new church with a new identity and they responded to it.

Fifth, the congregations past and present *sense of community/unity* should be examined. "Community is God's desire for us—and a sign of a mature faith. Because at the end of the day, when we grow in our relationships with others, we're growing in relationship with Him!"[135] Hebrews 10:24 says "And let us consider how we may spur one another on toward love and good deeds, not giving up meeting together, as some are in the habit of doing, but encouraging one another—and all the more as you see the Day approaching."[136] When I speak of community I speak of

---

135 The Stewardship Team, *"4 Reasons the Bible Calls Us to Community,"* (February 3, 2017}, accessed October 18, 2018, https://www.stewardship.com/articles/4-reasons-the-bible-calls-us-to-community.

136 Hebrews 10:24–25 NIV.

the church congregation not the surrounding community. When community is in disunity the church will not last very long. A study of past divisions, splits and factions can be quite revealing when diagnosing the problem in a church. Usually it reveals the presence of a matriarch, patriarch or some other power broker that has caused the disunity and the death of the church. Then Matthew 18:20 says, "For where two or three are gathered together in my name, there am I in the midst of them."137 God honors true fellowship and community in the local church.

Sixth, the *effectiveness of pastor and staff* must be considered. There is a place for the assessment of their role in the church's health or lack thereof. It seems that in many cases of dying churches, there is the presence of a lazy pastor and/or lazy staff. There presently seems to be an abundance of uncommitted church staff. Many are not committed to real discipleship, evangelism, caring ministry or even solid Biblical preaching. Some have their own agenda and refuse to work as a team.

A church and its pastor in eastern North Carolina contacted a church revitalization group to help bring the church back to life. The pastor had a reputation and history of indecisiveness and poor leadership. His way of dealing with a failing church was to leave it and go kill another one. In the initial revitalization meeting the churched seemed very responsive and a willingness to change its direction. At the close of the meeting the uncommitted pastor went to the revitalizer and handed him a manila envelope. The revitalizer asked, "What is this?" The pastor replied, "It's my resume...can you put my name in some churches that you might know that need a pastor?" The revitalizer replied, "No. When you called us here to help, you indicated that you wanted to see this church flourish once again. You have

---

137 Matthew 18:20 KJV.

wasted our time. I will not help you move. Plant yourself here and lead this church." He handed the envelope back to the pastor and left. A few months later the pastor moved and left the church in a lurch not knowing what to do. This kind of thing is happening in churches all over America. Pastors and staff are key to a church thriving. If they are ineffective or unconcerned, the church will fail. The pastor who truly cares about the future health of his church will plant himself for the duration of his ministry. The church deserves a constant and consistent leader that will not abandon the church when the going gets tough.

Seventh, the church's past and present *financial solvency* must be examined. A study of the past and present giving, budgeting and spending patterns of a church is a great revealer. Most churches that are in difficult straits and on their way to a death spiral begin to cut budget items that are vital to the spiritual well-being of the church. Usually the first thing to go is the missions and evangelism budget.

Art Rainer reports, "Church budgets are incredibly important, and they often get a bad rap. A church budget is not only vital for a church's financial health, but for their mission. A church budget is an essential tool for every church leader. It should not be ignored or avoided."[138] The budget of a church is important because it tells where the church places value. It reveals what is important to the people. It clearly shows where the priorities lie. A close examination of the finances and budgeting of the church are vital to diagnosing the health of a church.

Eighth, the history of past and present *growth, baptism, additions and salvations* will be very revealing. This is probably

138 "3 Reasons Why Church Budgets are Really Important," Art Rainer, accessed September 17, 2018, http://www.artrainer.com/3-reasons-why-church-budgets-are-really-important/.

one of the most important parts of assessing and diagnosing the health of a church. This is the most revealing area as to why a church gets into a death spiral. Growth doesn't just happen. Barry Cameron says in his article titled *The Twelve Mistakes Dead Churches Make,* "They (churches) mistakenly believe growing churches are nothing more than the result of being in the right place at the right time. Even the perfect garden in the perfect place won't stay perfect if you just walk away and leave it. Before long, it will be overgrown with weeds. Most growing churches grow in the hardest of places in the most difficult of times. They are the result of hard work. The Bible does not say, "God helps those who help themselves." However, God does have a way of blessing those who do everything they possibly can to build His kingdom and aren't afraid of hard work."139 The movie tag line "Build it and they will come," certainly does not apply to the church. Churches grow because of the ministry of the people. Individuals are saved because members are witnessing. The past records of baptisms and additions are sure signs of the healthiness or unhealthiness of a church. When baptisms and addition are absent it is a sure sign that the church is unhealthy, and the diagnosis is bleak.

Ninth, the church's past and present *willingness to change* should be investigated. Carey Nieuwhof said, "One of the tensions many of us wrestle with as leaders who are trying to navigate change happens when people tell us: I want our church to grow. I just don't want it to change. Isn't wanting to grow but not really change like saying "I want to lose weight, but I really want a bacon cheeseburger"? Well, yes, it's exactly like that."140 While speaking at a meeting in a local

---

139 Barry Cameron, "The Twelve Mistakes Dead Churches Make," *Crossroads,* March 10, 2017, accessed September, 13, 2018.

140 Carey Nieuwhof, "What to do when people want a church to grow…but not change," Carey Nieuwhof Blog, June 8, 2018, accessed

church on the necessity of change, the revitalizer was confronted by an elderly lady who was the Matriarch of the church. She stopped him and said, "I'm 86 years old. I've been in this church all my life and they are not changing a thing until I die. Then they can do what they want to do." Wow, what a frightening thing to say. The fact of the matter is, at the age of 86, that is a real dangerous statement because God can fix that. It seems that every church and every person is resistant to change if the change is drastic. However, resistance to change is a death knell for the church. Our culture and communities are changing so rapidly but the church has not kept up with the change and is losing many opportunities to reach the lost. As stated in a previous chapter, the one thing the church should never change is its message, if it is Biblically based. If that changes it will die a quick death. It must, however, commit to necessary change to keep up with the community it ministers in. The Southern Baptist Convention reports at least 1000 churches close every year. Other entities say that the number is far higher. One thing all the reports agree on is that they close because they are not willing to change. Every church needs to ask the question, "Lord what is it that we must change in order to reach our community with the Gospel?" How a church accepts or rejects change will determine the final diagnosis. Unwillingness to change will give the church a dark future.

Tenth, the past and present *internal relationships* of the church are vital to understanding the existing problems in the church. Is there infighting in the church? This infighting can be between the pastor and other leaders. It can be between members of controlling families. It can show up when the patriarch or the matriarch is challenged. It can even show up when members of the same family get at odds with each

---

September17, 2018, https://careynieuwhof.com/what-to-do-when-people-want-a-church-to-grow-but-not-change/.

other. A perfect example is a church in central North Carolina that went through the process of a collaborative weekend. During a one-on-one conversation with a volunteer staff member, the truth and heart of the disunity began to creep out into the open. The staff person had, for several years, been at odds with his own brother who was a member of the church. They brought their disagreement into the church and aired their dirty laundry, constantly, before the congregation. This conflict brought a horrible disunity into the congregation because members began to take sides. As a result, the entire church was drawn into a battle that should have been worked out in the family unit and not the church.

Disunity is closing church doors by the hundreds in America. The church is called to unity and is to promote unity not only in the fellowship of believers but also in the individual family units that make up the congregation. Ephesians 4:25 says, "Wherefore putting away lying, speak every man truth with his neighbor: for we are members one of another."141

Assessing for Reality

A church assessment is a necessary step towards making a proper church health diagnosis. It focuses on learning the needs of the church and gaining a clear picture of the churches strength and understanding of the church's "present reality." Assessing for reality is necessary to make decisions about the future of the church.

Most Church Revitalizers have developed their own diagnostic tools. Some work well, others not so well. The basic assessment should always include how well the church is doing in the six major character traits of a healthy church. These traits have been mentioned previously in another

---

141 Ephesians 4:25 KJV.

chapter, but they need to be reemphasized. These traits are evangelism, discipleship, worship, fellowship, ministry and prayer. These six traits should be categorized into four sections that cover the entire life and function of the church. Those sections are: Worship and Word, Body Life, Inside the Walls and Outside the Walls. Listed below are the various areas of ministry of the local church that included in each category.

Worship and Word - This section of the assessment deals with commitment to the Bible, effectiveness of worship, utilization of spiritual giftedness, the productivity of preaching/teaching, and the empowerment by the Holy Spirit. The main ingredient in the life of any healthy church is its worship and its stand and understanding of the Word of God. Every healthy church understands the giftedness of individual Christians and that every Christian has been gifted for ministry. Furthermore, it understands the importance of preaching and teaching the Word of God in such a way that Christians will grow in grace and that lost people will hear and respond to the Gospel. All of this must be saturated with the presence and power of the Holy Spirit. This part of the assessment reveals the churches understanding of what a New Testament church ought to be. This is the foundation of the healthy church. If the church is lacking in this area, there will be no spiritual health in the church. It will surely die if an intervention doesn't take place.

Body Life includes the availability of encouragement in the congregation, the presence of enthusiasm, and the truth about friendliness, unity, conflict and influence. This is a crucial element in the health of the local church. How the church conducts its life as a body of believers determines how healthy the church really is. Most churches that are plateauing or declining seem to have little or no real encouraging times within the fellowship. In fact, churches that are unhealthy are usually in a state of discouragement and even despondency. Discouragement seems to set off a chain reaction that is difficult to stop. Discouragement leads to loss of enthusiasm which results in the church losing interest in their community, mission and purpose. In turn, a lack of enthusiasm results in an unfriendly atmosphere where visitors and church members alike don't relate well with each other. When the church becomes unfriendly to the needs of the lost community, death is sure to follow. Then disunity sets in and conflict erupts. This is portrayed in the many church splits that occur every year in the evangelical church world. The result is the loss of influence in the community and area. The church becomes a nonentity to the community and its testimony is lost while the community remains hopeless and without a Gospel presentation. The finality of it all is death.

Inside the walls includes the work of assimilation, the clarity of communication, the structure of administration, the commitment to stewardship, presence of organization and the regularity of prayer. When a church gets in an unhealthy state the work of the church within itself seems to falter a bit. When a new member comes into the ranks of the church often they are not assimilated into the life of the church and they leave. In many ailing churches, there is little or no communication between the leadership and the congregation and this always causes problems and often disunity. Failure to communicate usually comes from poor administration and leadership. Sometimes the church is organization directed rather than leader led. Two other signs of a fatal direction in the church are present as well. The **first** is the lack of stewardship which insinuates that there is no understanding about the worship aspect of stewardship. **Second,** is a real misunderstanding of the purpose and priority of prayer. The health and vitality of the church is always revealed in this area of assessment. If this area is unhealthy it will lead to all kinds of problems for the church.

181

Outside the walls includes missions involvement, the work of impacting lostness, the foundation of discipleship, the work of ministry and presence of God given vision. This is where the so called "rubber hits the road." Walls are confining. Walls divide. Walls separate the church from its real purpose and objective. Hiding behind the four walls of the local church causes real spiritual blindness. The church ceases seeing the needs and the culture of the people they have been commissioned to reach with the Gospel. It causes the church to lose its objective of winning the lost. Jesus never confined himself to the walls of the synagogue. He never removed himself from the needs of the people. He came to minister to and serve. He went into the "highways and hedges" to seek and to save the lost masses. The church can never be a true New Testament church while it remains inside of its four walls and ignoring the needs of a lost world.

The church that moves outside its walls measures its effectiveness in reaching the lost not by numbers or programs. Its number one desire is to be an effective witness to those who need a savior. The "outside the wall" church delights in serving people who seem to have no hope or direction in their spiritual life. It delights in meeting needs of needy people.

Assessing with Right Questions

It is no secret that churches in America are not experiencing the growth in salvations, baptisms and additions as in the past years. This is not a single denominational or a single church problem, it is a problem in every denomination and church and the end is disastrous as the church dies a slow death. Here are twelve probing diagnostic questions every church must answer to diagnose its future:

First, *is your church engaged in "need" focused evangelism and discipleship?* Romans 3:9-20 says *"What then? Are we better than* *they? No, in no wise: for we have before proved both Jews and Gentiles, that they are all under sin; As it is written, "There is none righteous, no, not one: There is none that understandeth, there is none that seeketh after God. They are all gone out of the way, they are together become unprofitable; there is none that doeth good, no, not one. Their throat is an open sepulchre; with their tongues they have used deceit; the poison of asps is under their lips: Whose mouth is full of cursing and bitterness: their feet are swift to shed blood: Destruction and misery are in their ways: And the way of peace have they not known: There is no fear of God before their eyes. Now we know that what things soever the law saith, it saith to them who are under the law: that every mouth may be stopped, and all the world may become guilty before God. Therefore, by the deeds of the law there shall no flesh be justified in his sight: for by the law is the knowledge of sin?"*[142] Did you get the pointed conditions of a lost person listed in this scripture text? It points out that none are righteous, none has spiritual understanding, none seeks after God, none that does any good, their tongues use deceit, they shed innocent blood and they do not know or understand peace because they do not fear the Lord.*

Because of the condition of the lost world, every church that is aspiring to be a healthy New Testament church will always have evangelism and discipleship as top priority. The purpose of the local church is to win the lost and disciple them into the likeness of Jesus Christ. When a church fails in this task it has signed its death warrant.

When a church is being assessed for spiritual health, a sure sign of spiritual health or spiritual illness is seen in the answer to this question. The key to a church being evangelistic is found in the pastor. If the pastor is not a soul winner, the congregation will see no real usefulness in soul winning. If the pastor is not a soul winner there will be no urgency for evangelism to be a priority in the church.

---

142 Romans 3:9-20 KJV.

Furthermore, when there is little or no emphasis on evangelism in the church the programs of the church will have little or no evangelistic intentionality. When a church is void of evangelism and discipleship it will become void of Gods blessings and the soon end will be death.

Second, *is your pastor a visionary leader?* Isaiah 40:11 says, "He tends his flock like a shepherd: He gathers the lambs in his arms and carries them close to His heart; He gently leads those that have young."143 Any pastor aspiring to be a Godly leader will be visionary in his leadership. God has called the pastor to take the church to a higher level. He has ordained the position of pastor to lead the flock to greener pastures. The pastor who understands his role as a visionary will be the pastor who leads the church to accomplish only what God can do through the congregation. Statistics show that few pastors really understand their role as a vision catcher, caster and connector. It is imperative that the congregation be led by a God called, God anointed under-shepherd who walks close to the Lord and understands and executes the vision God has for His church.

The argument for visionary leadership has been made in a previous chapter, however, it is important to emphasize again the realization that if the church has no visionary leader, the church will flounder, have no direction or purpose and will soon fall prey to ineffectiveness and eventually death. The question of visionary leadership is very important in a true assessment of the future wellbeing of the church. This leads to the third question.

Third, *if the leader is visionary, has the congregation bought into that vision for the future?* Or simply put *does your church have a clear vision for the future?* Proverbs 29:18 states *"Where there is no*

---

143 Isaiah 40:11 KJV.

*prophetic vision the people cast off restraint but blessed is he who keeps the law."*144 It is a good and Godly thing to have a visionary pastor, but it profits nothing if the congregation is unwilling to follow that vision. As stated previously in this book, the process for receiving a vision is as follows…God possesses the vision for the church. He gives it to the man of God. The man of God gives it to the people of God. They, in turn, live out that vision to a lost and needy world. So, the result of a God given vision must always be evangelism. For the Man of God to be visionary he must be a transformational leader. He must be one who has first been personally transformed and can be transformational in his leadership. This means taking the church to a higher level of existence and service for the Kingdom.

The main purpose for visionary leadership and a visionary church, then, is not for the church itself but for the lost world around the church. The vision is not for the people of God but for those who need a savior. "Without a vision, the people perish." They go in all sorts of ungodly directions. Their paths are crooked and perverse. They remain lost without Christ. It is simple: a pastor without a vison and a church without a vision is merely playing church and will have no effect on those who need the Lord. This is an essential part of any church health assessment.

Fourth, *has your church developed an immunity to the effect of conflict and disunity?* Jude 17-19, *"But, dear friends, remember what the apostles of our Lord Jesus Christ foretold. They said to you, 'In the last times there will be scoffers who will follow their own ungodly desires.' These are the men who divide you, who follow mere natural instincts and do not have the Spirit."*145

---

144 Proverbs 29:18 MSG.
145 Jude 17-19 NIV.

The web site, Church Mediators, cite several alarming statistics from the Duke University's National Congregations Study 2006-2007 and the American Congregations 2008, Cooperative Congregational Studies. Even though these are several years old the statistics still stand true and are in some ways even worse.

- 25% of churches experienced conflict in the last two years that resulted in people leaving;
- 1,500 pastors leave the church every month because of conflict, burnout or moral failure.
- Every year more than 19,000 congregations experience major conflict.
- During the last 5 years 75% of churches in America have experienced conflict; 25% of which indicate the conflict was severe enough to permanently impact church life.[146]

One of the great tragedies every Church Revitalizer faces is the realization that dying churches have often become immune to the effects of conflict. In fact, this is the most useful tool Satan has in his arsenal for destroying churches. Many churches are so conflict-oriented that some people will leave and never return, and others will stay and try to weather the storm but, in the process, become hardened to the disunity and conflict that plagues the church.

What would ever cause a church to become calloused to conflict and disunity? One writer said it this way, "The church seems to think that it will get hurt if they take a stand against these troublemakers. Often these controllers have longevity in the congregation, or they're perceived as

---

146 "Surprising Statistics," Dispute Mediation, accessed September 20, 2018,
http://www.churchmediators.org/pages/page.asp?page_id=353899

irreplaceable financial supporters of the church, or they hold a powerful office. To confront or remove them seems counter-productive to peace and harmony or detrimental to the church budget. A second reason the church does nothing is that it takes passages from the Bible out of context and applies them to this situation. *"Turn the other cheek"* (Matthew 5.39) and *"Love your enemy"* (Matthew 5.44) is interpreted to mean "be a doormat" and "put up with evil," but nothing could be farther from the truth."[147]

If a church has become "immune" to or "tolerant" of disunity and conflict, it will become ineffective within itself and in the community. People outside the church will no longer tolerate infighting and bickering in the church. Many are leaving the organized church because of this problem. For the people who remain in the conflict-ridden church, the conflict generates all kinds of fear. Some become afraid of being rejected by those in authority. Some fear losing the confrontation and/or causing hurt feelings among their peers. Still others don't like anyone thinking badly of them, so they tolerate the conflict rather than be confrontational to redeem the situation. Some conflict specialists call this "confrontational phobia" which reveals a fear that causes one to not disagree with another's opinion in fear of being ridiculed, ostracized and disliked. This tends to cause the individual to avoid confrontation altogether and, in a sense, become immune to the conflict. When a church tolerates disunity, it is on its way to death.

Fifth, *does your church recognize the giftedness of the members and allow them to serve in those gifted areas?*
Romans 12:6-8 says, *"Having then gifts differing according to the grace that is given to us, whether prophecy, let us prophesy according to*

---

147 "Pressure Points: Conflict," Christian Crusaders, December 7, 2914, accessed September 20, 2018, https://christiancrusaders.org/pressure-points-conflict/.

*the proportion of faith; or ministry, let us wait on our ministering: or he that teacheth, on teaching; or he that exhorteth, on exhortation: he that giveth, let him do it with simplicity; he that ruleth, with diligence; he that sheweth mercy, with cheerfulness."*148

The big question here is, "Are the people who understand their spiritual gifts being given an open door to use those gifts?" Often churches become closed communities where only a few people are given the opportunity to exert their giftedness into the life of the church. Often the ones who are given the open door to exercise their gifts are from an elite group of people in the church; the "in crowd", if you please. Sometimes this group is closed to anyone outside their realm of relationships hence resulting in members not being given opportunities to serve. An anonymous writer once said, "A church can become a graveyard if its members bury their gifts." Every member should be given the opportunity to use their God given gifts whether it is encouragement, teaching, leading, or simply serving. When members are not given the space to exercise their giftedness, the church suffers, individuals suffer and the effectiveness of the church lacks. The squelching of giftedness in the church effectiveness will be crippled.

Sixth, *are your worship services exciting and enthusiastic or dead and lifeless?* The scripture has much to say about worship. "Worship is so integral to the life of the church that when we say we are "going to church," what we most often mean is that we will be attending a worship service. Worship is mentioned in Scripture, from the first book (the difference between how Cain and Abel worshipped God in Genesis 4, Noah and his family worshipping after the Flood in Genesis 8:20-22, and more) to the last book, where much of

---

148 Romans 12:6-8 KJV.

Revelation is a vision of heavenly worship."149 Clearly worship is important. In the Old Testament Psalm 66:4 says, "All the earth shall worship thee, and shall sing unto thee; they shall sing to thy name. Selah." Psalm 99:5 says, *"Exalt ye the Lord our God, and worship at his footstool; for he is holy."*150 In the New Testament Mark 5:6 says, *"But when he saw Jesus afar off, he ran and worshipped him."*151 Revelation 4:10-11 declares, *"The four and twenty elders fall down before him that sat on the throne, and worship him that liveth for ever and ever, and cast their crowns before the throne, saying, Thou art worthy, O Lord, to receive glory and honour and power: for thou hast created all things, and for thy pleasure they are and were created."*152

A sure sign that a church is quickly becoming unhealthy is when worship becomes dry, lifeless and lackluster. Worship is at the heart of why the church exists. It builds fellowship with God and fellow believers. Worship declares our allegiance to God and recognizes His authority and omnipotence. Everything about worship focuses on God and when the church falters in worship it falters in its acknowledgement of who God is. A healthy church will have exciting and enthusiastic worship experiences.

Seventh, *is the congregation engaged in real ministry "outside the walls" or are they simply "pew warmers?"* Hebrews 10:24-25 describes the sort of congregation that moves outside the walls. It says *"And let us consider one another to provoke unto love*

---

149 Jim Hawkins, "Why is Worship Important," *Ministry Matters,* (July 27, 2015), accessed October 4, 2018, https://www.ministrymatters.com/worship/entry/6205/why-is-worship-important.

150 Psalm 99:5 KJV.

151 Mark 5:6 KJV.

152 Revelation 4:10-11 KJV.

*and to good works: Not forsaking the assembling of ourselves together, as the manner of some is; but exhorting one another: and so much the more, as ye see the day approaching."*153 Question, is your congregation an audience of onlookers or are they an army of soldiers of the cross? This simply means that the church must go beyond the boundaries of its walls and reach out into the community in which it sits. An "outside the walls" church is mission-minded and evangelistic. It seeks opportunities to impact those who are not part of the congregation. It is the part of any healthy church's ministry. It is what feeds the future of the church by winning the lost and integrating them into the life of the church. This part of the church's ministry is always motivated by compassion on the world around the church. It occurs when the church really gets passionate about ministering to anyone and everyone it possibly can. Without a doubt, any healthy church will understand the importance of ministry "outside the walls."

Eighth, *does your church know and understand the different people groups in your community to better reach them with the Gospel?* Many churches fail to grow and minister outside the walls because it does not understand the culture of the community where it ministers. Communities are changing and as a result the culture is changing. The church must work hard at understanding those changes and resolve to adjust to meet the needs of the present culture. This, however, does not mean compromise. The church can never change a culture if it becomes like the culture. The Bible teaches that we should "come out from among them" but that does not mean we neglect them. We can never win the lost by living like the lost. A good example of this is how some pastors who seek to identify with the existing culture in their community have no problem going to a bar and drinking an alcoholic beverage with a person they are seeking to minister too. This is not

---

153 Hebrews 10:24-25 KJV.

ministry, it is compromise. It is not fruitful but instead damaging to the Kingdom of God.

The changing culture in many church communities calls for an understanding of attitudes, lifestyles and positions in life but it never involves compromising the truth. Ed Stetzer says that as the church lives out its life in the community "it should have certain biblical marks and should be focused on eternal purposes…it must also take the faith it believes and live it out in context."154 If a church does not seek to understand and minister to its community in a Biblical way, it will never become a healthy, thriving church.

Ninth, *does your church exercise extreme faith, natural faith or no faith?* What is "extreme" faith? Extreme faith is not knowing that God can, but it is knowing that God will. St. Thomas Aquinas said, "To one who has faith, no explanation is necessary. To one without faith, no explanation is possible." Many churches have forgotten that God on His throne can be trusted. The loss of faith is a symptom of a far greater problem. That problem is the fact that many churches have as Revelation 2:4 says, "left their first love." A clear by-product of loss of faith is seen in a total dependence on human wisdom and human intellect. Human thinking and intellect cannot match the wisdom of God and when the church makes decisions and carries on its work, void of faith, but engulfed in human wisdom, the church gets into real trouble. The church must exercise extreme faith to survive and thrive in this perverse world. "Natural faith" is faulty and human in nature. It is faith in what man can do. What man can see, feel, hear, touch or smell. It focuses on the tangible. Of course, "no faith" is self-explanatory.

---

154 Ed Stetzer, "Engaging an Ever-Changing Culture With a Never-Changing Gospel," (August 1, 2014), accessed October 4, 2018, https://www.christianitytoday.com/edstetzer/2014/june/avoiding-church-culture-pendulum-swings-engaging-ever-chang.html.

Tenth, *how important is living in accordance with the Great Commission to your church? Is your church mission minded and soul conscious?* When a church gets into decline or a death spiral, the first thing to be deserted is its missions and evangelism budget, commitment and efforts. When a church begins to ignore the Great Commission, its services, programs and life will reflect an unconcern for lost people in the community, and the world. Missions and evangelism will take a back seat to programs and survival. The church will be void of any training in evangelism and discipleship. Jesus commands his disciples to go. It is not a suggestion or an invitation, but it is a command. Go and make disciples. When the church fails to take seriously, for whatever reason, the Great Commission, that church is headed for a slow death. It is clear from the scripture that the church is directly responsible to Christ for the fulfillment of the Great Commission. He will hold the church accountable for how it seeks to fulfill the commission. "The Church is the primary agent ordained by God to accomplish the Great Commission. Yet, after 2000 years, many churches neglect this fundamental truth. For many churches today, global mission is something that happens once a year, sometime between VBS and the youth summer camp. It seems that the local church hasn't always lived up to the example that we see in the book of Acts."[155] If the church fails in the Great Commission it utterly fails and will become ineffective and impotent.

Eleventh, *does your church use Matthew 18 as a Biblical approach to church discipline?* Many churches find themselves in desperate times because they fail to discipline wayward and stubborn church members who are constantly causing discord among the church members. As a result, they lose

---

155 Paul Akin, "The Local Church and The Great Commission: One Mission, Two Contexts," (January 20, 2011), accessed October 9, 2018, https://baptist21.com/blog-posts/2011/the-local-church-and-the-great-commission-one-mission-two-contexts-2/.

their testimony in the community where they reside. Most churches do not exercise any type of church discipline. Matthew 18 gives clear guidelines on how it should be carried out. Church discipline is about redemption not alienation. The first step is to visit the trouble maker one on one and confront them about their sin. If the person does not repent go and visit again with two or three witnesses. Still if the person does not repent then the church, Biblically, is bound to consider the matter as a congregation always seeking to redeem the person. If this fails, the church should break fellowship with them until there is repentance. The key to church discipline is and must always exercise "Redemptive Love!"

Thom Rainer says that "no church discipline is a key reason for disunity in the church. Most churches with which I have familiarity have no process for church discipline, or they have a process in place in theory only."156 Rainer says in another article, "…there should be little debate about the biblical mandate for churches to exercise church discipline. Yet the topic of church discipline seems to be primarily reserved for the theologians and a few pastors. Those of us who write about practical ministry and church health rarely mention this topic, even though it is a clear biblical practice."157

The clear facts are that the goal in church discipline should never be vindictive in nature. It is not a punishment

---

156 Thom Rainer, "Fourteen Reasons for the Breakdown of Church Unity," (May 13, 2015), accessed September 26, 2018, https://thomrainer.com/2015/05/fourteen-key-reasons-for-the-breakdown-of-church-unity/.

157 Thom Rainer, "Seven Observations on Church Discipline," (January 25, 2014), accessed October 1, 2018, https://thomrainer.com/2014/01/seven-observations-on-church-discipline/.

but rather a time of redemption and repentance. Most churches that need a restart exercise no church discipline no matter the severity of the offense and God will not honor compromise and tolerance of known sin in His bride.

Twelfth, *has your congregation's wishes and desires become more important than Gods will and the Gospel?* This portrays and inward turn in ministry. Some pastors have decided that it is easier and safer for them and their future to simply let the church do as it pleases. Therein lies a real problem. If God has a plan for every church, and He does, and if the Man of God knows that plan, then he is responsible to God to receive, develop and carry out that plan. To allow churches (church members) to become "islands unto themselves" is plain and simple compromise. Churches become wayward and rebellious when they cease to seek after and do the Will of the Father. All of this is based on man's desire to run his own life apart from the wisdom and guidance of God and it always ends in disaster. There are two basic problems with this. **First**, it puts the pastor in a position of compromise and forces him in many situations to do things that God has not ordained to keep his position. **Second,** it will cause the congregation to grow weary of following the leadership of the Holy Spirit because it attends more to their own human intellect than they do God's wisdom. When this takes place in the local church the church is doomed to failure and will die a slow and painful spiritual death.

Applying Right Solutions

Any diagnosis void of a prescribed solution is no diagnosis at all. However, every church is unique as is their varied possible solutions. Because of this there are only two prescribed solutions that would fit for every diagnosis. Since every church is different and possesses different reasons for their downward spiral, each church will have its own special solution set. These two specific solutions are applicable to every situation and both are vital to the recovery of any dying church.

First, the most important solution is the need for the pastor or designated leader to call the church to genuine, Holy Spirit powered "prayer" for the future of the church. Not the kind of prayer that most churches engage in but the kind of prayer that grips the throne of God. The kind that moves the hand of God. This writer has been taught all my life that the "church always moves forward on its knees." The church must get serious about seeking the face of God for the future of the church. When the church fails to properly pray for power to move forward it stops the progress of the Gospel in that church. It has been said, "So goes the church, so goes the nation" and this is a true depiction of the importance of the church praying. Any church that has no compelling influence of the Holy Spirit in the matter of prayer will have only their human ability to resort to.

Prayerlessness is not mere human weakness. It is sin. Since it is sin it must be repented of and confessed. Prayer is crucial to the life and well-being of the church. Prayer binds the fellowship together. It brings new life back to the church. It begins to move the church to follow God's wisdom rather than man's intellect. Prayer keeps the church unified and secures the power of God. It opens the door for the Holy Spirit to rule and reign in the church's life.

Corporate prayer is an important key to turning a church around. However, most churches are deficient in the area of corporate prayer and are unwilling to face it. In the building blocks of bringing new life to an ailing church, there must be a solid foundation and that foundation must consist of both personal and corporate prayer. Because of the desperate times some churches find themselves in they tend to lose a prayer mindset if they ever had one. Prayerlessness must be replaced with God anointed, Holy Spirit powered prayer if the church will be salvaged.

Second, there must be a calling of the church to repentance. Most churches hear very little about repentance these days from the pulpit. Such verses as Luke 24:27 which reads, "And that repentance and remission of sins should be reached in his name among all nations beginning at Jerusalem," and Luke 13:3 which reads, "I tell you nay: but except you repent, ye shall all likewise perish," are rarely heard from the pulpits of America, and we wonder why our churches are dying. The true meaning of the word "repent" in the New Testament is "to feel remorse and self-reproach for one's sins against God: to be contrite, sorry; to want to change direction." It is marked by a Godly sorrow. Our churches must be called to this Godly sorrow. Sorrow over of sinfulness. Sorrow for our failing to be the church Jesus bled and died for. Failure of changing our world with the greatest message that has ever been. The message of salvation through the shed blood of Jesus. One important thought about repentance is that without repentance the Christian cannot grow as a disciple. If the church fails to repent it will never grow and become fruitful. These are only two solutions, but I'm convinced they are the most important.

Conclusion

There are numerous symptoms of a sick and dying church. Not every church will have all the symptoms. Since a diagnostic procedure is an examination to identify specific areas of weakness and strength to determine a condition or illness. The diagnosis will be somewhat different for every church but many of the symptoms mentioned previously in this chapter will be present.

Let's recap some of what we talked about in this chapter. The church that is filled with disunity and division is a sick church. Any church that refuses to change things to better the future of the church is a sick church. The church that has turned inward is on its death bed and death is not far behind. When a church ceases to hold a high view of Scripture and the Gospel, it is experiencing the "death rattles", and its future is bleak. A church that has lost its desire to win the lost and its desire for missions is spiritually sick. A church that is led by spiritually inept leaders, whether lay leaders or ministry leaders, is headed for stagnation and death. The church that is unwilling to use Biblical discipline is a church that will experience uninterrupted conflict and disunity in the fellowship. Finally, a church unwilling to face its own "present reality" is caught in that deadly death spiral and will end in a deadly crash.

Just as in human illness, the patient cannot treat himself; the ailing church cannot treat itself. Intervention is necessary. Revitalizers who have been called to this type of ministry are required. New life and better spiritual health will be difficult and painful. Even with treatment the church may die but without any intervention the church will surely die.

Chapter Nine
Avoiding the Cul-de-Sacs in a Church Restart

Write this to Smyrna, to the Angel of the church. The Beginning and Ending, the First and Final One, the Once Dead and Then Come Alive, speaks: "I can see your pain and poverty—constant pain, dire poverty—but I also see your wealth. And I hear the lie in the claims of those who pretend to be good Jews, who in fact belong to Satan's crowd. "Fear nothing in the things you're about to suffer—but stay on guard! Fear nothing! The Devil is about to throw you in jail for a time of testing—ten days. It won't last forever.[158]

Have you ever driven in a subdivision where at the end of each major road there is an off shoot which is a cul-de-sac? These communities usually have one or two main streets running through the subdivision with cul-de-sacs running off of the main streets. I lived on a cul-de-sac when I lived outside of the Atlanta beltway. Life in general in society has had far too many dirt roads paved and far too many off shoots, but they remind us all that life can at times be bumpy. At the end of most cul-de-sacs lives a wonderful Airedale Terrier named Reeses that waits patiently for you to return from school. At the end of the road kids play and spouses wait for your return at the end of the day. Our values were healthier when our roads were worse. People did not worship their cars more than their kids. Cul-de-sacs slowed one down and taught patience. You walked to a neighbor's house not drive there. At the end of a cul-de-sac you made a new friend. A cul-de-sac is a street or passage closed at one end.[159] The word cul-de-sac comes from the French language which means "dead ends." Dead ends stop you at the moment in

---

[158] Eugene H. Peterson, *The Message: The Bible in Contemporary Language* (Colorado Springs, CO: NavPress, 2005), Re 2:8–10.

159 "Cul-de-sac." Merriam-Webster.com. Accessed June 25, 2018. https://www.merriam-webster.com/dictionary/cul-de-sac.

time when you are moving forward only to lock you in your tracks and cause you to become immoveable. A church cul-de-sac is one that is at a dead end or an impasse. Some churches are on cul-de-sacs proverbially and struggle with the fact that their glory days are over unless something significant is done right away. Those churches are in need of a restart. Have you seen any church cul-de-sacs?

The Status of the Status Quo

Kenneth Priddy has developed a wonderful assessment tool designed to understand the church in terms of its culture, its atmosphere, and its psychology. It is called "The Status of the Status Quo." The philosophy of the assessment is to assess those remaining within the church while allowing them to discover for themselves if they are a viable church for a restart process. This tool asks seven simple yes or no questions. Each question deals with a particular issue and is accompanied by the follow-up question, "How so?" Priddy forces those who are taking the assessment to stop wavering and answer in a definitive way. The follow-up question calls for an explanation of the previous positional answer. The seven questions are:

Question 1: Can the activity of God be discerned? How so?

Question 2: Is the leadership moving the church in a positive direction? How so?

Question 3: Is the church in a state of qualitative and/or quantitative decline? How so?

Question 4: Is there a cultural match or mismatch between the church and its community? How so?

Question 5: Has survivalism set in? How so?

Question 6: Are negative emotions running high? How so?

Question 7: Does the church have a sense of hope for the future? How so?160

The Church Cul-de-sac

Churches that live on a proverbial cul-de-sac often lose count of the cars (and people) that come near the church as if to stop but they simply make a U-turn and disappear. These potential prospects and church members come in close to the church only to turn away in the last second. A cul-de-sac church teaches you something about life. Most churches which get to the place where they need to be restarted have done so because people were coming in close and taking a U-turn just before you reached out to them and embraced them. Cul-de-sac churches have reached the dead end because they have failed to offer anything subsitive at a specific point in time and found themselves with nothing more to add to make a lasting impact. Cul-de-sacs are the detractors from the appointed goal which delay us or even worse detract us from the real goal of restarting the church and bringing back vitality and renewal. How many churches have you seen that are declining - if not dying - that have entered the cul-de-sac and find themselves going around and around? There are small cul-de-sacs and there are big ones. But regardless of the size, all of these church cul-de-sacs are a huge waste of time and a tremendous waste of resources. Resources in people, prospects, and priorities for the restarting church. Restarts often face these cul-de-sacs because there are individuals within the existing church who do not want to see the

160 Priddy, Kenneth Earl. *Restarting the Dying Church* Doctor of Ministry Dissertation, Reformed Theological Seminary, May 2001. Pgs. 76-79 .

changes necessary to renewal take place, so they will attempt to lead you or push you into one cul-de-sac after another until it wears you out. Cul-de-sacs in church revitalization are where you as the Church Revitalizer work, and work while nothing changes. Things do not get better and surprisingly things do not get worse. It will take bold leadership of the Church Revitalizer to get the declining church off stuck. Habitual cul-de-sacs keep your from doing anything significant. Most church revitalization gurus will not tell you what I am about to tell you because they have never been in the trenches of revitalization and renewal. Here it is: If you are going to invest your life and ministry in the work of revitalization do not go to or remain at a cul-de-sac church because the cost and investment is too high for a church that does not want to be revitalized! People that lead revitalization from the sidelines often state that one quit that church. Quite to the contrary. The Church Revitalizer instead of awaiting around for no eventual solution left the church to their own demise and moved on to a church which was worthy of a Church Revitalizer who would be allowed to lead the revitalization efforts and help the church climb out of the doldrums. If the church has a chance of renewal then certainly rededicate yourself to the effort but if it is unwilling to make the changes and take the steps towards renewal then go to a church that wants to get healthy. You are not quitting church revitalization, you are going to a church that deserves revitalization over one that only sits on the sidelines waiting for the eventual demise. If the cul-de-sac church is on a dead-end journey it is alright to move on. As a Church Revitalizer it is essential that you move on from revitalization projects that have no chance of success or the reward of a renewed church. Besides you are not abandoning the strategy of revitalization, you are moving on to a church that wants revitalization over a church that does not. cul-de-sac churches must decide if it is wise to keep the church open in hope that new people begin arriving or let it close and then restart it.

Cul-de-sacs wear the revitalization leader out and the church seeking renewal out as well. Energy that is needed for things like outreach, evangelism, and restructuring of the vision and goals of a church are tapped out. The perpetual loop in some churches in decline keep it from over getting out of the cul-de-sac. Leaders who are not pure Church Revitalizers often get trapped in these circles of nowhere and become stale lacking the drive to lead the church to a new horizon. Many churches which are needing to employ a restart strategy, find themselves in some sort of cul-de-sacs realizing they are going nowhere and are in a perpetual dead-end. In these churches the thoughts of wanting to quit become more the norm than the exception. There is good news for you as the leader of a declining church and there is good news for that local church you serve. You do not need to allow the church cul-de-sacs to detract you form your desired goal of church revitalization and renewal. How do you know if you and your church is in a cul-de-sac? Let's take a look:

As the Church Revitalizer you find yourself working really hard but see little or no return on your investment.

Your lay leadership works endlessly but they see very little return on their investment of time and their talents.

Both the Church Revitalizer and lay leadership sense that the rank and file of the church have a greater desire to be entertained than they do for doing the work of the ministry.

There is a high degree of the "you serve us" syndrome going on in the church.

In spite of all the effort put into the ministry, things do not get better, they only get worse.

The feeling of drift surfaces in the church where participants are happy with status quo and prospects avoid you like the plague.

Visitor attraction and prospect retention are at an all-time low.

There is a sense that you as the Church Revitalizer are spinning your wheels and unable to lead the church out of the perpetual loop of the cul-de-sac.

People within the church begin to sense your frustration and become uneasy about your commitment to their church.

You as the Church Revitalizer are hesitant to challenge your membership to make the necessary changes to bring about a spirit of renewal.

When you experience the perpetual loop of the cul-de-sac as a church and the Church Revitalizer, your only hope is to be true to your people and if they are unwilling to make changes for the betterment of the church to jump off the roller coaster and look for a church willing to change. Dead end churches declare that they want to change, but in reality, and practicality, they do everything in their powers to not change. If you want your ministry to count for something you might, as a Church Revitalizer, need to leave this church that really only wants a person in the pulpit weakly (not a typo). As a Church Revitalizer the cost of investing one's life in something that is not going to get better is just too high. Perhaps the best solution for that church which desires too little is to allow a retired pastor hold their hands a little while longer. These churches have a mindset that the last one alive should please turn the lights off.

The Church's Dip in Revitalization

Seth Godin in his book: *The Dip: A little Book That Teaches You when to Quit (And When to Stick)* says that what most of us are experiencing is the "Dip" which is the "long slog between starting and mastery".[161] As one is avoiding the cul-de-sacs in church restarts there will be dips for sure. What is a dip? A dip is the portion of our work where things get hard. It is those times in ministry where it is just no fun. A dip are the moments which there seems to be no win for the church nor for the Church Revitalizer. It can be those times when you want to quit. There are some dips which you as the Church Revitalizer need to avoid at all cost. One dip to avoid are the showdowns where only one wins out. A dip is when you have painted yourself as the leader into a corner where others are saying their way of the highway for you and your vision. A dip could be when a patriarchal powerbroking lay leader refuses to embrace change. It could even be matriarchal members which see nothing wrong with killing the church. Recently I had a man who professes to be a strong Christian say to me: "I would rather see my church die than to see it become more contemporary in order to reach a younger generation!" That broke my heart. Should a professed committed actually believe that? I do not think so. Christ died for all not just our generation. Dips can become cul-de-sacs if you let them. Dips lead to beneficial ends while cul-de-sacs lead to the exact same spot over and over and over again. Time after time you will find yourself back at the original starting point if you allow dips to become cul-de-sacs. There are many churches locked in a cul-de-sac. Are you pastoring one right now? Dips take time to climb out of while cul-de-sacs are a never-ending series of wasted energy where a pastor and the church back find themselves at the initial place where

---

161 Godin, Seth. *The Dip: A Little Book that Teaches You When to Quit and When to Stick.* New York: Penguin Group, 2007, pg. 17.

they begun. How do you know if you and your church is in a dip? Let's take a look:

For the Church Revitalizer what was initially fun and exciting has become a drudgery.

Engagement has been replaced with an attitude of withdrawal from the work.

The Church Revitalizer is merely going through the weakly motions of pastoring in public yet receding from the ministry during the week.

Patience in the renewal effort has been replaced with shortcuts seeking closure.

Church revitalization has become quick-fix focused not journey deployed.

Doing things to appear busy has replaced effective effort towards revitalization.

You and your church forfeit a learning climate and replace it with a maintaining environment.

Decisions which were initially easy have become more difficult as a lack of trust in your leadership has developed.

Here is a revitalization lesson for you: Church Revitalizers who are successful do not just ride out the hard times of renewal. They actually lean into it. They work harder, stretch further, change up the structures keeping them from breaking through, and refuse to quit and coast. They know they are in the dip but do not act like there is nothing they can do about it. Instead they work systematically to whittle them down one piece at a time until they have moved all the way through the dip.

The Cliffs

Many a pastor has found themselves on the cliff of ministry as they try to renew a declining or dying church. Knowing where you are and how you got there is the beginning. It is vital to know where you are in your effort towards revitalization. There are times when you want to throw in the towel or jump of the proverbial cliff because ministry is so hard. These cliffs challenge us to embrace our trust in the Lord first and foremost and secondly to ponder whether or not we trust our instincts for renewal. Think about the first time you preached. Was there an uneasiness? Yet, God was right there in the middle of your challenge and even better, at the end you realized His willingness to see you through. Overcoming the fears in ministry when encountering the cliffs all begin the instant you as the Church Revitalizer take the first step. What was petrifying a second ago now is replaced by an assurance that the Lord has a plan and we follow obediently His will and His plan for our church renewal effort.

Granted, until you have confronted the cliffs of your ministry a few times, it is never a completely nerve free experience. I have always been afraid of a fall. The cliffs in ministry make us uneasy. But over the few years I have realized that the best way to overcome your fear is to face it. The more you try to run away from your fears all the more it will come back at you to haunt you. How do you know if you and your church is facing the cliff? Let's take a look:

First acknowledge that cliffs are usually the last resort and that is why you are considering a restart.

The cliffs often precede a line in the sand type of decision as to what you and your church will do next.

While rarely will you face such dilemmas as the Church Revitalizer, usually issues have led up to such an encounter by ultimatum, by either the pastor or the lay leadership's unwillingness to work together for resolution. A cliff's present junctures in the destination for the church are potentially destroying encounters that ultimately make future resolution impossible to avoid. For the Church Revitalizer, the cliff causes the form and function of your church worship appear impossible to abandon because you have done it that way for so long that most of the participants are unwilling to change, and the new prospects are unwilling to settle for the status quo.

The eventual outcome will be that either the church lay leadership will come to an impasse with the pastor or the pastor will encounter a stalemate with the church's direction of its lay leadership. The end result is that this church will eventually fall apart terribly while trying to hold on until it is too late. A wise decision will be to consider a restart before it is too late and you have loss any chances for retaining critical mass. This is endemic of the church's unwillingness to change on the part of one or more parties. It is tremendously vital that you discover which situation you are in. Your church's outcome and your outcome as a Church Revitalizer is a life and death concern.

So Where is the Direction?

Cul-de-sacs and cliffs are the opposite of the dip because they are seeking to be permanent. These will eventually lead to ministry failure. The hardest thing for a Church Revitalizer to do is to tell the church that it has not changed, does not want to change, and the final, last option is for the church is to make a change. Now not later. You actually know it is not going to get better and yet you hang on, lacking the conviction to do something about it. Many a pastor of a rapidly declining church has a preference to not rock the boat but the boat is sinking and you lack the commitment to challenge others to see the eventual outcome. Why should a Church Revitalizer stick it out if there is no eventual benefit of a changed church seeking a new direction? As a Church Revitalizer do you have the stuff necessary to say, *"I would rather lead a smaller church over leading a larger dead one?"* As a Church Revitalizer, if it does not cost you a commitment of your complete life, you are not on the pursuit for church revitalization and renewal but only a ride!

I love reading Seth Godin's blog. Recently he had one about lessons you can learn from a Woodpecker.[162] There is a lesson for Church Revitalizers within this blog. He says:

> A woodpecker can peck on 500 trees 50 times each and find nothing! But stay busy. Or, a woodpecker can tap 50,000 times on a single tree and discover dinner![163]

Our world is changing and we must wake up as a church. Many churches needing a restart strategy have failed to keep up with the changing environment around its ministry area. Many are closing and that sometimes happens, yet it is much better to leave a legacy and give your facility over to an association and allow it to utilize it for a restart or a new church plant. The very moment you sell your church you have hurt the cause of Christ in that target area due to the increasing costs of property and some new churches' lack of sufficient funds to purchase the property. You then sell it to a business or developer and the property which God had given you for the work of Christ is lost because of lack of

---

162 Go to: https://seths.blog/page/2/ to subscribe to his blog.

163 Ibid.

understanding of the potential options. Many churches needing to consider a church restart have memberships that are growing old and many of the formerly active participants have passed away. Young people are not drawn to your church and once they come, they do not stay due to differences in what is relevant for present participants over what is relevant for newcomers. Many of the younger ones in the church are there because of a family member and they feel stuck. Many younger prospects for the church are absent from the ministry or are there with a sense of disgust because they are powerless to change the rank and files idea of a culturally relevant church. Many of these churches needing a restart strategy are not keeping up financially, numerically, nor spiritually. These churches are becoming dead in their forms as the lifelessness of their ministry is no longer attractive to the community it is called to serve. Many of these churches no longer have the ability to make disciples of others. It is time for the rapidly declining church to develop an intentional church revitalization paradigm. Slowly cul-de-sacs turn into habitual patterns and we go on repeating the same problematic patterns on and on. That is where many a church gets in trouble. The learning, even if it does not stop, it does slow down significantly. With time, we as renewal leaders, are bound to feel trapped and frustrated. For the Church Revitalizer, it is always in one's best interest to come out of the cul-de-sac and go out to learn more. Unless you learn, you cannot grow and finally end up withering away. Maybe, now is the time to start a new journey for your church through a restart. As the leader you should challenge your membership to take the U-turn and get out of their cul-de-sac. Failure to act only continues to forfeit critical mass and endangers your church's chances of survival. You have a choice right now. Instead of waiting and eventually being forced to give your church away to a church planter, you can keep your church and begin the work of restarting it. I know it is going to be very painful. But then it is also true that when you accept pain without any fear of rejection, it is no longer a pain. It becomes acting upon quality changes that are filled with a new vitality. Neither should a Church Revitalizer nor a church stay in a cul-de-sac or perpetual loop. Get out do something now that will give your church the greatest chance for survival. If not, you will never grow.

Developing A Fresh Intentional Church Revitalization Paradigm

The hard reality is this, Church Revitalization is important because so many churches are dying and/or are all but dead. It is also important because even today's healthy churches run the risk of developing the same illness that other churches are experiencing. God's people desperately need a biblical foundation for church revitalization!

Why Consider a Restart?

Restarting is about deciding to give the present church new life. It is about having the courage to begin differently so that others might join in the work of renewal. Restarting is about honoring the past but refusing to live in it any longer. A church seeking to not die must begin dealing with the challenges of those who can't let go of the things destroying the church's chance for a new future. Restarting is about seeking a day where the church might be resuscitated and resurrected. The church must forge forward on unknown paths, trusting the Lord to see you through. When a church is ready to face the realities of their current situation of rapid decline, restarting will become more about allowing God to do what needs to be done. There are so many Churches that need to embrace a restart strategy today not tomorrow. Restarting is about choosing between life or continuing towards death. For the Church Revitalizer it is about being frank with present members about their difficulties and challenges. Restarting is about forgetting traditions and following Jesus. Restarting is about stopping the lies to one's self about the current realities of the church. It is about taking what is dying and making it alive once more. When a church will look realistically at itself and see its nearness to death, it is often more ready to take the necessary steps to avoid the situation. The rapidly changing culture of the United States is leading to many church deaths. The church, being slow to react to the ever-increasing rate of change in this country, falls further and further behind in cultural relevance. Rather than adjust, adapt, and update, the dying church seems to resent the changes and the culture, alienating itself further from the people it is called to reach.164

Restarting is about realizing you must die somewhat if you are going to survive. Restarting is about realizing that the Lord is in the restarting business. A dying church needs to be made aware of their critical condition. But awareness is not enough, they must become convinced that they need major surgical treatment. As the Church Revitalizer, we must recreate the mindset of the remaining members within the renewing church that something significant can come out of the challenges before us.

What Churches are Good Candidates for a Restart?

What kind of church is a good candidate for revitalization using the restart strategy? There are some churches with a better chance of living again through a restart. There are five types which are most often found:

The Church has no debt and few bills.

The Church is still in a strategic location for a work.

---

164 Priddy, Kenneth Earl. *Restarting the Dying Church* Doctor of Ministry Dissertation, Reformed Theological Seminary, May 2001. Pg. 81.

The Church who is not in the first two types might want to sell property and use the money through the local association to fund a new church plant or fund a church revitalization opportunity.

The Church that sells the building might offer it at a reduced rate to a new church plant so both sides win and Jesus is honored.

The Church might be used for a new group of people previously not ministered too.

Here's a cautionary note: often by the time the majority of dying churches comprehend that they are dying and in grave trouble, the issues for revitalization are too deep, and leadership too tired and worn out with the overwhelming mindset of the congregation who is too trapped in the past and in mere existence mode to grip the harrowing issues requiring a change through a restart.

What Does Restarting Entail?

There are five initial concepts which, if your church can work through, will give you a greater chance of survival. If you balk at any of these, you lessen your chances for survival. Here they are:

Charge
Change
Charter
Church
Control

When you begin working in the area of church revitalization there will be at least three to five things, depending on how your church is structured and the polity it works within, that will need to be surrendered by most participants if your church has a chance of revitalization and renewal. Notice I said a chance! Letting go of two out of five will not cut it. Giving up three but holding on to two might still mean your church's demise! In working with churches, I have found that these are the five areas that must be given up if your church is going to move towards a revitalization mindset. The five things listed above are the things that need to be relinquished in most churches when beginning to move towards church revitalization. Let's take a brief look at them:

Who is in Charge?

The call for revitalization often begins with the first item that needs to be relinquished within the church and that is who is leading the revitalization effort! Most if not all successful revitalization efforts are led by a single solitary leader directing the cause. It might be the pastor who has heard from God and has been renewed or it might be a new leader whom God raises up to assist the church. Often churches get stuck with an array of leaders (both public and some private) all trying to do their thing and lead in the way they believe is necessary. As churches in need of renewal and revitalization begin to decline there will often become a little bit of a power struggle with long time members and those who are called (or think they are) to lead the effort. Determining who is going to be in charge of the renewal effort is a big deal and yet it is one of those initial things that can or could stall any real effort towards revitalization.

Change ($)

Perhaps the hardest area for the church in need of revitalization to relinquish is that of letting go of who runs the financial arenas of the church! This is because the continual decline of the church has led to an extreme caution towards the use of money within the church. Those who have been there for a long time will often resent the use of finances on new ideas that have never been tried before! There has become a protective mindset of keeping what dwindling funds we have. People of habit in churches often cannot see other ways of doing things and this shows up often when a new idea that could help the church attract new prospects costs an amount that those "holding on" are unwilling to accept. When you do the work of revitalization, you will encounter this aspect and how you deal with it will either allow the church to move towards renewal successfully or it will be hindered in anything it does. Some of this struggle in a historical review of the church might be one of those reasons why the church constantly struggled to do anything new in its ministry.

Charter (Constitution stuff)

The church's charter (legal constitution & bylaws stuff) is another area that is hard for the existing church to let go of. Though it is not a document that is utilized daily there is still much difficulty for long time members to see the need to examine the documents and perhaps adjust items should there be a need. Adjustments to these "sacred" documents, is a no-no in some churches. While it is not actually a sacred document, many view them as such. There are churches that are hindered in their growth by what they thought was a good idea one hundred years ago! Examples such as no one can teach a bible study class until they have been a member for five years might have been a good idea one hundred year ago, but now it is simply part of why your church cannot attract new prospects. Your charter documents might need to be updated and yet some will struggle in this area.

Church (The reins of the Church)

Long time members of a church, even one that is in rapid decline, find it hard to relinquish the reins of the church. Only a small percentage of churches in need of revitalization can do so at this point. If a church is going to be revitalized it must allow the new leadership to do things that will allow it to draw a new group of prospects. If the church refuses to let someone else lead, it will make the eventual funeral of its members only a prequel to the eventual funeral of that local church. Within the western mindset there appears to be a dangerous and infectious thought that it is actually alright to allow God's church to have a funeral just like its members. That is not why God plants and grows churches. HE wants them to thrive and not die. He wants life and to have it in abundance.

Control

Where the first item dealt with the one who is in charge as in a single leader, this item focuses on who will come alongside the leader and help him grow the church. New blood needs to be infused into the revitalizing church! New leaders need to lead the new programs and work with the various ministries to give it new energy.[165] Long time charter members often find it difficult to allow new and might I say it younger leaders to take over the control of the church. Even those who are tired and have grown weary might give over control in word only, yet retain the veto power brokers should the church actually take off in a direction that long time members are uncomfortable with.

Can you do it? The question that first needs to be considered is to what degree are you as a church willing and open to see if you can restore and revitalize your church? Can you work towards new ideas and activities that can help you get off the plateau and get growing again? Are you willing to let new leaders lead even if you don't like some of the changes in order for the church to get healthy and begin

---

165 For more on this check out *The Repotting & Restarting Strategy for Revitalization* by Tom Cheyney at www.renovateconference.org.

growing once more? These are some of the challenges that need to be discussed and considered when working towards initial steps in a restart towards new health and revitalization.

Nine Reasons Your Church Might Fail

Not every church is a viable candidate for a restart. Here are the nine most common reasons your church might fail to restart.[166]

You and your church run out of time and quit.

You and your church run out of money and quit.

You and your church run out of followers and quit

You and your church get scared of all of the changes necessary and quit.

You and your church loose interest in church renewal and quit.

You and your church settle for mediocre and quit.

You and your church think short term not long term and quit.

You and your church think it will be an easy thing and quit once you see the work involved.

You and your church think of dabbling in renewal and eventually quit.

Realize that those churches locked in the cul-de-sac circle of turning left or right never to come out of the perpetual motion of going nowhere, are excellent prospects for a church restart.[166] Rebecca Barnes and Lindy Lowry declare: "188,000 orthodox churches in America today are in need of a restart."[167] Churches that have bounced from one

---

166 A great little book on the subject can be found by: Dottie Escobedo-Frank entitled *RESTART Your Church* (Abingdon Press).

167 Rebecca Barnes and Lindy Lowry, "Special Report: The American Church in Crisis," *Outreach*, May/June 2006, The Missional Church Network,

cul-de-sac to another for years have the chance to do something significant for Christ even in its waning years. If these churches can set aside the traditions of a few for the focus of the many which need to be reached and need to come to Jesus, then they can begin again and have one more chance for life. A fresh restart is often the very thing which can give life to a community that has grown weary of the existing church. Restarting is about understanding that the world is still quite hungry for the Lord God while the church is trapped grieving over the past. In Revelation chapter two John declares:

> *"Remember therefore from where you have fallen, and repent and do the deeds you did at first..."*[168]

That is the three-fold emphasis of the paradigm: Remember...Repent...Recapture the first things. I believe that within the next fifteen years there will be a growing shortage of pastors willing to fill our declining churches that have low renewal potential. In my own denomination we have 6,000 Southern Baptist Pastors who leave their ministries each year. More than 200 pastors are fired each month. In one recent article from LifeWay Research there are 70,000 vacant pulpits in America. If you are going to consider a restart or even a relaunch for that matter there are seven paradigm or model shifts for church revitalization that addresses the current crises of leader quantity and quality. A paradigm is simply a new and fresh way of thinking. When our lives come into alignment with Romans 12:2, our way of thinking gets re-aligned with God's thoughts and ideals. Paul says:

---

http://missionalchurchnetwork.blogspot.com/2007/10/american-church-n-crisis.html.

168 Revelation 2:5.

"Do not be conformed to this age, but be transformed by the renewing of your mind, so that you may discern what is the good, pleasing, and perfect will of God."

Any restart that will survive must develop a commitment and an entirely new goal of redeveloping sustainable critical mass. There must be the embracing of new methodology for rebirthing something new from the rapid decline. A new ministry design developed from church assessment and leader assessment. Restarts that are successful implement an all-inclusive process that gives strong and cohesive attention to four dynamics for church renewal:

They Seek Spiritual Transformation First

The first key to the process is seeking spiritual transformation. This reconnection allows a union with Christ Jesus and is the center of a truly transformational restart revitalization paradigm. Restarts must get away from the age-old standard of being pew sitters and become community walkers hitting the streets sharing Christ.

Successful Restarts Require Relational Journey

Developing Church Revitalizers who achieve success requires relational journey. These churches are transformed by a new and fresh structure which places a high degree of emphasis on developing deeper relationships. These churches and Church Revitalizers need a daily dose of relationships with mature fellow revitalizers, role models, and examples. They need spiritual Paul's, in the context of normal daily life and ministry. In the encouragement, support, challenge, teaching, discipline and accountability of these relationships, the shepherd's character is built, marriages are strengthened and spiritual life is nurtured.

Watch One, Do One, and Teach One

I learned well over thirty years ago from John Maxwell the importance of the medical model for learning. It has allowed me to gain experiential transformation as I stretched in my understanding and learning in church revitalization and renewal. When leading a restart, it is clear that developing Church Revitalizers learn more by doing and not only by listening. Activity is the new norm not audience observation. They are transformed through the fires of trail and pressure. The Church Revitalizer is stretched by challenging tasks that focus on church revitalization and renewal.

It is Not Your Father's Oldsmobile

Bringing back a dying or near dead church takes a new outlook. A restart can easily become derailed when the church begins to be turned around and the lessening of pain dulls the membership into thinking all of the hard work is done. One of the things that must be considered is in the arena of preaching. Developing Church Revitalizers must work on new ways in teaching of the Word of God – in an engaging way, and woven into the ongoing daily realities of life, family and ministry.

Churches in decline and pastors of declining churches both need an assessment. Shepherds need to know what the strengths and obstacles of the church may be and the church needs to know if the skill sets necessary for a turnaround are within the leader's ability to learn or possession already.

Restart Churches Develop Other Restart Leaders

Interesting in my work with churches needing a restart is the observation that the majority of the time while the church restarter is leading his own restart, often he is training others who will move on eventually and restart another church.

Church Revitalizers that have the heart and skills for restarting a church always are embracing and building up new Revitalizers. They understand that they face the personal responsibility for embracing and building new Revitalizers as a core part of what it means to be a restart leader. This single shift alone has the potential to raise up a new army of missional pastors equipped for the task of revitalization and renewal. In a day where church planting is on the decline the need for the church restart specialist has never been greater. Understand that not every declining church wants to give away their property to a church planter that is an unknown and unexperienced leader in revitalization. It is far better for the local church to work hand in hand with a local or regional association which will keep the property from being sold to a grocery store development company or land developer. People sacrificed greatly for that church and it needs to remain a church. The restart strategy allows for this to happen. Restart churches develop other restart leaders. In fact, biblically, the primary place for the development of new Church Revitalizers is the local church or a cluster of restart churches. When restarting churches and restart revitalizers building new revitalizers, it is a move from an old Church Growth Paradigm of the 1980's to a restored emphasis on a biblical paradigm. Some of the benefits of churches building restart revitalizers are:

Reproduction

If you are going to take the necessary time required to restart a church it is only wise to take others with you. Intentionally seeking to multiply oneself is strategic for your initial restart but as you progress, what becomes a learning lab for future restart leaders is so valuable. Such a restart strategy and approach provide a paradigm or model that can be multiplied virtually endlessly with every local church or cluster of churches offering a church revitalization-learning environment for their new leaders. If every local church would build only one or two new restart leaders for church renewal, the quantity crisis would be over!

Local in its Context

The learning process for restarting churches becomes significantly more effective since the local church provides the spiritual, relational and practical context for the development of the restart revitalizer. The three-fold development of a future restart specialist could be the very thing that could bring a great awakening to our nation. Think about this: We have been doing the strategy of church planting for well over fifty years and intensely for the last twenty-five years. We have thrown big money at the effort of planting and yet no huge move of the Lord has come. Granted we have added many a great church across the land but have not seen a ground swell like the great awakening of the past. There has been no great awakening. I sense if we are to see one in our nation it will come through church revitalization and renewal and not through church planting. There are so many churches which need a restart. Imagine what might happen if we actually sought to help churches in decline before it becomes too late.

Training the Right People Over Those Retooling

When you become selective in your efforts to train the right people over any and all of those who want revitalization training, you have a greater chance for success. I have people come up to me all the time and ask how they can get into the revitalization and renewal gig. After some conversation, I often sense they are more about finding something to do in retirement over having the skill sets that are transferable to the next generation of Church Revitalizers. Church revitalization is not church growth. Church growth often comes after church revitalization. Church revitalization is not church health. Church health often comes at the end of the revitalization journey and immediately before substantial church growth. The right people should receive training. The emerging restart revitalizer and existing church pastor who need training the most are those who are already engaged in some stage of renewal ministry. With the training focused in the church we move from training the wrong individuals to training and equipping the right people.

Adaptable and Flexibility in One's Approach

My friend Gray McIntosh is right when he says it takes all size churches to reach the nation for Christ. When it comes to Church Revitalizer development, "one size" does not fit all. Around the world, Church Revitalizers from a vast variety of cultures, backgrounds, experiences, education levels, need to be fostered. Our renewal approaches must be flexible and customizable. In addition, the environment is rapidly changing around the church today so flexibility in our approaches to renewal is required.

Keep Focused on the Three Self's

While most of us know this idea from the field of church planting, a restart effort must focus on becoming once again self-supporting, self-sustaining and self-propagating. The local church provides the financial support for the learning process, thus maintaining both the responsibility for and control of the development of its own emerging restart revitalizers. The church must also become self-sustaining so equipping future revitalizers for the work of the ministry is essential. Then the local church must become self-propagating in its effort to regrow the work of the Lord in their setting.

Skill Development through Monthly Cohort or Lab

In Orlando where I live and lead a missions organization, we work at equipping future Church Revitalizers through a layering process we have developed. Because so often in the revitalization of churches, process and strategies must be sequentially layered upon the previous one, it is important to implement a monthly cohort or lab to begin the training of Church Revitalizers. Church Revitalizers must get in a regular time of training and remain in it. There are ongoing skills that need to be not only encountered but emblazoned into one's heart and ministry. Such development takes a long time but while you are learning you are doing so not to waste the journey the Lord has for you and your church. We have Church Revitalizers around central Florida that have done a tremendous job of turning around their churches. Yet these are the ones that are always at the cohort meeting. Conversely, those who come sporadically often misstep in the process because they have not given it their full effort. The equipping and training is not limited to a certain period of time but continues throughout the Church Revitalizers lives. Church Revitalization Leaders are built over lifetimes. That is why I am so glad to see so many of my former doctoral students in church revitalization still at the task of learning, equipping and growing.

Ongoing Assessment

The restart leader must be constantly assessing the path the church is on. Moving too fast is just as detrimental as moving too slowly in revitalization. Pace is required.[169] There will always be seasons of evaluation in a restart. Members of the local community who know the emerging Church

---

169 For more on the pace of church revitalization and renewal see, *The Church Revitalizer as Change Agent* by Tom Cheyney. Available through Amazon books or www.renovateconference.org/bookstore.

Revitalizer and who work with him on a regular basis are the best ones to help him both establish clear goals for his development and evaluate his growth toward those goals. The right restart leader is there to the end. They are not on the pastor visitation tour that moves a pastor every three year somewhere else.

Wrapping it Up!

While I would be among the first to acknowledge that you must honor the past in order to move into the future, never let it be said that you should live in the past. Churches that need to be restarted have come to this place and point in time because too much emphasis was focused in what the church had done in the past and not what it was doing right now. Restart churches must embrace new forms. Restart churches must get ready for new people both young and old alike. Restart churches must get out of the rut and raise the bar towards growth. The leader who leads the effort must be allowed the freedom to try new things. Raise the level of influence of your restart pastor so that there will be a clear message about whom the church should follow. There can only be one shepherd so follow him and pray for him early and often. Here is a lesson for the restart leader about putting those you have to work. Remember this, groups leading ministries, which are left on their own, will usually justify the plans that long-time members have invested in regardless of their outcome for growth. Then you will lose any chance of a successful restart.

Chapter 10
The Congregational Life Cycle and Intervention

Solomon declared in Ecclesiastes 3:2, that there is *"A time to be born, and a time to die; a time to plant, and a time to pluck up that which is planted;"*167 He declares that there are two main events that all will experience...birth and death! In the book *Legacy Churches,* the writer states, "...that all humans must move through a normal life-cycle that begins with conception, celebrates birth, grows and blossoms into maturity, and moves into the final stages of decline and death. What is true of the human body is also true of organizations. These same principles of birth, growth, development to maturity, decline and death can also be applied to the church."170 However, the church as Jesus founded it as not intended to die but to endure until He returns to catch it away as His bride so that it will ever be with Him. (I Thessalonians 4: 16-18, Ephesians 5: 25-32) While the church, as an institution of God and the Body of Christ, will never die; it is a sad truth that local congregations do die every year unless there is intervention. That is what this chapter is all about.

Many congregations will close their doors and cease to exist this year. Many others will not be around another three years. This does not have to be! The church and its leaders must begin to seek to understand the importance of their church's life cycle. The church is the only hope for future generations and if the church fails our nation is doomed. Jim Futral points out that, "According to Jesus, the church is not only significant; it is vitally important. In fact, as you see Him establish the church, you come to realize that it is the most significant institution on the planet. This gathering of born-

---

170 Stephen Gray and Franklin Drummond, *Legacy Churches* (St. Charles, Illinois: ChurchSmart Resources, 2009) 53.

again, transformed people reaching out to tell the Good News of Jesus was founded by Him and will be rescued one day by Him. In Matthew 16 Jesus said, 'Upon this rock I will build my church; and the gates of hell shall not prevail against it' (Matt. 16:18). The church building is not just a meeting place, but for amalgamating newly transformed lives with other transformed lives to create a fellowship that literally is a force to move against everything that Satan would force upon them."171

Any type of Life Cycle, whether it be a human body, a secular organization or a church always reveals what that body, organization or church goes through during its life. In some cases, it is a very slow process and the changes occur gradually. In other cases, the process seems to be rapid and swift. No matter the speed, it is always a process of change.

Every year this writer works with churches in the area of church revitalization. Because of several years of pastoral experience, I have found the basics of the church life cycle to be true and of great benefit to the local church pastor and leadership. It has become an important tool for giving direction to the pastor and the church's leadership in the area of church health and revitalization.

One of the earliest proponents of the importance of the church life cycle was Robert Dale in his book *To Dream Again.* Keith Williams said in his article titled, *A Church's Life Cycle,* that Dale's illustration "shows a bell curve with labels at different places. On its bottom left side sits the word "dream." On the opposite end sits the word "dropout." Some versions of the illustration (not Dale's) use the words, "vision and death" instead of "dream and dropout." Between the two

---

171 Jim Futral, *The Life Cycle of a Church,* Mississippi Baptist, April 19, 2018, accessed November 20, 2018, https://www.mbcb.org/archives-list/life-cycle-church/

far ends of the curve lie the stages of a church's life. The words "dream, beliefs, goals, structure, and ministry" label the upward side of the curve. On the bell curve's downward side are printed the words "nostalgia, questioning, polarization and dropout." Those nine words describe the life cycle of a church."172

All living organisms have a life cycle and so does the local church. When a church understands its life cycle it can better understand its future and its spiritual health. As a Church Revitalizer I am frequently asked, "What can be done to change the direction of our church?" The only answer to that question has to do with helping the church understand where they are on the Life Cycle.

Ron Edmondson says concerning the church life cycle and its effects on the church and its leadership, "Every organization goes through life cycles. This includes the church. Theses cycles can be natural or forced, but part of leadership is recognizing them and adapting leadership to them for continued health and growth. Each stage has overlap but understanding this can help a leader decide how best to lead…which is different in each life cycle."173 Here is the version of the church life cycle that I have developed after years of working with the local church. Let it be said, however, that while the local church may die, the church as an institution and Body of Christ will never fail!

---

172 Williams, Keith. *A Churches Life Cycle,* June 9, 2016 and accessed November 21, 2018,
https://gobnm.com/perspectives/a_pastor_s_viewpoint/a-church-s-life-cycle/article_7d1f67ce-2cbe-11e6-a530-8b1d8cc3347a.html

173 Edmondson, Ron. ChurchPlants.com, *5 Must-Have Stages of an Organized Church,* accessed November 21, 2018,
https://churchplants.com/articles/5754-5-must-have-stages-to-an-organized-church.html

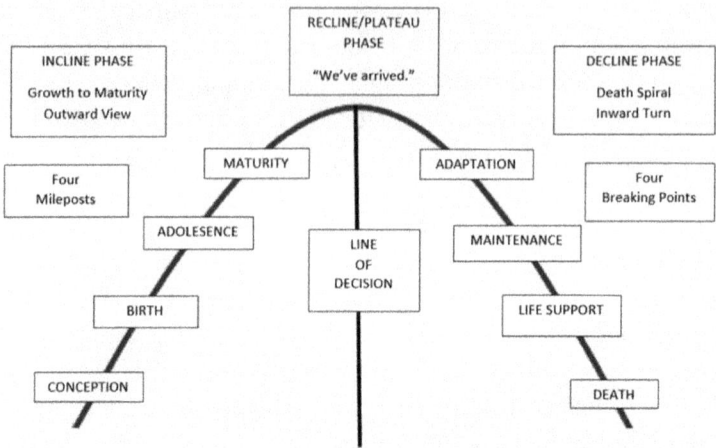

It seems that all Church Revitalizers have their own version of the life cycle but most all of them have similar elements. There is, however, a clear understanding that when a church finds itself on the declining side of a life cycle there are only two options left or death will be certain. These two options are "Intervention" or "Restart." Both options will be explained in the following pages.

First, it is important that the reader gain a general understanding of the terms "Incline, Recline, and Decline." These are the three main phases of a church life cycle. Each of these phases represent a different development period in the life of the church. In each of these phases there are specific tasks and mileposts that determine the future ministry and health of the church.

INCLINE (GROWTH) – The main character traits of a church on the incline are clear. The church is future focused because of a God-given vision for the community it ministers to. The church in this phase is not afraid to do new and challenging things for the Kingdom and they are not afraid of failure or taking risks. This is a phase when the church is full

228

of vitality, enthusiasm, and excitement. It is marked by an increasing effectiveness of ministry. It is in the process of building its approach to the community and the quality of the ministry is being developed as well. This phase begins to mark the churches identity and its reputation in the community where it resides. It is a time when the church is maturing into the church that most resembles a New Testament church. It is focused on the needs of its community and the preaching of the Gospel message to impact the lostness around it. It shows the progress the church makes in the first half of its existence. This is when the church is growing and healthy. When the church is in this early phase it generally has an outward focus, meaning it is striving to reach its community with the Gospel. It understands the Great Commission found in Matthew 28: 19-20. Furthermore, they take seriously and live out Acts 1:8. In this phase the church focuses most of its resources, whether it be man power or finances, on reaching the community and winning souls to Christ. The focus of the church is on "them and not us."

RECLINE (PLATEAU) – The main character traits of a church in this phase of life are evident. The church that is in recline or plateau focuses mostly on the present and is controlled by the programs that it has been using for years and, in some cases, even decades. It has turned its attention to its present members and pays little attention to those outside its ranks. Ministry becomes boring and habitual and people begin to become dissatisfied and leave. Furthermore, it refuses to do anything different, especially those things that would call for them to take a risk. This is a phase when the church thinks it has arrived and this is the most dangerous time in the church's life. This is called the plateau phase of the church. The church becomes comfortable with who they are and what they have accomplished. The church is marked by repetitious ministry. Doing the same thing over and over no matter what the results might be. In this phase the church becomes more and more averse to any kind of change, and goals that had been set in the past have been accomplished and they are happy with the results, so much so that they sit back and gloat about their past accomplishments. Instead of becoming comfortable in this period, the church should begin to revision itself and set a new course to accomplish new goals and new priorities. Instead it becomes a mediocre self-satisfied congregation that has no real impact on anyone, let alone their community. This usually results in a numerical decline as people who really have a desire to serve the Lord decide it is time to leave and seek a place of worship that really cares. This place in the church's life is characterized by a comfortability that slows momentum and brings about a need for revision and refocus, but that does not usually happen. Dale Roach says in the article, *How to know the Life Cycle of Your Church,* "This is when things seem to settle down for the church. This is the stage where a congregation has lost their desire for new visions and goals. Everyone seems happy with the way things are. This is the starting point for church decline."[174]

DECLINE (DEATH SPIRAL) – The main character traits of a church in this phase of life are quite tragic. Churches in this phase always live in past failures and past successes with no thought of the future. This kind of church is living a visionless existence. Its attention is given solely to the core of the congregation and it caters to their wants and desires. It is apathetic about everything that really matters in the church and becomes complacent and faithless. This is a phase when the church begins its "death spiral." It begins to decline spiritually as wells as congregationally. The church becomes unhappy with leadership and with each other as members. Disunity sets in and everyone begins to ask the

---

174 Dale Roach, *How to know the Life Cycle of Your Church,* accessed November 20, 2018, http://likeateam.com/how-to-know-the-life-cycle-of-your-church/.

question "whose fault is this?" and the blame game begins. Apathy sets in and the congregation that used to care about reaching the world comes to a point of not caring at all. One writer puts it this way, "the church doesn't care, and it doesn't care that it doesn't care." The church becomes more like a club rather than a church. It turns INWARD and only seeks to satisfy those that have remained. It goes into survival mode spiritually and financially. In this phase of the church's existence doubt sets in. Doubt about purpose, priorities and position in the community. The church becomes more focused on their program of survivability than they do on the needs of the community. This phase, if there is no intervention, will lead to certain death of the church. The vision of the church has long since been lost and survival is the main objective. There is a point in this phase that a church will reach the "point of no return". Sad to say, death usually follows. It may be slow and agonizing or it might be fast and swift, but death will follow! When a church finds itself in decline it loses its sense of security. Often, however, the members refuse to admit their problem of decline and the situation becomes direr than before.

The life cycle consists of three main PHASES, twelve STAGES and numerous STEPS in those stages. We will examine these in detail in this section.

Stages in the Incline Phase

In this phase of life, the church truly understands the importance of the six Biblical traits of a healthy church. The church is heavily involved in **evangelism** and **missions.** The church understands the importance of **ministry, discipleship** and **fellowship.** It builds its program based on **prayer** and **worship.** It greatly resembles the New Testament church. There is a clear growth stage on the incline side of the life cycle. It is the "glory" days of a new church. This phase is always **outwardly focused**, meaning that the church has one objective and that is to preach the Gospel and win the lost. Here are the stages that are evident in a healthy church. There are four main stages in the incline phase.

The Conception Stage

The most important stage in this phase of the church's life is the conception stage. As in all of life, real life begins at conception. Every church has its beginning in the heart of God. So, it is first conceived in the heart of God before He imparts it in the heart of the Man of God.

Step one is *the Imparting of the Vision.* This is God planting a vision into the heart of an obedient servant. He imparts that vision in the heart of someone who will take seriously the need that has been revealed. God is faithful to show this leader just exactly what He wants done, how to do it and when to do it. When God imparts a vision, you can be sure that it can be earth shaking in its ramifications. The visionary always understands who God is and how powerful He really is. As a result, the visionary leader is driven to attempt and accomplish the impossible.

A real, God-given, vision inherently expects God to do what man cannot do. A true vision from God motivates the visionary to step out on faith and attempt the seemingly impossible. God given vision is the stimulus that drives the visionary to accomplish the work God has assigned.

Step two is *the Reception of the Vision.* Just as a baby is conceived in the mother's womb, the church is conceived in the heart of an obedient servant of God. Any church that had its beginnings in controversy, division and church splits probably did not come from the heart of God. Rick Warren says, "You get God's vision by saying, 'What do you want me to do? How do you want me to do it? And when do you want me to do it?' You need to stop praying, 'God, bless what I'm

232

doing.' And instead start praying, 'God, help me to do what you want to bless.'"175

Arlin J. Rothauge writes about the formation of a new church concept when he said, "A new congregation springs from nothing because someone believes in the possibility of it coming into being. That person, or core of people, gathers others around the vision and begins to make transitions from one size to another. They form a history, traditions, and a distinct identity. If their resources permit, the congregation acquires property, buildings, and salaried staff."176 Every New Testament church exists because God put a vision into a leader's heart for a community. The Bible is filled with examples of great leaders who received a vision from God to do a work for God. For a New Testament church to have a beginning there will always be a man of God with a vision.

Step three is *the development of the Vision.* "Vision is one of the most critical elements in the success and effectiveness of the local church. The Bible is clear, 'Without vision people cast off restraint.' To keep the church traveling down the right path, it is important for its members to have a clear and shared vision."177 The vision is developed by keeping attention on God.

---

175 Rick Warren, *Three Aspects of the Vision God Has for Your church,* Pastors.com, January 20, 2017, accessed November 19, 2018. https://pastors.com/3-parts-of-vision/

176 Arlin J. Rothauge, *The Life Cycle in Congregations,* accessed November 21, 2018, https://www.episcopalchurch.org/files/Life_Cycle%281%29.pdf

177 Steven R. Mills, *Developing Vision in A Smaller Congregation,* Enrichment Journal, Accessed November 13, 2018, http://enrichmentjournal.ag.org/200001/046_developing_vision.cfm

Ecclesiastes 5:3, *"For a dream cometh through the multitude of business; and a fool's voice is known by a multitude of words."*[178] Just like in child birth, the most painful time comes just prior to the child's birth. So, it is in the birth of a church as well. It takes time and commitment to know what God wants in any vision for a new church. The development of the vision is painful, but well worth the effort, when the vision of a new church becomes unchangeable reality.

The Birth Stage

From this dream/vision that God placed in the leader's heart grew a simple possibility into a living organism. After conception follows the birth of the church. This is an exciting time because everything is new and full of potential. It is a time of great enthusiasm as the future is focused on by a new congregation. With this stage comes some very clear steps toward a mature, viable and productive congregation.

Step one is *infancy.* This is the step that formulates the future of the church. The first year of a human's life is the most important stage in the future development of a human. The first year of life is when the most amazing changes occur. These growth changes come so fast that they are noticeable every month in the first year. These growth changes are similar, in the early infancy stage, to the new born church.

Step two is *basic body development.* This step ensures that the church will be successful in ministry. Just like the physical changes that occur as the child begins to gain control of their body there will be changes that will be made along the way as the church body develops. The child begins to develop the self-confidence that will help them child stay motivated in order to achieve. The child begins to develop and try new skills and learn how to make correct decisions. The new born

---

178 Ecclesiastes 5:3 KJV.

church, guided by the leadership of the Holy Spirit, will also learn to develop new skills and make correct decisions as it grows.

Step three is learning to *depend on each other and God.* Babies learn that they must rely on others to meet their needs and as a result must learn to trust those that are caring for them. This is the most important step in the development of a new church. The church must learn to depend, not on self, but on God. It is a time when the church becomes a "community" in the sense that trust and dependence in and on each other is developed. This is a must for a new church. All of this brings a real sense of security for the future both physically and emotionally.

The Adolescence Stage

This is a time when the church begins its efforts to adapt to the community it resides in. It begins to see the cultural landscape and the needs that the community possesses. The dream/vision begins to take shape and the church begins to develop as a worshipping congregation. It begins setting goals and training leadership.

Step one is *refining the vision.* This step is marked by the development of an evangelism and missions strategy, Bible study system and worship style that will coincide with the original vision of the church. Every vision is a work in progress. God gives the vision and sometimes He leads us to refine it and tweak it in certain areas. It is an ongoing process. This is a time when the church gets excited about finding and doing the will of God. The church family works from the vision that God has given it to accomplish the work of the church.

Step two is *goal setting.* This is when the church decides what it will do to change its world. Goals for future growth are determined in the areas of attendance, baptisms, finances and facilities. Setting clear God given goals is a part of the process of an adolescent church. The greatest challenge most churches have today is the ability to keep the main thing the main thing. Without clear understandable goals the church will flounder. Every church that ever started had a leader that knew the importance of goal setting. In the early stage of the adolescent church it is important for the church to set clear, attainable realistic goals that can ensure a measure of success in the early days of its young life.

Step three is *developing its values and beliefs.* This is when the church begins to ask itself the question "Who are we and why are we here?" What the church believes is very important because it will determine its approach to missions, evangelism, worship and discipleship. It is a time when the church welcomes individual ideas and is open to trying new things. It operates out of true harmony and unity among the congregation. Very little self-centeredness exists because everyone is working toward a common goal.

The Maturation Stage

Finally, the church begins to shape its own identity. Its missions and evangelism strategy are developed and put into motion. They become priorities in the life of the church.

Step one is the *development of a stable ministry program.* This is the time when the church is becoming effective in ministry. This is when the church organizes around the set goals and vision by implementing programs and activities in order to get the Gospel message out to those in the community. This addresses the question "How will we change our world?" The church has become innovative in accomplishing its task. It is marked by cooperation and achievement by the congregation. It is a church full of faith with a desire to succeed even to the point of sacrifice.

Step two is the *development of an evangelistic and missional approach*. This is when the spiritual needs of lost people become the priority of the church. Winning and discipling new converts becomes the priority of the congregation. Missions at home and abroad become the objective of the church. Budgets and programing reflect the commitment to missions and evangelism.

Step three is when the church begins to *shape its own identity*. Somewhere along the way during the process of "becoming" the church began to form its own identity. Somehow an identity emerges in the leaders and the congregation. The personality of the church is set, and the church's kind of worship and ministry become the trademark of the church. In this step the church becomes visible to the community and begins to build a rapport with those living there. It sets priorities that begin to set the church apart from other churches.

After the structure for the church ministry is put into place and the church is actively pursuing its goals through that structure, it can be said that the church is coming to maturity. The church, at this point, will usually stay in this stage for years and even decades but then something happens. It gets too comfortable.

Stages in the Recline Phase

There comes a time in the life of every church when something happens that changes the course of the church itself. It comes to a time when ministry becomes the rule of the day. The attitude that "we have arrived" begins to prevail. The church becomes happy with itself. It has reached its goals. It has reached people. **It has plateaued**. Now it has reached a dangerous point in its existence. The time frame for a church arriving at this point varies according to the church but every church will reach this point sooner or later and when it does ministry and being a New Testament church takes a back seat. This begins the decline of the church. This phase is unique in that the church cannot remain in this decline position forever. Neither can it revert to the incline side. It must change its course, or it will begin the trek into the dreaded "death spiral." One writer said it this way "Recline is a tepid, tread water stage featuring decreases in membership, attendance, giving and overall impact in the community."179 This phase is marked by the church having **no real focus.** What are the stages of the recline phase?

The Contented Stage

This is the stage when the ministry of the church becomes so comfortable that it makes no real difference in anyone's life. It settles into ministry that, despite its ineffectiveness, is done repeatedly getting the same mediocre results. When a church is in plateau it thinks only of the present not the future. It is driven by its programming and quickly becomes focused on the members and not the community. Services become mundane and have little appeal to outsiders. Real faith is at a minimum and nothing happens that will challenge the faith of the members. It usually is led by the established leaders that have been serving in the church for many years. Any growth that comes to a plateaued church mostly come from switching members from one church to another. Very little conversion growth takes place in a plateaued church.

In **step one** a *pattern of routine develops.* The church reverts to its tradition rather than true ministry. Every church will find itself content with its accomplishment sooner or later

---

179 *The Church Revitalization Lifecycle: Three Primary Stages.* Accessed November 9, 2018. https://outreachnorthamerica.org/wp-content/uploads/2015/06/The-Church-Revitalization-Lifecycle.pdf

but for some this step is where the real danger for the future of the church lies. It is a time when the church relaxes all its efforts to reach the community in which it resides. The major task of the church, of course, is to reach the community with the Gospel but somehow things begin to change at this point. A church cannot and will not remain in the recline (plateaued) phase of existence forever. Herein lies the danger. What is the church to do?

Step two is *when the church has a sense of having arrived at their desired destination.* It begins to bask in its past accomplishments. It seeks to stay in the "safety zone" and never take a risk on anything. It is easy, at this point for the church to get "at ease in Zion." They have been at the task for years, maybe even decades, to do ministry. Now, however, the congregation seems to be happy with their present position in the Kingdom and ministry to a lost community is no longer of importance to the church. It takes upon itself a "we deserve a little rest" attitude and the church begins to go downhill spiritually and ministerially. Because it has accomplished much of what it set out to do, the church relaxes its faith principles and fails to attempt anything that involves a risk.

Step three is *when the goals of the growth period have been accomplished.* This contented step is only realized after the church has reached its present potential as outlined in their vision and set goals of the past. After goals they set have been accomplished, it seems as if nothing else needs to be done. On the contrary, this is when the church needs to go back and revision and retool for the next period of ministry and growth that God has for it. Sadly, most churches do not revision. They settle in where they are and begin to die.

The Settled in Stage

Step one is when the church *turns inward.* A sure sign that the church is in this stage is when the church turns all its attention, budget and ministry efforts to only include the present membership. It focuses on not only what the needs of the congregation are but also it majors on what the congregation wants. This is usually done because of an effort not to offend anyone. The leadership develops the mindset that "we can't afford to lose any more members." So, everything in the church reflects that attitude. The budget reflects it in the fact that money is allocated to inner church activities and efforts. Evangelism and missions seem to have no place in the budget. Programs also reflect the same attitude. Ministry programs are geared to meet the needs of those already present and very little effort is given toward reaching those outside the walls of the church.

Step two is when the church *becomes comfortable in its accomplishments.* When a church gets to this stage it usually reminisces about its past and most of the time it is about its past accomplishments. Statements like, "I can remember when we had a youth program with 50 youth in it!" or "I can remember when we had 500 in Sunday school and worship!" "I can remember when our budget was $500,000." There is nothing wrong with remembering how it used to be if you allow the memories to spur you on to do greater things for the Kingdom. There is, however, something wrong with living in the past as if the past cannot be improved upon. This is where 90% of Evangelical churches find themselves today. After the church begins to live in the past it begins to lose, at the present time, any momentum it had for ministry.

The Loss of Momentum Stage

Step one of this stage is when the church gets *set in its ways (I shall not be moved).* When a church loses its momentum it usually gets "set in its ways" to the point that it refuses to be moved from its place of comfortability. It is a place of complacency and disability. It becomes a dysfunctional church. It no longer is structured like a New Testament church. It no longer functions as a New Testament church. It becomes as mediocre as any secular/civic organization. Then step two kicks in.

Step two is when the church *loses its direction*. This is the final stage in the life of a church before it enters the "death spiral." It has no direction. It has no distinctiveness. It has no message. It has no ministry. What a tragedy! The church that loses its direction is like the Christian that is described in Matthew 5:13-14, "Ye are the salt of the earth: but if the salt have lost its savor, wherewith shall it be salted? it is thenceforth good for nothing, but to be cast out, and to be trodden under foot of men. Ye are the light of the world. A city that is set on a hill cannot be hid."180 The church that has no direction is a floundering church that has no impact on the lost community. It, for all practical purposes, has become null and void of influence for the Kingdom. It is then that the church enters the decline phase (death spiral).

Stages in the Decline Phase

In this phase the church has entered the "Death Spiral" and is picking up speed toward its own demise. The church loses its equilibrium and begins to veer off course. The concepts of a New Testament church begin to fade, and the church becomes the possession of the people rather than God. This phase is marked by an **inward focus**. It becomes self-centered and goes into a self-preservation mode. "Too many churches experience decline without an exit strategy and end up flat lining without a proper burial and poisoning

---

180 Matthew 5:13-14 KJV.

everyone they come into contact with."181 There are four major stages in this decline phase. One must keep in mind that the church can change direction at any point in this decline, but the further it goes into decline the more difficult it will be to change, and the more drastic the action needed to make the change.

Thom Rainer says about the decline phase "The church not only declines numerically; it declines in spirit and unity. The congregation often looks more like a spiritual country club doling out perks and privileges, rather than a biblical church where all of the parts of the body are working in a self-sacrificial manner."182 So, what are the stages in the decline phase?

The Questioning Stage

It is in **step one** that the church becomes *problem focused*. This step begins to ask, "What is our problem?". This has a paralyzing effect on the congregation. Most of the time the answer to that question is obvious but the church refuses to face the answer. Often churches don't want to face the truth about their situation because they know that understanding will require action and they are too satisfied with where they are to act and change anything. Usually this leads to an even graver direction which is found in step two.

---

181 *The Life Cycle of a Church.* Elevate Church in Vancouver, Washington, May 20, 2013, accessed November 10, 2018, http://www.elevatew.tv/leadcast/2013/5/20/the-life-cycle-of-a-church.html.

182 Thom Rainer, *Understanding Where Your Church is on the Congregational Life Cycle,* January 3, 2018, accessed November 10, 2018, https://thomrainer.com/2018/01/understanding-where-your-church-is-on-the-congregational-life-cycle/.

In **step two** the church begins to *play the blame game!*
Often churches in decline begin to place blame on
someone…anyone who can become their "scapegoat." After
all, someone must be at fault for the church's failure. Usually
the pastor is that person who is blamed for the church's
failure, even though he might have been the only one doing
anything to keep the church alive. This is a time when
differences of opinion are usually not tolerated, and the result
is division. This attitude of intolerance gives way to disunity
and a whole new battlefront erupts.

In **step three** the church begins to *grow accustomed to a
non-caring attitude.* This final step in the questioning stage is
usually a tragic sense of apathy. When a church becomes
apathetic, the power brokers in the church take control and
the church becomes a bureaucratic mess. Its leaders often
become quite inflexible and domineering. The frightening
thing about apathy is that it is a killer. If you understand the
true meaning of apathy, you will realize that it is not simply a
careless attitude. It is when someone does not care, and they
don't care that they don't care! This is the tragedy of apathy
and it will destroy everything it touches. Many of the 90% of
declining churches today are steeped in apathy. This attitude
will result in the church being so sick that it will be almost
impossible to heal its wounds and return it to the state of
health it once enjoyed.

The Maintenance Stage

This stage is a milestone in the demise of the church.
Anytime a church comes to this point in its existence and
solutions have not been sought, then the church charts a
completely new course of action to stay alive. Money is tight.
People are leaving. Visitors do not return. Disunity and
conflict prevail. Here are the logical steps in the maintenance
stage.

Step one is the church acquiring a *survival mentality*. At this point, all the church can really do is seek to survive from one week, month and year to the next. When a church reaches this point, it is well into the "death spiral." This is when budget cuts are made. This is when power groups take control. At this point, the pastor becomes a pawn in a horrible game of church chess. The pastor will become personally and financially challenged because of the church's financial problems. These financial problems will affect the total effectiveness of all the ministries of the church. The pastor becomes the "whipping boy" of the church because several people in the church family believe that he must be the problem. Often, the pastor resigns and leaves the church in the early beginnings of this step.

Step two occurs when the church *works to preserve what it still has*. The natural thing for a person or a church to do when they get in survival mode is to try to salvage what they still have. We are not talking about money or programs. We are talking about position and dignity and influence. However, at this point, these are very hard to hold on to. A special effort is made to avoid doing anything that will ruffle the feathers of the people who are still in the congregation. That's where step three comes in.

In **step three** leaders seek to *make the existing congregation happy*. So, instead of demanding accountability on the part of the congregation, compromise is usually made. Programs that keep people happy are maintained. Any program that will call for action or commitment is usually deleted. Money is spent on the existing congregation to entice them to stay. When this happens, it is reflected in the program and the budget. These actions take the church to a whole new level of demise.

The Life Support Stage

This is the stage when the church is on the verge of death. The congregation that is left finally realizes that the church probably will not continue to be a viable entity. As a Church Revitalizer, I have dealt with several churches that waited until they got to this stage which was too late for revitalization. The church's only hope was to do a restart. That's what this book is about. It would be nice if there could be an intervention phase in the life cycle of any given church but tragically a church will usually wait too long to seek help.

Step one is when the future of the church *becomes terminal.* All hope is lost. The church is careening toward a tragic end. Thom Rainer says, "As many as 100,000 churches in America could be dying. Their time is short, perhaps less than ten years."183 The number of churches that are terminal in America is staggering. If the tide is not turned, we will lose our civilization as we know it.

Step two is when the church *begins to face closure.* The church begins to lose any connection it ever had to its community. It loses its testimony usually because of infighting with each other and an uncaring attitude toward the community. Finally, when it is all said and done, it becomes a disgrace to the Kingdom.

The Death Stage

The church then begins to implode, and more people leave and even staff members begin to seek other positions. This is the time to plan the funeral. It is the time to decide what will become of the church's assets. It is over. Or is it?

---

183 Thom Rainer, *Autopsy of a Deceased Church: 11 Things I Learned.* April 24, 2013, accessed November 1, 2018, https://thomrainer.com/2013/04/autopsy-of-a-deceased-church-11-things-i-learned/.

The only hope for a church at this point is intervention. Intervention can take one of two directions. Intervention with re-visioning and re-tooling, or intervention with a re-start to leave a legacy.

There seems to be a "point of no return" on the decline side of the cycle. That point of no return would fall between the maintenance stage and the life support stage of the life cycle. It is next to impossible to turn a church around that is beyond the maintenance stage. If the church is still viable and has a possibility to survive, then positive intervention must happen before the church reaches the life support stage. This is the time to take the church back to be re-born, have new dreams for a bright future, and set new goals. A new vision from God should be sought and a new, Holy Spirit led, structure of programs and ministry should be implemented.

What is this process? Simply stated it is a forced interruption of the downward trek of the church. The ideal place for the intervention is at the top of the curve where plateau and recline become reality or in the very early stages of decline.

It is a new beginning with the things that matter. It is starting over by going back to the early stages of the church's life and beginning again with a new vision and dream. The church is the same church, but it takes on a new direction. It sets new goals, organizes to accomplish those goals and once again makes evangelism and missions the priority of the church.

Every great, growing church understands this principle. Every time the church reaches plateau and recline, they begin to dream new dreams for the church. It is sort of like a step ladder. You get to the top and you erect another ladder. Ladders are built upon ladders to have a constant climb upwards. This climb upwards guards against stagnation, staleness and complacency in the church. This principle helps to grow a vibrant and healthy church. If the church is vibrant and healthy, souls are won, and the Kingdom is expanded. It can't get any better than that!

However, it is sad to say that intervening in the life of a church at this early stage does not come easy because at this stage most churches have not faced "present reality" about their church and they think that somehow everything is going to be ok.

When a church crosses the "point of no return" the only option left is to intervene with a re-start. The diagram below helps us to understand the preferred intervention in the life cycle.

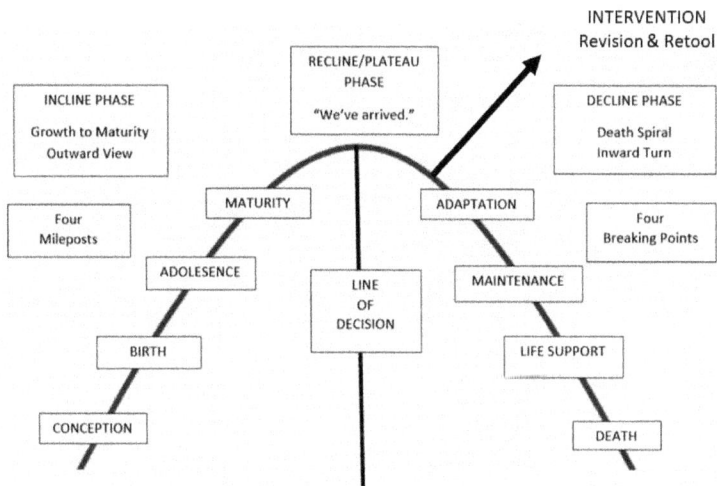

Here are the steps that will generally be used in a re-start.

1. Rejoice and honor the former church's history.
2. A Church Revitalization Team is formed; made up of individuals outside the existing church.

3. Consideration must be given to the potential for success in the former church's setting!

4. If possible, a church revitalization restart contract will be developed between the old church and the new restart.

5. The church property must change hands.

6. The Church Revitalization Team will make all decisions from the beginning.

7. Research must be done about the declining church's ministry area for what type of new work will have the greatest chance for survival.

8. Dissolve the membership and close the doors of the church for a time.

9. Begin seeking God for a Church Revitalizer for the new restart.

10. Change the church's name and give it a new identity.

11. Develop a fresh vision for the community.

13. Begin outreach activities and develop a new church core group.

14. Call a new church Pastor who has energy and faith.

15. Start the countdown to the new church restart launch and grand opening!

16. Finally, when you launch, reach forward, draw a line in the sand, and do not look back.

During a re-start intervention there will be only two teams at work. The Church Revitalization Team will be the primary decision-making group during the process. The core group will be made up of people who come to the church and have a real interest in the idea of a new church. This core team is accountable to the Church Revitalization Team and they make no decisions on their own.

Conclusion

Nearly all churches will go through this life cycle. If a church is to remain healthy and Kingdom focused, it must have leaders that understand the significance of how a church lives, grows and yes…thrives. It is imperative that pastors and leaders keep in constant contact with what the church is doing right and what it is doing wrong. They must pay attention to the successes and the failures and know how to adjust the ministry in such a way that the church will move forward and not get bogged down in the trivial. Tony Morgan on his Blog site Tony Morgan Live said, "It's true. Most churches start, grow, thrive, decline and eventually end. But I believe God's plan for our churches is that they grow in maturity towards a peak of sustained health, and that as methods and traditions and culture change, they continually reevaluate and refresh, finding new ways to lead people towards Jesus."[184] I would echo those words and make them my own if I could but the reality is that most churches are headed toward death and we need to be ready to intervene with a re-start process when faced with the opportunity.

---

184 Tony Morgan, *Understanding the 7 Phases of a Church's Life Cycle | The Unstuck Church.* April 2017, accessed November 12, 2018. https://tonymorganlive.com/2017/04/10/phases-church-life-cycle/.

Chapter Eleven
When a Church Restart Strategy is Your Only H.O.P.E.
in Revitalization

Praise the God and Father of our Lord Jesus Christ. According to His great mercy, He has given us a new birth into a living hope through the resurrection of Jesus Christ from the dead 4 and into an inheritance that is imperishable, uncorrupted, and unfading, kept in heaven for you. 5 You are being protected by God's power through faith for a salvation that is ready to be revealed in the last time. 6 You rejoice in this, though now for a short time you have had to struggle in various trials 7 so that the genuineness of your faith —more valuable than gold, which perishes though refined by fire —may result in praise, glory, and honor at the revelation of Jesus Christ. 8 You love Him, though you have not seen Him. And though not seeing Him now, you believe in Him and rejoice with inexpressible and glorious joy, 9 because you are receiving the goal of your faith, the salvation of your souls.185

The restart-based church revitalization model is being used all across North America. Any group planting churches or working in the area of church revitalization should have a restart strategy if it is going to be a wise steward. I never sought to write a step-by-step process for doing a church restart. Yet, so many have used this material over the last twenty years that it has become such a process. Sometimes I get kind notes of encouragement thanking me for the bold stance and unwavering advice offered within this strategy. A few times I have been ripped apart by those not brave enough to consider such drastic steps to move their local church towards a new expression of health and vitality!

Rick Lawrenson declares: "There is no need to replant a dead church. I've learned that when first responders find a body is cold or stiff, CPR is a waste of energy. Dead means totally lifeless. But, few churches that were once truly

---

185 The Holy Bible: Holman Christian Standard Version. (Nashville: Holman Bible Publishers, 2009), 1 Peter 1:3–9.

alive are truly dead. The heartbeat may be faint, the breathing shallow. If you find the life points, you have somewhere to begun. Mostly dead is still alive."186

The idea of a church that is dying taking the necessary steps to provide it the best chance for survival is not an easy idea to consider. For those who have been part of the setback, admitting that they have hurt the church is hard indeed. Those who will take over also have a challenge in that it will be under their watch that they seek to change those traits, now embedded in the local church, for the betterment and opportunity to turn around a church that is in rapid decline.187

It is amazing to me today that many individuals that attend a dying church see nothing wrong biblically with allowing their church to die along with them. It is as if there is a secret message, which reads: "The last one alive, remember to turn the lights out!" Humorous? Possibly! Tragic for sure because the local church is the very thing for 12which Christ Jesus gave His life and yet we treat his local church with such irreverence that it is no wonder churches are dying all across the world.

This restart strategy is a vital piece for anyone working in church revitalization efforts and for those who possibly lead church planting efforts. If the two disciplines could join forces at this point perhaps it will be the local church that wins. Change is going to happen within the small rapidly declining church and this strategy offers an opportunity for a turnaround that is working, has been working for decades,

---

186 Rick Lawrenson. *The Replanted Church: Leading a Dying Church Back to Life*, (Nags Head, North Carolina, 2018), pg. 19.

187 There is a new book just out by George A. Thomasson that has helped many in this area of restarting churches. The book is entitled: *RESUSCITATE: How to Breath New Life into a Gasping Church*. Go to: RenovateConference.org/bookstore to order your copy or Amazon Books today. It is a great companion to this resource.

and needs to be reconsidered in light of the advancing decline and plateauing of our churches today.

It is a journey of hope for the local struggling church, which is facing hard decisions in light of its future and what it will do to insure a Gospel lighthouse remain in the community it was placed for many more years until Jesus comes to take all of us to Glory. Take the journey with those in your area, which are working to revitalize churches for the sake of Christ. Become willing to embrace the opportunity for your church to survive rather than close down in failure. Allow the Lord God to bring forth a miracle for your church as He transforms the work of ministry within your midst. Pray that the Lord will rise up a group of committed new leaders with the energy to work and turn your church around. Ask God to bring new families into your worship center that have never heard the gospel message and are now drawn to hear the glorious message of salvation in Christ Jesus. Seek transformation not stagnation. Ask the Lord to transform your church, each one of you as individual worshippers and Christ followers. Watch how God will transform your individual families and bring a new expression of "church" right where you live.

Not Every Church is a Candidate for a Restart

Interestingly, many laymen often ask me if I think that their church could be a candidate for a restart. Usually they share of the need for their church to be revitalized. A series of questions frequently follows of which I will answer each and every single one. Once they wear out in asking questions, I ask one. That question is: "How willing are you and your lay leadership willing to let go of the controls of the church for the next three years and allow someone else to make the decisions necessary to restart your church?" One of two things happens at this point.

No Need to Bleed

The first response is that the individual and his co-leaders see no need to make such a drastic decision. There is no real need to make those necessary decisions that will stop the bleeding of the exodus. After all they have been leading the church for over twenty years and see no reason to make this change despite the decline they are facing. Failure to admit one's weakness and need for a restart is often the initial response. Their emphasis on former glories over present or future glories is a key to the polarization and stuckness they face.

As a layperson, you have more to do with the church in its present state then you often take credit. Whether the congregation in which you belong is thriving or declining, it is ultimately up to you and your fellow members and because of you and your fellow members. Pastors are called to equip the saints for the work of the ministry and they can teach, inspire, train, and lead! But when the rubber meets the road, your church's health is a function of how you and your fellow members relate to one another, to the community in which the church is located, and to how they respond to God's leading within their lives. John 10:10 remind us that Jesus said, "I came that you might have life, and have it abundantly." We need to be reminded that as laymen we are the church!

When a local Church is spiritually journeying as a vibrant Church:

- Church members willingly work together!

- The community finds hope from the church!

- There is a sense of belonging and togetherness!

- Members easily and frequently forgive others!

- The laity find their individual and corporate sense of purpose!

- God's leading and direction is apparent to everyone!

Your pastor can be the greatest pastor and preacher, but his message only has the power to the extent that the people of God within the specific local church live it and practice it with each other!

Is There a Guide to Stop the Slide?

The other response is less common and that is when the leader asks how this could happen and who would assist them in considering such an option. The question was once asked this way, "Pastor is there a guide we can follow in order to stop the slide we are facing?" Some laymen desire to stop the near-death throes of their dying church and take the drastic steps necessary to help it become healthy and vibrant once more. They are more concerned about the future needs by allowing the Lord to bring about a resurrection of life the way God wants over what man has become comfortable in.

The church dying or in rapid decline must face the hard realities and wrestle with the biblical passages dealing with reinvention, realignment, and restarting. Scriptures speak of the message of death and resurrection and for rapidly declining churches it is a testament that God can bring life out of something that was once dead. You do not begin in the Bible with new life. You begin with life, death, and being raised in newness of life. Rapidly declining churches often want to skip the journey and jump right to newness of life. Jesus is a fitting example of not missing the process necessary to embrace newness of life.

Ten Reasons Churches are Challenged When Making the Necessary Changes

There is a guide to stop the slide and it is found in the Bible. This material is about helping those ninety plus percent of churches that are in need of church revitalization and renewal. When a church has allowed a deep state of slumber to creep into the work and ministry of the local church it is challenging to make the necessary changes necessary for revitalization. Here are ten reasons:

- All around us the world has changed but the local church has lagged behind these changes and fallen far behind.
- Our world is growing every day and the local church in decline is purging itself at alarming pace.
- The world embraces the young but in declining churches the young are feared.
- The younger generations are returning to church but the rapidly declining church sits on the cliff of fatality refusing to change to embrace this new church attender.
- In the rapidly declining church, there is a void of individuals in the populace. The young are in minute numbers, the middle age worker is absent, young families are few, and the late middle age and older individual are many.
- Older members are in disgust about what younger people want in worship while the younger individual looks at the older as irrelevant.
- The rapidly declining church is unable to keep up numerically, financially, spiritually, and physically.

- The local expression of church has allowed deadness, un-resuscitated, lifeless form to exist without an attempt to turn the expression around.
- Disciple-making has become a thing of the past while gathering together for socializing has replaced the idea of growing deeper and more spiritual Christ followers.
- The world sees a need for change in the local church yet those within have become so comfortable that they miss the need of the lost world for it to remain relevant.

What Does Church Revitalization Mean?

Every place I go people ask me for a definition of church revitalization. Here is one I have used for at least the last ten years:

Church Revitalization is a movement within protestant evangelicalism, which emphasizes the missional work of turning a plateau or rapidly declining church around and moving it back towards growth. It is led through a Church Revitalization Initiative, which is when a local church begins to work on the renewal of the church with a concerted effort to see the ministry revitalized and the church become healthy. Church Revitalization means that the local church knew how, at one time previously, to renew, revitalize, and re-establish the health and vitality of the ministry. One of the challenges for the laity in the day in which we live is that they have lost the knowledge of church renewal and no longer want to cultivate the skill sets necessary to see their church experience revitalization. Even sadder is when a congregation does not have the corporate memory that there was a day when the local church was reaching people for Christ Jesus and active as evangelistic witnesses into their community.

Some church revitalization restarts originate from the decline of others due to failure to remain on the threshold of community transitions. Sometimes our memories of how things use to be hinder us from seeing what we could become. I know that death is painful yet Jesus Christ can bring something new out of the sorrow. One critical point from the start is a complete change of lay leadership and direction is a must for this model to be successful.

When we are talking about a true "church revitalization restart," I am not referring to the typical small, struggling church that finds fresh life and growth, nor am I looking at mergers or relocation of existing churches. A church that is a candidate for a church revitalization restart has already sought advice from the local association leader or district leader about disbanding or is almost ready to disbanded. The church has dwindled down to about twenty or thirty survivors who are too tired to continue on. They no longer possess the critical mass necessary to get the church healthy once more. The leadership which remains, is too tired, too ineffective, and too small in numbers to bring about the changes it will take to make the turn. Those left are at the end of their rope and often want to make decisions that are unwise or lack any chance of success.

A church in need of a restart is a church that must have leadership and resources from outside of itself. Within these churches God often uses the local Association Director of Missions or a district superintendent leader to help bring back to life what I am calling a "church revitalization restart." These leaders will look for healthy churches to parent the restart for a time. When a parenting church or field partner seeks to aid a dying congregation with a solid revitalization strategy, reality must be squarely faced and decisions must be made that are often hard for the declining church. It is hard to admit sometimes but the concept of letting the declining or dying church die is huge if you are going to restart it and make it a growing new work. For good healthy change, there needs to be a spiritual death for that former church. There is mixed opinion in the area of whether a church revitalization restart should close up for a time or continue on. I believe a significant case could and should be made for closing if not for even a short time. Some, to be fair, say that a rebirth of vision is all that is needed. That may be too optimistic and in my individual experience too unrealistic as well.

Some Restart Stories

Northwest Community Church in Washington, DC

Pastor Dan Turner is the founding pastor of Northwest Community Church which is a church restart. Dr. Turner was big on reconnecting with the local community. The church has seen lives transformed and has had over sixty individuals baptized into the church in the last ten years. Today the church has an attendance of over two hundred and averages about eight percent growth annually. It has grown much younger and multicultural. Formerly the church was known as National Memorial Church of God. Turner is a leader in the Wesleyan denomination.[188]

A Coastal Savannah Church

A Church in the coastal area of Savannah had dwindled to just a handful of members. They finally decided to die, deeding their property over to the local association and relinquishing control of the church to a revitalization restart steering committee which included members of other churches, pastors, and state denomination leaders. Since the

---

188 Wiens, Greg and Dan Turner. *Dying to Restart: Churches Choosing a Strategic Death for a Resurrected Life.* (Columbia, SC: Harrington Interactive Media, 2018) Pg. 119-120. This is a wonderful book of restarting churches by two Wesleyan church leaders.

restart steering committee called a church planter as the restart pastor two years ago, the church has grown to 198 in attendance on Sunday mornings. Additionally, the church, which never had morning Bible study, now also has 84 participants!

The Church @ Oaklevel

Jason Cooper "Coop" became the lead pastor of Oak Level Baptist Church in February 2007. During the years leading up to his arrival, the church had reached a critical point of decline and the members had considered renting the existing facilities to another congregation. Jason embraced God's call to begin a revitalization effort at Oak Level in order to restore Jesus' mission to the church. The church began to take steps to refocus on the community surrounding the Ocoee campus. God began to bring leaders together from all over West Orange County and the revitalization effort was in full swing. In the first 3 years of Jason's tenure at Oak Level Baptist Church, more people who had placed their faith in Jesus were baptized than had been baptized in the 10 years leading up to his arrival put together. It has been a remarkable turnaround.

In August of 2010, Oak Level Baptist Church celebrated its 50th anniversary as a church. The very next weekend, the church became known as "The Church at Oak Level," in an effort to remove the barriers of religion that accompanied the name "Baptist" in its name. However, the church remains affiliated with the Southern Baptist Convention and the local association as they partner together to reach the world for Jesus. Jason's hope for The Church at Oak Level is that it would be a family of followers of Jesus who know God intimately, worship Him passionately, and seek His will tirelessly in what has become the church's finest hour. In October of 2012, Rev. Jason Cooper and the folks at the Church@OakLevel received the Church Revitalizer Award for Church Revitalization and Renewal from the

Greater Orlando Baptist Association for its amazing turnaround.

Bethlehem Church in Bethlehem Georgia

This church is a church which has at the heart of its church revitalization strategy the restarting of churches in the northeast portion of Georgia over near the University of Georgia area. Jason Britt I the lead pastor and he has a heart for revitalizing churches. Jason recently did a restart by taking over a declining church in the area and restarted it as the 211 Campus launch in 2017.

Lockhart Church in Orlando

Pastor Rob Arnold is an incredible church planter and becoming a significant Church Revitalizer of Lockhart Baptist Church in the Lockhart community of central Florida. Rob is faced with the daunting challenge of turning a church around that is focused inward on what is comfortable to moving it outward while it seeks to embrace the younger population of central Florida.

Grace Journey Community Church

Coleman Pratt is the pastor of Grace Journey Community Church a restart church that formerly ministered as the old First Baptist Church of Union Park. In early February of 2013, Pastor Pratt led the church to close down as the former church and reopen as Grace Journey. A church running at best 80 people launched its first Sunday with 150 plus people in attendance. The new church had no members and at the end of the first launch service the altar was opened for those wanting to join GJCC. People were moving from all over the sanctuary as the invitation to become part of this new restart in Orlando.

The Summit Church in Durham, North Carolina

The Summit Church, led by J.D. Greear, was formerly known as Homestead Heights Baptist Church in Durham, North Carolina. Serving as the youth minister when the senior pastored retired, Dr. Greear was asked to become the lead pastor in 2002. The Summit was restarting with a new name and a new focus. During the three plus years before he became the lead pastor, the church had gone through a lot of people leaving, dissension and division. Out of the original 450 people within the church, 150 church members refused to make the shifts necessary to reach new people. In 2001, the church had just about gone bankrupt. Still, from the time J.D. became the pastor, a committed core of the people who stayed were ready to get involved. In 2012 Outreach magazine named The Summit as the fifteenth fastest growing church in America.

A Los Angeles Suburbs Church

A Church in the thriving San Fernando Valley of Los Angeles had dwindled to just a handful of members. They finally decided to die, deeding their property over to the local association and relinquishing control of the church to a steering committee, which included members of other churches, pastors, and state denomination leaders. Since the restart church planting steering committee called a planter as the restart pastor three years ago, the church has grown to 70 in attendance on Sunday mornings.

Regardless of the Terminology a Restart is a Restart!

When I began working in church revitalization there was only a single word for the single strategy of restarting a dying church. It was the term *restart*, which meant just that. Then two friends out west wanted to coin a new term for a church restart and they came up with a new term *repotting*. Repotting is a very organic term and for those who think systematically this way it works. I had one pastor tell me that he preferred the term to restarting because it was a kinder term that did not offend Church people. My response was that it was important to shock them and the last thing we ought to be is concerned if they like a term that speaks of a rapidly declining church during their watch. Another term that a few utilize when considering a restart strategy is the term *resurrection*. A resurrection strategy brings a church from death to life. A fourth term that is often used is *restore*. When a church is restored is may sometimes be through a restart but often churches facing rapid decline will try everything else before they consider a restart. Many try to restore the church by fixing processes and systems to eventually realize that is not the best way to revitalize the church. *Realignment* is the fifth term for church restarting some use. It is an effort to speak to the new structure, which will be required to see a church restarted. The term *restoration* is an effort to address the need for something old to become new. The danger is that some believe that by throwing on a new coat of paint it will revitalize a church, it will not. Nearsighted fixes in facilities never has and never will revitalize a church. A seventh term used by some is the term **rebirth**. Granted the dead church must have a new birth and the term rebirth is one that is a viable term for what a restart strategy is all about. Yet, some think of it as just rewrapping the rapidly declining church and while some degree of wrapping the restart in swaddling clothes is necessary, restarting is more than nursing an infant. It is resuscitation. A restart is a strategy that necessitates resuscitation. The paddles have been gelled and there is only one more opportunity to bring back life to the patient.

Principles for Considering a Church Revitalization Restart Strategy

If you are ready to consider the church revitalization restart strategy there are several principles that should be considered. While leading church revitalization efforts all across North America for the RENOVATE National Church Revitalization Conference, I have had the opportunity to work with many who look at the restart strategy as their last and only hope. This is a strategy that works and is effective if the present church cares deeply still about reaching the community it has been placed. Things change and communities change and hopefully the church's desire to change so it can continue to reach it ministry area for Christ Jesus. So just how do you go about restarting a dead church? In talking to restart pastors and denominational leaders across the country, these fifteen principles come up again and again:

Rejoice and Honor the Former Church's History.

Before the former church passes away, gather together to rejoice, honor and celebrate its victories and historical past. One of the best lessons any Church Revitalizer could learn is the importance of honoring the former churches past while moving the restart into the future. During one service I participated in of a church that was closing and in a few months would restart as an entirely new church, a longtime member was asked to formulate a historical timeline of the significant accomplishments of the former church for distribution at its final worship service. The closing church and the local church revitalization transition team helped them put together a service, which was a time of thanksgiving for the past and a time of anticipation for the future. Members shared about joyful memories of significant events where God had displayed His marvelous blessings. Five to seven members from various stages of life took part in this portion of the celebration service. Some had been members for a long long time; others were recent leaders who had worked diligently to try to turn around the closing church.

The Restart Strategy Works Best when a Church Revitalization Transition Committee is made Up of Those Outside the Existing Church.

Many terms work for this type of team to assist the local church in transition from closing and reopening as a restart. Where I lead church planting and church revitalization efforts, we use the term Church Revitalization Assistance Team. Others utilize the phrases that speak towards a restart transition committee. It is wise to consult your local Director of Missions for assistance in this effort. He should have the necessary experience to lead the former church through an exit strategy leading towards a closing and reopening as a new restart church. His advice, while sometimes difficult to share, will give the former church the best chance of surviving as a new work that can minister to the ever-changing community. Such a team usually is made up of more individuals from outside churches helping the weaker rapidly declining church. A sponsoring church will embrace this process and take the lead in this effort. The local association will have one or two individuals who work with the church restart pastor. One will usually be the church-planting leader and the other will be an individual who works in church revitalization within the association. As the church closes remember it is not the old church opening under a new leader but an entirely new church so there is only the need for a single leader from the former church to serve on the transition team.

Consider if there is Still Potential for Success in the Former Church's Setting!

Not every rapidly declining church is a suitable candidate for a church revitalization restart. Those which refuse to allow a strong organization in to lead them through the restart, are poor opportunities because often what they desire is for someone to merely pay the bills and get them out of danger of closure. Those which will not allow a new

Church Revitalizer to come in and lead the new restart, will be poor candidates for a restart. Churches where the lay leadership has run the former pastor's life and refused to follow the pastor shepherd will be poor candidates for a restart. When a church is guided by comfort over evangelistic fervor those churches will be poor candidates for a restart. Rural areas that are losing population base, areas of ethnic change, and deteriorating neighborhoods are very difficult to restart. The area around a church restart needs to have a definable target group of sufficient size, which may be effectively reached by the type of ministry that the local association, or state convention has to offer. It is amazing often to discover what a Church Revitalizer has done to move the church towards growth, then when he leaves, it only takes a few months to revert back to the past stagnation by changing everything it took three to five years to change. Remember church revitalization is a minimal investment of one thousand days.

To Use this Model, it is Critical that a Church Revitalization Restart Contract be Developed Between the Old Church and the New Restart.

By having a contract or covenant agreement between the former church and the new restart it will help avoid any conflicts that arise once new changes and structures begin to be put in place. Many will be all for having another church take over the responsibility for financial and day-to-day operations. But once new changes and ways of doing ministry become the norm, without a contract or covenant agreement the restart could become sidetracked and lose any chance for a successful restart. So important is this issue that if a church refuses to agree to a contract or covenant agreement the embracing church ought to walk away immediately and allow the struggling church to continue to diminish. It is not worth the risk of putting in large sums of money only to see the vocal minority sabotage the new restart and cause one disruption and disturbance after another.

Empower the Church Revitalization Transition Team to Make all Decisions from the Beginning.

When a transition team is empowered initially there is less chance of power struggles impeding the new church revitalization restart. This team can allow the best prospect for developing new systems, structures, skill sets and services for the restart. Also by moving all leadership issues away from the former rapidly declining church and placing it in the hands of the transition team it is much quicker to pass the baton on to the embracing church. Additionally, when some of the key decision makers of the former church are transferred to new Church Revitalizer leadership any fallout is focused on the transition team and not the new pastoral leadership. Remember you only get once chance to do it right so utilize a Church Revitalization Transition Team and you will benefit from that single decision many times.

Research the Declining Churches Ministry Area for what Type of New Work will have the Greatest Chance for Survival.

The reason a restart is even being considered is due to the fact that the former church has experienced plateau then decline and is now faced with the realization it does not know how to revitalize the church. Before any other church considers embracing the candidate for a restart research the ministry is to determine what type of new work will have the greatest chance for survival. Sometimes a restart will focus on a niche while other times it will emphasize a younger more relevant model more in tune with those who currently live in the community.

Close the Doors of the Church for a Time.

Many Church Revitalizers, when working on a restart strategy, often wonder if closing the doors might help the restart. Comments are usually the same and surround ideas such as:

> "We are not sure we ever expired or stopped being the old church."

> "The old rapidly declining church never closed so we grappled with change because there was no finality and closure."

> "Our services continued under interim leadership. To older members, it feels like we went through an illness and a trauma, which we have now come out. If we had closed the church for a time, renamed it, and done some renovation, the community would have realized what was happening. In the business world we would have put out a sign that said "Under New Management."

Here is the issue:

You lose every and all opportunity to say something completely new to the community.

One Church Revitalizer said it this way, "I question if we ever really disconnected, disengaged, and detached with the past? If we would have just shut down, let the building take care of itself, and kept the electric bills paid, perhaps we could have crossed these obstacles better."

A wise Church Revitalizer will see the need of a transition time to allow separation from the former and the restart of the future. Pressure will come from those wanting to hold on to the past glories hoping to see resurgence though none will come.

Begin Seeking God for a Church Revitalizer for the New Restart.

Church Revitalizers are becoming a new breed of pastoral leader that is equipped for the difficult task of revitalization and renewal. Not every pastor has the skill sets necessary for becoming a Church Revitalizer. This is partially due to the evangelical community no longer having the knowledge of what it takes to transition a church out of decline into a healthy renewing church. Most pastors in declining churches when asked if they know what will turn around their ministry are unable to provide more than a wish list. On the other hand, a Church Revitalizer while understanding that there is no single magic pill to instantly cause a church to become healthy, has been trained with various tools, which might give the declining church the best opportunity for revitalization. There is a new minister out there which desires to become part of the revolution to see the decline reversed in the American church.

Change the Church's Name and Give it a New Identity.

One church in Georgia decided to change their name as they entered the church revitalization restart process. One of the things that was most symbolic for this church in giving up their identity was to change its name. By taking this measured step the people within the community could see that it was not just the same old group wobbling along, but a new church restart. Something new can compel and draw individuals, which would never have given a thought of visiting the previous church and ministry. Wise revitalizers will say the name of the new church often as it moves towards the restart and once the initial worship service commences utilizing the new name while allowing it to ring in the ears of the congregants moves the new away from the old.

Another important symbol might be transferring ownership of the property to the local association office for a period. While this seems drastic, death is drastic. It should be done for the right reasons, though. The protection the weak and vulnerable church receives from being taken over by outside groups is secondary to its symbolic value of death and breaking of power. When a church is facing rapid decline, it is desperate and often makes poor decisions, which lead it to neither being a possible candidate for a restart, nor a church that can survive. By transferring ownership to the local association, it allows its heritage to continue by allowing the church to be utilized for a church plant. Usually some type of covenant that the church will be a church plant for at least five years is a good way to insure a mission heritage that will honor the former church.

Transfer Control from Local Church Power Brokers to a Steering Committee of Mostly Outsiders!

One of the most common barriers and roadblocks to growth in a rapidly declining congregation is leadership that is closed to faith and a vision of the future. Often these entrenched old timers have run off the very people who could have provided vital ministry. They are more interested with their personal preferences over what it will take to see renewal come back to "their" church. The need for a leadership transplant is paramount in a restart strategy. The failure to successfully change the leadership contributed to the failure of a restart of an old urban church in Kansas City. "The nucleus of old timers were still trying to call the shots and were not willing to see change," recalls a state denominational member. "When the few new people showed up, they were intimidated by the older core of people. Right from the beginning," he counsels, "make sure you have the cooperation of the church people involved. Here was an indication that the church people were only half-hearted about cooperating." So many churches will say they want to change until change begins to take place. Restarting a church takes a deep commitment of those joining the new restart. Be sure the steering committee is fully empowered.

Another church revitalization restart in south Florida did not use a steering committee. Here is what they shared during a recent conference in West Palm Beach. They said, "We did not follow the guidelines for a restart as advised, and we believe that was a catastrophic misstep. What we discovered after it was over was that we never actually closed the former church. One week we were the old church and the following week we were the old church with a new name but nothing else. The congregational leadership of both clergy and laity never changed. We were supposed to be a new restart but what we were was the old trying to put a face lift on someone unwilling to change. This has been one of the greatest obstacles to growth. I wished we had never done this because it repelled the new people who were coming hopping for something new and vibrant only to find the same old thing. They felt cheapened because they were used, and once they saw no change they left hurt and disappointed."

One pastor from Dallas says, "The people from the church revitalization restart on the steering committee are part of the old power group. There is no change only someone else to pay the bills." Another church member from North Atlanta commented, "Some of the former members of the dying church have been quite reluctant to embrace any sort of change. They were allowed to become leaders in the new restart and they are already exerting a powerful influence on those deciding if they should join or not. Their practice of negativity on everything new is hurting our opportunities for success. They are domineering and despite more people joining you keep losing momentum even though they are not in the majority they stall almost everything with pessimism.

What we have learned is that a steering committee of outsiders dilutes the stakeholders power base that has blocked growth and allows time for a new dream to grow. The restart leadership meetings should be very focused avoiding the same old tiresome rhetoric, the same old troublesome conflict, the same old dismal discussion over the same never-ending issues of pacing blame on those not happy with the tried and true. Restart leadership must be more visionary and exclude looking back without seeking some forward direction. Understand that even a steering committee may not break all the negative power struggles.

Develop a Fresh Vision for the Community

Without a mission beyond its own survival, a church revitalization restart is neither new nor viable. The word "restart" is not fully appropriate. Remember you are not going to restart the old ministry. You are there to make a new beginning. You will have a new name, a new vision, and a new purpose.

Begin Outreach Activities and New Church Core Group Development.

Developing a new thrust for evangelism in the restart is key as a fresh core group begins ministry and outreach. Those joining the church from the former church must join just like any new person coming into the congregation. Focus on what the church will look like in the future and how it will draw and reach new prospects and bring them to Christ.

Call a New Church Pastor with Energy and Faith.

Church revitalization restarting takes mountains of energy and the faith in God's power. This deep faith and abundance of energy is necessary to ward off discouragement. One of the common ailments in a restart situation is the people's tiredness. If the restart seeks to bring most of the old church with them, there becomes a sense that the new church is not energized because the former members of the rapidly declining church are worn out. Their inability to rise above the negativity and weariness will hamper the work. There is a sense where they say; "You fix it for us pastor." Trying to do it all will burn out a Church Revitalizer. The Church Revitalizer's energy must be focused on growth and advancement.

An old mainline denominational pastor living on the East coast recalls, "When I first moved here, I thought the denomination had done the right thing by not closing the church. There was a great facility and all I had to do was come in and begin to reach out into the community. I believed that I could build on the church's standing within the community. Previously I had been successful in connecting with community leaders in my former ministry assignment so I believed this would be the same thing in this ministry. It has taken me two years to see that you should not just make cosmetic changes such as a name but real changes that can give the new ministry the greatest change for success."

One Church Revitalization Restarter from New Jersey said, "If the rapidly declining church does not die, the new life brought in by a Church Revitalizer which is expected to revitalize the old rituals. It takes so much energy to make the transformation from the ceremonial there is not adequate energy left to do something new and vibrant."

The single theme which I hear again and again from Church Revitalization Restarter is be certain that the church is genuinely willing to die and help it to seal this decision with significant new symbols such as a name change, new leaders in control, property transferred over to new ministry, former leaders not able to be in leadership positions for the next three years.

Start Countdown to New Church Restart Launch and Grand Opening!

While working in the background as the rapidly declining church celebrates its past and closes its doors, the new restart begins a countdown towards launch day. Though public ministry is not yet happening, core group meetings, home groups, and preparations towards the kick off of the new church are functioning. New assimilation strategies must be developed as well as launch strategy that embraces the new needs to be established. The best scenario is to close the old church after its final farewell service for about 90 days. I have had many people argue with me about this only to acknowledge later that shutting it down for a week was too little. You only get one chance to do it right so do not hurt this important opportunity by rushing too fast.

When you Launch Reach Forward, Draw a Line in the Sand, and do not Look Back.

All looking back usually does is giving you a sore neck! There is a great deal of pastoral momentum that is gained by drawing a line in the sand proverbially and saying we are moving forward. Honoring the past is one thing but living in the past is another. Church Revitalizers need to spend all of their time moving and looking forward. Looking back will drain you do keep the throttle on and advance strategically. Too much effort is spent by inexperienced pastors looking back trying to fix old systems that cannot be fixed.

These fifteen principles will be most helpful in your church revitalization restart. Church Revitalizers have practiced these principles for years. Those who feel they are too harsh often live in regret that they had not followed these principles.

What Kind of Church is a Good Candidate for Revitalization Using the Restart Strategy?

There are some churches with a better chance of living again through a restart. Five types are most often found:

*The Church that has no debt and few bills

*The Church that still is in a strategic location for a work

*The Church who, if it is not the first two, might want to sell property and use the money through the local association to fund a new church plant.

*The Church who, if it sells the building might offer it at a reduced rate to a new church plant so both sides win and Jesus is honored.

*The Church that might be used for a new group of people previously not ministered too.

Final Church Revitalization Restart Observations

The desire to see the church grow once again is not the main reason churches seek assistance in church renewal! The main reason is that they fear the church is dying, near death, or the members have waited too long to do something about it! A reduction in the church's ability to offer ministries usually prompts its desire for a church revitalization restart. The desire to avoid the deathblow of a church compels many congregations to consider church revitalization efforts! Yet, most laity find it hard to allow someone to assist them and reveal the very things that caused their decline.

A Church Revitalization Lesson

When a local church refuses to trade its fear of closing the door for a desire to see life come back within the congregation, the church revitalization experience will end promptly as soon as the danger of death has been eliminated. What happens next may mean another recycle of decline until it is bad again. Churches only experience renewal when their people experience renewal! Unless a churches leadership wants renewal, it will not happen. There must be a commitment to lead the church towards revitalization. If not, nothing will be changed. Church renewal must shift from a few being interested to eventually a full effort of the entire congregation. Revitalization is not a secret journey but a public one.

Preachers of the Word are called by God and even with their giftedness, renewal will not happen unless the laity is willing to experience a new and better journey. If the laity refuse to change, refuse to repent of unconfessed sins which are keeping the church from experiencing God's blessings, and refuse to allow the shepherd to lead the flock, there will be no impetus for renewal.

When a church is more interested in self- conservation, it develops a barrier towards the community it is called to serve, which declares our needs are more important than your needs. Many a church is not interested in serving its community until it is in trouble and then it is done for survival reasons. People will see right through this approach and feel cheapened.

Key Paths for the Local Church

A key factor in congregational decline is the failure to introduce new members to disciple making and equip them in the disciple- making mission of the church. Observe a few key paths for the local church seeking revitalization and renewal:

Place a larger emphasis on disciple making.

Show your faith in and to your community (Acts 2:42).

Share your life within the community (2 Cor. 8:3-5).

Remember the church is people and they are the key to renewal (1 Thess. 2:8).

Equip others for the harvest field.

Develop new leaders for leadership.

Move past self-preservation to self-sacrifice for the cause of Christ.

Avoid copying others' renewal efforts and begin listening, discerning, and responding to the Lord's leading.

Develop ways for the laity to give themselves to others.

The church must face the current realities of its ministry. Truth is not an enemy of the new.

Discover what has changed around your ministry area during the last 20 years. Most churches do not know.

Help your people dream a little about what could be.

Do not wait too long to begin to revitalize your church.

Understand that there is a huge cost involved in church revitalization and it will take a combined effort of laity and ministers to see renewal come to fruition.

Items to Be Addressed in Renewal

You must have a *"begin the journey point in time"* with church revitalization. It is easier to go to meetings and talk about church revitalization than to begin working in church revitalization. If you are not careful the task force can spend more time talking about what "we are going to do" than getting to doing it. The Church must begin to address some key issues for revitalization:

The need for new initiatives (new avenues)!

The need for new entrance points into the church!

The updating of present ministries and programs!

How the church will care for its new and present participants!

The long-term development of disciples!

The present and future staff equipping!

How the laity will be matured in the faith and enlisted in the work of the ministry.

The examination of any areas of work that are becoming dead weight to renewal efforts.

How to let go of ministries that are no longer serving the church.

Remember that groups leading ministries, who are left on their own, will usually justify the plans that long-time members have invested in regardless of their outcome for growth.

Church Revitalization is a long-distance relay run by marathoners not sprinters. You must be willing to invest a minimum of 1000 days into church renewal. Anything less, do not get involved.

Ideas for the Closing Service

Use those who have been there the longest. Consider using some type of candle ceremony asking the oldest (length of membership) members to light a candle then working down to the newest. This is a very significant way to symbolize that their ministry meant something and that they were appreciated. Conclude the worship service with great hymns of faith and the Lord's Supper. Then move into a period of "Starting Something New" led by the local Association Director of Missions.

Such a service is not easy to develop and it takes much thought before that final day of worship. Even your weakest unattached church member will find that they have memories of the former church. Questions the weeks before that allow those members of the church that is closing to vocalize their feelings will be helpful. Some questions you might want to utilize might be:

What are your personal memories of the ministries from this church?

Is there something harder about letting go than you had expected?

What individual recollections would you share with fellow members during these final days?

In your view what were some of the most historical events that were part of our church's life timeline?

What were the significant events that took place in the lives of the children of the church?

How were the youth impacted within the community through this church?

During each pastor's tenure what were the significant events that took place?

What were the ministries that impacted the women of the church most?

How were the men impacted though the church?

There are probably many more questions, which you could come up with, but this serves as a means to prime the pump of your creative memory to begin thinking about your church as it moves towards closing and a restart.

Ideas for the initial restart service

When a church revitalization restart launches its first initial service, it is vital that new direction and tempo is set. If this is the former declining church with a new hip name you will be in trouble from the start. This is a time for the Church Revitalizer to share a new and compelling vision for the restart that is very different from the former rapidly declining church. During the great day of vision, it is wise for the new church to ask for members to join the church as founding members and prepare to go through a new members class as an initial step towards commitment and membership. This is a way for those, which were in the former church whom decide that this new restart is for them to join right away. For those stakeholders who are not so sure, once the first month of joining is over they would need to join the church in accordance with the policies set forth by the new church.

As the Church Revitalizer give the restart participants constant hope. Your compassion for the former church members who now join with you and your passion for the vision God has given will be reassuring during the launch season for the restart. You as the leader must be the provider of hope in a church revitalization restart.

What is HOPE?

Hope defined by *Webster's II New College Dictionary*, is "to wish for something with expectation of its fulfillment." Hope means the confidence to trust in your actions and reactions. There is a desire connected with hope to see something good come about as a result of one's efforts. One of the most powerful, energizing words in the English language is the word "hope." It's a power that energizes us with exhilaration and purpose, as we look onward to the future. Hope takes our everyday obstacles and converts them into opportunities. Hope gives us motivation to live. Hope is a muscle that keeps us moving in the hardest stages of life.

It's been said that a person can live 40 days without food, 4 days without water, 4 minutes without air, but only 4 seconds without hope. Hope truly is a power that energizes us with life.

Hope is the Ultimate Talent of a Church Revitalizer!

Hope has the power to make our renewal churches healthy in the detrimental world in which we minister. Our job as Church Revitalizers is to always be a provider of hope for those who need it the most.

Hope is the Winning Difference Between Turning a Church Around and Letting it Die!

This difference, while it appears small, is huge. A Church Revitalizer who can convey hope, has the innate ability to keep the morale up in a church that wants to function more like a previous failure than a glowing success. Hope give us a positive feeling and attitude about the future and if you lack this hope there will be and cannot be any power in the present.

The Church Revitalizer is the One Responsible for Providing Hope.

No one else is responsible for providing this hope. It is the calling and duty of the Church Revitalizer to be the one which imparts hope on a regular basis. A friend of mine Tom McEachin, many years ago talking about my nature towards providing hope, said that even my lowest days are still so full of hope who would ever know when I am down! Every Church Revitalizer must have the skill set of being an encourager and provider of hope. Churches that are being renewed must place people on staff that ooze from this skill set. You cannot have negative people serving on a church revitalization staff because it is just too hard to turn around the church anyway. These negative skunkers just cannot be part of the forward charge. *"Skunkers"* in church revitalization efforts are those people who spray negativity all around the good things that are helping turn a church around. As Church Revitalizers we are dealers in hope and you just cannot feed hope for your new congregation without you possessing hope yourself.

How Does a Church Revitalizer Offer Hope to Others?

When I was thirty-two year of age I was at a meeting in Upper Marlborough, Maryland where John Calvin Maxwell the great leadership guru was speaking. He said something way back then which has stayed with me all of these many years regarding hope. I wrote it in my Bible that day and it has been there ever since. I know John could do a better job at this but here is what has stayed with me from that significant encounter. It is a HOPE acrostic that has served me well. I have adapted it for revitalization a little:

Help Your Restart: Change Their Way of Seeing and Thinking

People of habit have a hard time seeing new things. In fact, the biggest difference between creative and reactive people is how they use the letters. A Church Revitalizer will often work among individuals who are not able to think or see right most of the time and it will be a journey to patiently help them make the journey towards hope. People who do not possess hope do not think right most of the time. Turning around a restart church is why the Church Revitalizer will deal over and over again with low self-esteem and confidence. Church people often grow hopeless because they have faced decline for so long that they are not use to looking up. Hopeless church members need a Church Revitalizer that offers hope each and every day.

Offer Safety and Reassurance During Periods of Doubt

The passage to revitalization and renewal is not a short one and there will be periods where the rank and file just need to know they are safe and that their leader is assured of victory so that they can be reassured of victory as well. A Church Revitalizer that leads visually out front of others helps the rest see that the path is just ahead. I think about the priest that bore the Ark of the Covenant as they went into the Jordan river; it was a miraculous sign to the rest that God was providing safe passage and that they could be reassured of His wonderful presence all around them. Here was the army of the pharaoh behind them and the Jordan River in front of them and they were afraid. But the Lord our God and His leader offered safety during a significant period of doubt.

Put Some Wins Under Their Belt

Nothing helps the Church Revitalizer more than success for the leader and on behalf of the restart. Even little serendipitous blessings are ways in which the members see the hand of God upon each of them. Renewal pastors need these little wins and blessings because revitalization is a long-term effort and cannot be rushed. Small wins become middle size wins and in turn become large wins. Do not keep the little wins secret; share them humbly and continually. You will help the church and its membership by doing so.

Express Openly Your Confidence in the Renewing Church

Every strong Church Revitalizer shares the ministry and the blessings given. Expressing your belief in those who make up your ministry is a blessing to your followers and an asset to the work. Ministers who do not have the gift of generosity often struggle with this issue because they believe it is more about them than it is about the collaborative group. Openly sharing your faith and trusting in your fellow laborers is a great way to offer hope. Express these feeling often and unapologetically. Church revitalization is a going together movement not a movement form the general's headquarters.

A Short Sermon on Hope for the Church Revitalizer

The first epistle of Peter gives five wonderful promises of a living hope:

> *3 Praise the God and Father of our Lord Jesus Christ. According to His great mercy, He has given us a new birth into a living hope through the resurrection of Jesus Christ from the dead 4 and into an inheritance that is imperishable, uncorrupted, and unfading, kept in heaven for you. 5 You are being protected by God's power through faith for a salvation that is ready to be revealed in the last time. 6 You rejoice in*

this, though now for a short time you have had to struggle in various trials 7 so that the genuineness of your faith —more valuable than gold, which perishes though refined by fire —may result in praise, glory, and honor at the revelation of Jesus Christ. 8 You love Him, though you have not seen Him. And though not seeing Him now, you believe in Him and rejoice with inexpressible and glorious joy, 9 because you are receiving the goal of your faith, the salvation of your souls.189

1. **There is a Hope that is Imperishable (vs. 3-4).**

2. **Our Hope is Protected by God (v.5).**

3. **This Hope Leads to Joy (v. 6).**

4. **Our Hope Will Be Tested and Proved Sound (v. 7).**

5. **This Hope Fosters Faith and Belief (v.8).**

I love going to Washington D.C. It is a place where history leaps out from its many Smithsonian Institute collections. Wrapped around the Mall it is a wonderful place for a family to go and enjoy history and beauty. I just cannot keep from mentioning that it is also free to go into these museums as well, which always made it a great destination for our family vacations. Our family often enjoyed this vacation. I still enjoy walking the Mall and taking in all of its history.

When our nation was faced with a recent financial challenge they closed all of these family-friendly areas as the Park and Recreation was closed for a lengthy time. We were dismayed because we had counted on the museums being

---

189 The Holy Bible: Holman Christian Standard Version. (Nashville: Holman Bible Publishers, 2009), 1 Peter 1:3–9.

open so we could have a vacation that was affordable. Instead we walked all around Washington D.C. and explored things we would never have done if the nation had not been shut down. As we walked under one of the overpasses that had cars racing to and fro over our head, there was a sign which posted this little phrase:

> "Due to the present economic conditions of our nation, the light at the end of the tunnel will be turned off until further notice."

I remembered what I had been taught by John Maxwell some thirty plus years before:

> It is the Leader's Job to Turn the Light Back On!

As a Church Revitalizer that is your calling and your charge! Turn the lights back on in this dear church for which Jesus died. Keep the lights on and watch as many come to Christ through an individual salvation experience. Keep the lights on for Jesus' sake.

Chapter 12
A Proper Burial - The Trauma of Closing the Doors

That day about three thousand took him at his word, were baptized and were signed up. They committed themselves to the teaching of the apostles, the life together, the common meal, and the prayers.[190]

As the Doctor was relating the condition of her husband after a very difficult cancer surgery, he said "I'm sorry to have to tell you this but your husband probably has less than six months to live. His cancer is terminal. We did all we could, but the cancer is far advanced and there is nothing further that we can do!" A shock wave went thru Jenny's body. Her natural reaction was, "No, No, Doctor you have to be wrong. Jimmy can't die. He is my life. He is everything to me. He just can't die." This is typical of how often we humans respond to the news of impending death.

The fact is that this is also the way church members often respond when it comes to facing the reality that their church is terminal. Most churches fail to accept "present reality" about their future and try to go on with business as usual but then find the church in a death spiral it cannot get out of. In the book, titled *Finishing With Grace,* it says, "Declining congregations may not let go until the last member dies of old age, a long-term pastor retires or dies, the money runs out, or a serious conflict puts them 'over the edge,' disabling them permanently."191 This is a tragedy because some churches could be spared if they would face facts. However, those that will die should die with dignity. Involved in that is charting a course for the death and hopefully the restart of a new congregation.

---

[190] Eugene H. Peterson, *The Message: The Bible in Contemporary Language* (Colorado Springs, CO: NavPress, 2005), Ac 2:41–42.

191 Linda M. Hilliard & Reverend Gretchen J. Switzer, *Finishing with Grace* (Booklocker.com, Inc., 2010) 5.

Death is traumatic under any circumstances. Whether it is the death of a loved one, a friend and yes…even a church. Often the trauma of death will leave long lasting effects and sometimes it takes a long time to go thru the grief process.

When a church dies, it is not nearly as traumatic to the newer church member as it is to the member who has grown up in the church. To those who grew up in a church it is the place where they planted their life. They raised their children there. They saw grandchildren baptized there. They have the bulk of their fellowship there. When a church closes its doors, it leaves a void that nothing else, humanly speaking, can fill. It is much like losing a close friend or a loved one. In fact, it can be so overwhelming that those who were left without a church never attend anywhere else. Feelings of sadness and even depression can be a part of grieving over the closing of a church. They may even find it difficult to function in other church settings.

The question arises, then, how can the closing of a church be made more palatable and acceptable? How can it be accomplished with as little trauma as possible? A close examination of closing the doors of a church is important.

The Case for Closure!

Late in the winter of 2017 I received a call from a church in a small town near me stating that the church was on the verge of closing its doors. I was asked if our ministry, Operation Transformation, could step in and help them through the rough times. My initial meeting with them was discouraging and difficult. This church had at one time been a beacon for the Gospel in the small town but now it was struggling with finances, attendance and leadership. At one time the church had averaged 400 in worship but the day I met with them they were down to 17 on a good Sunday. The church was barely getting enough money through tithes to pay the pastor a part time salary and even at times had to take money from their savings. The savings account was dwindling each month and in my estimation they had only 6 months to survive. I helped the church with an honest assessment of their situation and suggested a restart, but the congregation would not accept that direction. I made it clear that they were in the throes of death and they must act soon. Nevertheless, I worked with them for several months endeavoring to help them face reality about their future. It was not until they had a savings account with only $1700 left that they decided to consider the restart. This church is so typical of many churches that refuse to face reality until it is too late. We finally talked them into doing the restart and the new church is up and active and reaching the small town with the Gospel. This church had all the typical elements of a dying church and it died.

Jack Wellman asked two important questions in the article titled' *What Causes Churches to Die and Close?* "Why do some churches close while others flourish? Why do churches die or close their doors?" Then he goes on to write, "Churches close every single day in this country, and even though some have been around for over a century some end up closing their doors, or they simply fade out of existence due to irrelevance, population shifts, societal changes, corrupt church leadership, and sometimes it's no one's fault at all. Some churches are like human beings. They are born, they live, they thrive, and then they die, but it's not the end of the world."[192]

---

192 Jack Wellman, *What Causes Churches to Die or Close?,* Patheos, July 3, 2017 accessed November 11, 2018, https://www.patheos.com/blogs/christiancrier/2017/07/03/what-causes-churches-to-die-or-close/.

What are the conditions present that would cause a church to close its doors? What has caused the church to reach this juncture? There are many reasons that churches reach this point in its existence. Some of the reasons are from external sources such as mass migration away from the church because the community has become an industrial community. There are other internal reasons for a church having to close its doors. Most church closings are because of internal reasons or problems. Here are just a few:

Probably the number one reason a church closes its doors is because of *a dwindling attendance and membership.* In today's culture people need to be and want to be a part of something that is healthy and stable and somewhat growing. When the attendance begins to dwindle it has a twofold effect on the church. First, it fosters discouragement on the part of the pastor and leaders which results in more people leaving. Strong leaders sometimes pull out because they have had enough of failure and hopelessness. Second, it always results in visitors never returning for a second visit and when the word gets around about the condition of the church, people simply chose to go elsewhere. Those who are looking for a church home will not settle for the deadness that is in many churches. In the book titled, *Legacy Churches,* the writers make this very valid point, "Weekly worship services provide the most visible public ministry of the church. Every church needs enough critical mass (that is, adequate attendance) to make it look, feel, and sound alive. When worship attendance drops consistently below those levels it is difficult for a church to continue."[193]

The loss of attendance is especially traumatic to the church that has for the most part been healthy. It seems to take a toll on those who remain faithful in the church after

---

193 Stephen Gray and Franklin Drumond, *Legacy Churches,* 70.

others begin to leave. L. Gail Irwin says in the book, *Toward the Better Country,* "When a congregation with a history of fruitful ministry experiences a downward spiral, the result is a profound disconnection and sense of failure."[194] The big question is why? Why are churches across North America experiencing such a decline in attendance?

Statistics vary when speaking of church attendance. Pollsters like Gallup report that about 40% of the population attends regular church services. These stats, however, do not add up to what David Olsen has discovered. His research shows that the rate of attendance is less than half of what the others report. He took his figures from surveys done with mainline denominations and the actual figure is that 17.7% of the population attend church on any given Sunday. These figures paint a much bleaker picture than the other pollsters give. Again…why?

The causes for the need to close a church are numerous and often complicated. There are however some common causes that every Church Revitalizer agrees on. Some churches have numerous causes and others only a few but usually the cause is fatal. These are listed below with a short discussion of each.

One of the most obvious reasons for church attendance decline is the aging out of the builder generation. These are the people that grew up in an era when the church was the center of a community's activity. Nothing was ever scheduled that would conflict with the work of the church. Lives were built around the local church and loyalty to the local church was high. Today's generation sees no need in that kind of loyalty so outside forces have entered the equation. Activities like "travel sports" have taken its toll on attendance. Family

---

194 L. Gail Irwin, *Toward a Better Country: Church Closure and Resurrection* (Eugene, Oregon: Resource Publications, 2014) 24.

outings and trips on the weekend takes people away from the church as well.

Because of the death of the builder generation, the younger generation, if they attend at all, seeks immediate change. This becomes a difficult task to a church that has been used to a certain type of worship style, etc... Barna says that most churches are 20 -30 years behind the modern culture they reside in. This may be true, but there seems to me to be a larger more ingrained reason for the decline. That is, simply put, a real lack of spiritual desire and commitment on the part of the present generation. This has developed over the years because there has been a shift away from the church as the center of community and activity. The world is full of entertainment that this culture seeks. This is seen clearly in the few churches that are growing because of their stage performances of music and theatrics. It is simply not the "happening place" in the community any longer.

The rise and availability of the internet has been credited as another valid reason for the decline in church attendance. People turn to the convenience of the internet even when it comes to worship, preaching and teaching. This is a tragedy because it lessens any contact and cooperation with other Christians as a community. There is no fellowship in worship through "social" media.

Rick L. Stonestreet sums it up well, "The church experience at some churches has caused people to lose interest in attending church. There is the unfortunate disorganization, irrelevant messages and lack of connection with people, which has had a dramatic impact on guests." He continues, "People today are influenced by the professionalism of television, Internet and high-quality video, causing people to view their world through a different set of eyes. Certainly, churches cannot, nor should not, seek to compete with these things, but we are competing for man's attention to spiritual truths."[195]

As a result of the dwindling attendance another sign almost always follows. Simply said, the *money gets scarce!* When finances are in jeopardy church finance committees usually make the decisions that will affect the entire congregation and often those decisions have fatal results. Those decisions usually end in deep cuts in the budget that usually begin with the church staff salaries, ministries and benefits being axed in such a way the church staff becomes ineffective. The next cut to follow is the missions and evangelism budget. This, for a lack of a better term, guts the entire ministry of the church rendering it completely useless to the Kingdom. Granted, often cuts are needed but how much and where the cuts are made will determine the effectiveness of the ministry in the future. Sad to say that often the actions of these finance committees lead the church further into a death spiral and the demise of the church is on its way.

Another very valid reason a church should close its door is when it *loses its sense of what its real mission is.* This includes its missionary and evangelistic zeal. If the church does not have a need to cut the budget in the areas of missions and evangelism there is still the present danger of the local church losing its vision for evangelism and missions. As has been stated in numerous places in this book thus far, when a church loses this vision it loses its bearing as a New Testament church and will surely meet and untimely death. Carey Neuhoff writes about the time when a church loses its sense of mission, "And when you do, it gets bad quickly. You start to see every new person as someone who can give and serve, rather than as someone to serve and introduce others

---

195 Rick L. Stonestreet, *Church Attendance is on the Decline.* Daily Republic, accessed Nove28, 2018, https://www.dailyrepublic.com/all-dr-news/solano-news/local-features/local-lifestyle-columns/church-attendance-is-on-the-decline/.

to Christ. You start to view every decision through a cost filter. You care far more about efficiency than effectiveness."[196] However, many times the local church ignores all warnings about this and ends in utter defeat and hopelessness. Then finally death comes.

A final reason for closing the church is when the church has grown to *tolerate sin in the congregation.* This subject has also been discussed in a previous chapter but it merits repeating. If a church allows known sin to persist in the congregation, the church will lose its effectiveness and reputation and it will surely die. It is important to remember that this postmodern culture and its insistence concerning tolerance seems to be influencing the local church. We live in a society that throws irrational judgements around like they mean nothing. Our culture is so judgmental that even pastors and churches are kowtowing to the threats and innuendos of those who would neuter the local church and take away its effectiveness. The result is compromise and steering clear of any ridicule or criticism. When the church refuses, for whatever reason, to deal with "sin in the camp", the end is certain death.

Benefits of Closure!

First, it is important to examine the benefits from closing a dying church. Why close? What's the point? The death of an unhealthy church can result in the launching of a new and exciting church that has a fresh vision and mission. There are several good benefits but none of them make it any easier to accept the closure by a congregation. However, the dying church should view it as a success as much as a failure because it has allowed a fresh new approach in the ministry activities of the church to blossom and grow.

---

196 Carey Nieuwhof, *5 Good Reasons A Church Should Close,* accessed December 12, 2018, https://careynieuwhof.com/5-good-reasons-a-church-should-close/.

The main benefit after closing the doors of a dying church is rooted in the purpose of the church itself. The New Testament church was designed by the hand of God to be salt and light to a lost world; to proclaim the Gospel to the nations and to disciple those who believe. When a church becomes derelict in that purpose it is time to close before more damage is done to the Kingdom of God. When a church ceases to be a New Testament church it is time to close its doors in order for a new church to restart with a new purpose and a new vision for the community and insure that souls will be saved and discipled in the Word of God. It truly is a matter of "life and death" not just for the church itself but for the community that, in the past, has depended on the church for spiritual guidance.

We find somewhat of a purpose statement for the church in Acts 2:42, "And they continued steadfastly in the apostles' doctrine and fellowship, and in breaking of bread, and in prayers."197 This verse clearly teaches that the purpose of the church is to instruct in Biblical doctrine in order to ground believers in the faith, give opportunity for fellowship and prayer. Ephesians 4:14 makes it clear that the church is to grow and help to mature new believers into servants of God. It says, "That we henceforth be no more children, tossed to and fro, and carried about with every wind of doctrine, by the sleight of men, and cunning craftiness, whereby they lie in wait to deceive."198

So, it is evident from the scripture that the main purpose of the church is the proclamation of the Gospel and involvement in missions to the world with that Gospel. Matthew 28:19-20 says "Go ye therefore, and teach all

197 Acts 2:42 KJV.

198 Ephesians 4:14 KJV.

nations, baptizing them in the name of the Father, and of the Son, and of the Holy Ghost: Teaching them to observe all things whatsoever I have commanded you: and, lo, I am with you always, even unto the end of the world. Amen."199 Then Acts 1:8 says, "But ye shall receive power, after that the Holy Ghost is come upon you: and ye shall be witnesses unto me both in Jerusalem, and in all Judaea, and in Samaria, and unto the uttermost part of the earth."200

One final thought about the purpose of the church is found in 1 Corinthians 12:12-14 when Paul talked about the purpose of the church. Paul said "For as the body is one, and hath many members, and all the members of that one body, being many, are one body: so also, is Christ. For by one Spirit are we all baptized into one body, whether we be Jews or Gentiles, whether we be bond or free; and have been all made to drink into one Spirit. For the body is not one member, but many."201

Simply put, the church should be doing the things that Jesus would be doing if He were walking among us today. The church is to be "Christ-Like" and seeking to be more like Him day by day. When the church ceases to be that kind of church it is time to close the doors and make way for a new exciting, enthusiastic move of God as a new congregation is established to become a true New Testament church.

The death of a church that has lost its vision and purpose can be the opportunity to launch a new move of God in the community. So, the death of an ineffective church can become the launching point of a viable church. In this

---

199 Matthew 28:19-20 KJV.

200 Acts 1:8 KJV.

201 1 Corinthians 12:12-14 KJV.

kind of situation, the death of a church can become a successful thing rather than just the routine failure of a church. It can pave the way for a church that hopefully will reach the community with the Gospel of the Lord Jesus Christ. That would certainly be a great success story. The dying church should aim for maximum Kingdom impact as it allows a new work to take its place.

One final benefit of closing a church is that it is an expression of faithful stewardship. Lee Ann M. Pomrenke says, "When the number of people dwindles, and resources start to run out, the tendency is to try to stretch them, even to the breaking point. But redirecting passions and resources into a ministry that can use them well is an expression of faithful stewardship." She further states, "We are resurrection people, but resurrection comes only after death. So, the death of a ministry requires a lot of faith in the promise of resurrection."202

Every dying church needs a playbook. When a football player is brought on to a football team, the first thing they are given is the play book. That play book maps out every play that the team will run during a game. Without that book every game would be chaotic, and the team would surely lose every game. So it is as well for the church that understands that it is dying and needs to close. A plan to implement the closure as effectively and efficiently as possible is needed. Most dying churches refuse to make that plan and chaos usually ensues. As a result, people are hurt and disenfranchised from church life in general. There must be a team established that will put the playbook into action and carry out the process. That play book will cover many aspects of the dreaded closure, but it will serve the remaining congregation well and make the

---

202 Lee Ann M. Pomrenke, *Closing a Congregation as an Act of Faithfulness.* Lewis Center for Church Leadership, February 7, 2018 accessed November 10, 2018, https://www.churchleadership.com/leading-ideas/closing-a-congregation-as-an-act-of-faithfulness/.

process much easier. Here are a few points that should be considered when formulating this play book.

A Blueprint for the Closure

Let me begin by saying that once the church has worked thru the emotional roller coaster of deciding to close, certain actions must be taken to create an atmosphere of peace, and even, at some point, celebration. It is important at this point to create a *"timeline"* with which the church will function until the church completes the process of closure.

The first thing that must be decided is the *effective date of closure.* This is important because there must be a sense of finality to the process. This decision should be made by the congregation, pastor and consultant (if involved in the process).

One of the most important steps on the time line is the *clearing of any outstanding debt* the church may have. This is vitality important because in its final days the church does not need to have a tainted financial standing in the community. It is a matter of integrity and honesty.

After the debts are settled the church should *begin the process of dissolving the corporation* if it is incorporated and *file all necessary documents with federal and state governments.* This also involves giving up the tax-exempt status and any federal application that applies to the church.

The next thing on the timeline should be the *transfer of the deed to the property and other assets* to the restart entity (whether it be another church, association, group of churches or revitalization group). At this point all bank accounts should be closed and the funds should be transferred to the restart. If the church has some seed money for the restart it will insure a good start and it will help with initial expenses as the new church begins to function.

Next, the church should deal with the *historical data* of the church. What is the church to do with its many years of documents and records? If the church is a part of a hierarchical church system in which there is an organization that oversees the church and its functions, then the church should contact that entity and provide those documents to be archived as required. Many churches, however, are not a part of that kind of hierarchical system. So, what are they to do with the vast collection of documents and records? These records will include minutes of the churches business meetings, giving or tithing records of the individual church members, bank records, cancelled checks and check stubs, church membership rolls, organizational rolls and a vast array of other documents, some of which should never get into any outsiders' hands. It is very important that any records remaining after the process of archiving should be disposed of properly.

The church must also decide how the *disposable property* such as equipment, furniture, vehicles and other furnishings will be handled. Many of these items can be donated to other existing churches, especially the restart that is taking the dying church's place. Any articles that are broken or damaged should be disposed of in the trash. If there are memorabilia to be disposed of, let the congregation know of a time for them to come and get any item they may have given to the church in the past. This is a good method that will help in the healing process of the congregation. Office equipment should be donated to the restart to help them in the startup.

If the church has a *cemetery,* a matter of integrity and respect is involved. There must be a plan put into place to handle this delicate situation. What is a church to do with the cemetery? How do you dispose of it? There are issues involved in the disposal of a cemetery that does not affect the disposal of other property. Because of the nature of the cemetery and families' expectations; plans must be made for upkeep and maintenance.

A major part of this blueprint for closure involves *any staff the church may have remaining*. How does the church minister to those remaining on the staff? When a church that has staff members closes, consideration must be given to some type of severance. Of course, this will be in accordance with the financial capabilities of the church. Staff should know of the closure well in advance in order to begin the process of seeking other ministry positions. This is a matter of integrity. The congregation will experience grief over the closure, but the staff will experience not only grief but the loss of a job and steady income. They must be considered in the early stages of the closure and the pastor and staff should be given a good recommendation for future ministry positions if desired.

At this point *a closure agreement* and *transferal of property agreement* should be prepared and signed by the leaders of both the former church and those who will be taking possession and restarting the new church. If possible, there should be a legal document prepared by a lawyer and registered with the proper entities to ensure no misunderstanding in the future. This will solidify the separation of the old congregation from the facility and open the door for the new church to take possession of the building.

Have a *celebration* of the past. Dr. Tom Cheyney writes, "Before the former church passes away, gather together to rejoice, honor and celebrate its victories and historical past."[203] This should be a time to begin the healing process.

---

203 Tom Cheyney, *When a Church Restart Strategy is Your Only Hope, Part VI.*

As stated previously, when the church closes, it is like a death in the family. The church goes through a grief process. There has been much written about the process of grief when a person experiences the loss of a loved one. Most psychologists agree that there are at least five stages a grieving person goes through. One writer says it best, "The five stages, denial, anger, bargaining, depression and acceptance are a part of the framework that makes up our learning to live with the one we lost. They are tools to help us frame and identify what we may be feeling. But they are not stops on some linear timeline in grief. Not everyone goes through all of them or in a prescribed order."204 It has been discovered that the grief process does not just apply to the physical loss of a loved one but can also occur when someone loses some significant aspect or influence in their life such as a church or the fellowship they experience in the church. This is the reason the congregation of the church that closes must be given time to grieve over their loss.

This celebration or service (will be discussed at the end of this chapter) should be a time of remembering. It should have some elements that will bring some finality and closure to the remaining congregants. It should be a time when the church worships and fellowships together for one last time. It should be a time of honest reflection. Remembering the successes and even the failures. The service should focus on what God is going to do soon with a new DNA being established with a new congregation. It is a time to remind everyone that this is truly a new beginning for the proclamation of the Gospel in the community. This is a time or a process of conclusion. It is a time of thanking God for the past and rejoicing in the future. It should never "sugar

---

coat" the churches past failures but should focus on the bright future.

This final service of celebration signifies the *disbanding of the existing membership and the closure of the church*. It brings some finality to the whole process. The previous church will exist no longer in the community. Staff has gone to other places of service. Membership has disbanded and gone elsewhere to worship. The building is empty. No services are taking place and the church facilities are getting prepared for a new beginning. All signs of the past church should be removed. Hymnals with the church name on them should be removed. Anything that has the name of the previous church on it should be removed and archived in a historical room. The past is the past. The old church is buried and gone, and it must remain such.

Process for the Restart

Any Church Revitalizer that has ever been involved in a restart process utilized, whether they knew it or not, Dr. Tom Cheyney's model or at least portions of it. As far as I am concerned as a Church Revitalizer, there is no better model. I have used it and it works. So, much of what you will read in the remaining part of this chapter is a repeat of his concepts and process with little variation.

After the closure of the existing church a plan or a process for the restart of a new church must take place. The biggest advantage of a church restart is that it has the opportunity for a fresh encounter with the community as it applies a new approach and vision. The past is eliminated, and the old failures of the past church have been put to rest. The creation of new DNA in the church becomes a reality and the old DNA is gone. It is like a resurrection of a sort. It "can only happen if something is allowed to die. An attempt at a new ministry that is really just designed to support the old one will not lead to rebirth."205 There must be a death for the new church to be birthed.

The new church has a glorious opportunity to make its mark with the Gospel to a community that probably had been neglected for some time. It is a fresh start for maximum Kingdom impact. It is an opportunity for the legacy of the previous church to live on. So, how do you proceed through a restart? What is involved in the process? Here is one suggestion for the process even though there are variations of it.

The first step in any restart project should be formulating *a restart transition team* that will work under the leadership, guidance and counsel of the revitalizer. This team will be the main leadership team to get the process complete. It should be made up of outsiders. They should be individuals with financial abilities (accounting, banking, etc.), retired senior pastors, retired church educators, Sunday school leaders and good solid thinkers. This team is vital to the future of the restart. Because there will be no one to do any of the work in the beginning, this team will help in leading out in teaching and training in the early stages of the restart. This team will make all the decisions from the beginning to ensure that no power struggles arise. The team must remember that they are not restarting the old ministry.

This team will be charged with doing the *proper studies of the ministry area* using demographics, past records, community logistics and population inventories. This study should include any changes that may have taken place over the past ten years in the community such as cultural, ethnic and geographic changes should all be addressed. This helps the team understand the kind of ministry that should replace the

---

205 L. Gail Irwin, *Toward the Better Country: Church Closure and Resurrection* (Eugene, Oregon, Resource Publications, 2014), 131.

old failed church. When evaluating the viability of a church restart in a community, the revitalizer must pay close attention to whether the community has grown or deteriorated in the past several years. Are people migrating out of the area? Is the community being over taken by industry and commercial entities? Is there a clear, definable target audience present in the community any longer? These are all valid questions the revitalizer must seek answers to before the consideration of a restart.

Another important task the team must consider before entering into the restart process is a *study of the condition of the building* (if one is present) and facilities of the former church. Many congregations that end in death have arrived at death's door because of years of decline. This decline reveals itself in buildings that have not been kept up and maintained. Many churches that die leave behind facilities that need much repair. This can be devastating to a restart process. The fact that the restart will have minimal funds makes it clear that not much money will be available for building repairs. So, any building that will be taken over by a restart should be in considerably fair condition when the restart commences.

The second and most important step is the *transferal of the property to an outside entity*. In some religious circles that could mean that the property be transferred to a local association or group of churches that would hold the property until such time the restart church becomes a viable congregation and then the property would be transferred back to the new congregation. Sometimes this becomes a complicated process especially if there are major repairs to be done on the property or if the former church has an outstanding building or mortgage debt. All of this must be determined before the possession of the property is considered.

The third step in a restart is *closing the church for a period*. After the transition team has been put into place the church must close to prepare for the future. Every situation is different, but the standard is 90-120 days. During this time repairs and cleanup of the church property should be done. Usually a church that dies leaves behind many needs undone because of the lack of funds and/or man power to get any work done on the building or property. Often repairs to the building need to be done. Painting, carpet cleaning and other face lifting projects will be completed during this period of shut down. Closing the doors for a season gives the church a time of separation from the past to prepare it for the future.

The fourth step is to *change the name of the church*. This is a very important step in the restart process. It shows the community that something new is coming to the area. Because of possible past failures, church fights and staff problems, the community needs to see something fresh. It helps to change the past perception of the church by the community. It wipes the slate clean and the community sees a new thing on the horizon. If the former church had a sign, the face of the sign needs to be changed. Most sign companies can customize a sign to fit almost any sign board. Until that can be done a vinyl sign should be draped over the existing sign if possible that contains the name of the new church.

The revitalizer and the restart transition team should *re-tool the church for ministry*. At this point a new ministry structure will be formed. The team will develop a new program and process for the ministry of the restart church. It will set the budget and plan the teaching and discipleship program for the new church. It will set policy and procedures for the new congregation and future staff. In the restart process there is only one opportunity for success. The restart transition team is the group that will give it that opportunity.

Decisions about the educational system the church will utilize (small home groups, small on sight groups, Sunday school, worship times and services, leadership qualifications and general structure of the new church) and how the church will function as a body with new DNA. If the church is going to apply for non-profit status this team will fill out all the applications necessary. This team will also put together a workable budget based on potential income and gifts. It should also write a pastor and staff job description to be used when calling a restart pastor and or staff. Basically, this team will do everything needed to start a new church. The old ministry failed. It is to work hard at developing a new ministry with a new name, a new vision and a new purposeful mission. If a new vision and mission is not formulated, the new church will not be a viable or different church. This team will develop a new commitment to evangelism and missions.

After the previous has been accomplished, they will turn their attention to **the fifth step** in the process. The restart church must begin to *seek and call a pastor.* This is the most strategic part of the process. The team cannot make a mistake at this juncture, for if it does, the restart will have no chance of success. As has been stated in previous chapters, it takes a certain kind of God called individual to be a restart pastor. I have learned that not everyone who comes forward to be considered will really meet the criteria for this kind of ministry. At this point there will be pastors who have grown weary where they are that will seek the opportunity to pastor a new fresh situation, but they are usually not the ones who have the qualifications and personality needed to pastor a restart church.

The process for the interview of a prospective restart pastor should be developed. That process must take into consideration every aspect of the church community research that has been completed previously by the team. This is not a time for considering pastor friends that may need to move or any that have itchy feet. The man who is called to this task must be clearly called and qualified by spirit and training.

After the restart pastor has been interviewed and has accepted the ministry assignment, the team must stick with him for at least a year by giving guidance, helping in ministry areas and in leadership roles in the new church. Some revitalizers make the mistake of stepping away from the process after the restart pastor is on the job. This is a grave mistake because the process of restart is so difficult that the new pastor needs and deserves all the help and assistance that can be given.

The final step in the process is *setting an opening date.* At this point the team should begin with *advertising the new work.* Yard signs, newspaper, radio and local TV stations will usually run these types of news as public service ads or a community information piece. The advertising should reflect the new vision and mission of the church as well as the restart pastor's name. The team should do as much of this as possible in the early stages of the church in order to free the pastor to get acclimated to the community and begin to build relationships with those in the area. This is an area where leaders should allot as much money as possible to do a good job of blitzing the area with the information about the new work. This will begin to entice new people to the work and you begin to build a core group that will, someday, possibly be the leadership for the church after its launch.

After everything has been put into place for the restart and the date for the grand opening or launch of the new church has been set, prepare a program for the opening service that is dynamic, enthusiastic and appealing to the community.

The Program at the Restart

This should be a celebration of new life. This opening service will be a picture of how the church will worship. It should answer the questions that may be in the seeker's mind as to how this church will worship and fellowship. Every different church denomination and style of church polity will have a different slant on the worship service but there must always be certain elements present in the service.

Rick Warren gives a wonderful definition of true worship when he said, "Worship is expressing our love to God for who he is, what he's said, and what he's doing. We believe there are many appropriate ways to express our love to God: by praying, singing, obeying, trusting, giving, testifying, listening and responding to his Word, thanking, and many other expressions. God—not man—is the focus and center of our worship."[206] When a church truly worships, it will be attractive to those who visit and attend. Every service must have a built-in evangelistic message and mechanism. If not, the church is defeating its own purpose.

The first service that the restart church has should be the one that sets the pace for the future services of the church. It should be well planned with the best singing and music that is possible should be utilized. The **sermon must be spot on** and there must be an element of excitement.

Who should be invited to this launch Service? Of course, the entire community that has been blitzed is invited. Denominational leaders, local and statewide, should be invited, especially if they have committed money for the new work. Those who initiated the restart and the restart team will

---

[206] Rick Warren, *The Evangelistic Power of Worship* (Christianity Today), July 11, 2007, accessed December 14, 2018, https://www.christianitytoday.com/pastors/2007/july-online-only/030527.html.

be there because they have helped plan the program. Local dignitaries such as the mayor, town council, police chief, fire chief and county leaders as well should be invited. This should reflect a celebration of "new ministry" to those dignitaries that attend and reveal to them the validity of the new work and its desired influence in the community.

How do you structure such a service? What are the elements of the worship time? **First,** the service must have a solid theological basis. The motive for an evangelistic worship service is seen in Isaiah 2:2-3 where it says "And it shall come to pass in the last days, that the mountain of the Lord's house shall be established in the top of the mountains and shall be exalted above the hills; and all nations shall flow unto it. And many people shall go and say, Come ye, and let us go up to the mountain of the Lord, to the house of the God of Jacob; and he will teach us of his ways, and we will walk in his paths: for out of Zion shall go forth the law, and the word of the Lord from Jerusalem."[207] Then in Psalms 12:18 says "This shall be written for the generation to come: and the people which shall be created shall praise the Lord."[208] Philippians 3:3 says "For we are the circumcision, which worship God in the spirit, and rejoice in Christ Jesus, and have no confidence in the flesh."[209]

Most churches struggle with structuring a worship service that is geared toward evangelizing unchurched guests and faithfully leading Christians in worship. Much has been written about the impossibility of a true worship service being evangelistic simply because of the two different approaches. However, all through the New Testament worship is depicted as being relevant to those who are seeking as well as those

---

207 Isaiah 2:2-3 KJV.

208 Psalms 12:18 KJV.

209 Philippians 3:3 KJV.

who are believers. My point of view is that you should not and even could not separate the two and be a New Testament church. So, the continuing services of the restart church should be based on evangelistic worship.

But now let's turn our attention to the elements that should be present in the launch service of the restart church. What element should be present?

First, there should be an element *of praise and worship*. This should be special music as well as congregational participation. One mistake that is currently being made in many churches in their regular worship time is the exclusion of the congregation from the worship experience. Those present should be invited to participate in a time when God is praised for His faithfulness in bringing about the restart of the new church. There could also be a small portion of this time given to testimonies that reflect how God brought the restart to fruition and even a thanksgiving element that the former church had the desire for the church to be continually used to proclaim the Gospel even after its death. This is a time when members of the team can share how God brought the restart together.

Secondly, there should be a time of *greeting* when the recognition of the new restart pastor and those who participated in the team's efforts to bring about the restart is given. Then attention should be turned to those dignitaries that may be present. Give denominational leaders and civic leaders an opportunity to give a short greeting. Whether they have a short spot on the program or not they should be recognized in the service.

In this greeting time a short presentation of how the restart came into existence should be shared. A brief history of the former church could be shared at this point as well. Those attendees that are looking for a church will be encouraged to see the newness of the work and may seek an opportunity to become a part of the future work of the restart. This should be a time when everyone present is made to feel welcome and appreciated.

Third, the *new DNA of the restart should be shared*. The new vision and mission of the restart are shared with those present. This is a time to present clearly the approach to restarting the church and a description of what the church will look like. Goals should be presented, and a short version of the budget should be shared. Basically, a roadmap for the future of the restart is presented with the hope that those attending will understand and buy into the process in the future. Core values of the restart church should be shared and highlighted during this launch service. The new philosophy of ministry should be clearly presented.

Fourth, a *time of worship* should be the highlight of the service. The restart pastor should be given the opportunity to bring this important message that should highlight the Gospel and the work of the local church. This should be concluded with an invitation to Christ and to service. The Church Revitalizer will then close the celebration with prayer and comments.

One Final Thought…

Again, I want to emphasize that when a church closes there is a multitude of feelings and emotions. It is not something to be taken lightly and the feelings of those who lost their church do matter. It is easy to become disconnected from the feelings of others, so any restart process should be carried out with kindness, love and compassion. It is important that the dead church close with dignity and with as little hurt as possible. It is a tall order for a Church Revitalizer to manage and merge the two congregations with grace. It's a tall order to resurrect a dead church. God, however, takes joy in this new life. The restart of a dead church brings new meaning to the scripture where Jesus said, "And I say also unto thee, that thou art Peter, and upon this rock I will build my church; and the gates of hell shall not prevail against it."210 When Jesus made that statement in Matthew, he was promising that Satan and his demons would not defeat the church. What a glorious thought...the Church Revitalizer standing strong against the forces of darkness and evil to resurrect a dead lifeless church. It is equally as important that the restart be born out of enthusiasm and excitement. It is a church of new life, new vision and new hope.

---

210 Matthew 16:18 KJV.

Chapter Thirteen
The Perils of Steeple Jacking in Revitalization and Renewal

"Wake up! Strengthen what remains and is about to die…"
Rev. 3:2

"Yet you have a few people…who have not soiled their clothing."
Rev. 3:4

Having pastored a church in New England I was familiar with the term steeple jacking. This old term refers literally to individuals who climb tall church towers and steeples to repair and maintain these visual reminders of a church's presence. A steeplejack is one who does the work on these structures. They are all over the north east. There's a new meaning to the word "steeplejack" creeping into the American lexicon, and it has nothing to do with muscular craftsmen who repair aging church spires. About seven years ago, Thom Schultz redefined the phrase to mean something entirely different.[211] On October 29, 2012, Schultz[212] coined the phrase to refer to declining churches which were being stolen away by unscrupulous church planters through either a hostile takeover or a quiet joining of the declining church by the members of the plant which will eventually vote to move

---

211 https://churchleaders.com/pastors/pastor-articles/163374-thom-schultz-steeplejacking-churches-is-foreclosure-a-legitimate-mission-strategy.html/2.

212 Thom Schultz is an eclectic author and the founder of *Group Publishing* and *Lifetree Café*. Holy Soup offers innovative approaches to ministry, and challenges the status quo of today's church. *http://holysoup.com/*. He first coined this phrase in his periodic blog when on August 29, 2012 he posted his views about why such practices were being considered by leaders of large churches and denominations.

the church into the plant and take over the property by vote at a church business meeting. Thus, steeple jacking became a less than dear term for church planting movements which steal churches from declining congregations. We see the truth every Sunday that there are many churches are dying. Many of these will be unable to support their facilities. While considering a restart for the existing church there are times when either merging or giving the facilities away to a mission's organization for the purpose of developing church planting centers is advised. That way they could utilize the Lord's facilities to help many potential new churches and not just one new church. Church planting centers allow for the facility to be a launch venue for multiple church plants over and over.

The average church in America has less than one hundred in worship. Churches with less than 50 people in worship make up 40% of all churches in America. The average age of the membership within these churches with fewer than 50 people in worship is over 65. Add to that less than 2% of these churches are growing and you have a formula for a major disaster over the next fifteen years for 40% of all the churches in America. Researchers indicate there are approximately 350,000 Protestant churches in the United States; 280,000 (80%) of which are either plateaued or in decline.[213] Twenties of thousands of churches today are declining to the point of unviability. Within my own denomination the rate of plateau and decline sits somewhere between 80% and 92.2 % depending on who is reporting the state of affairs. The economic recession had forced a lot of churches to reassess their long-term viability. Under prosperous times many churches were propped up by artificial life-support which no longer exists for many of

---

213 http://kairoslegacypartners.org/not-sure-where-to-begin/defining-at-risk/.

them. More significantly, other churches are seeing the synergistic benefits of joining with like-minded churches and a similar mission for greater Kingdom impact. Yet caution must be exercised if you are a church needing to be embraced by another. The church landscape is changing in North America as predatory practices which were once unthinkable are becoming common practice. Recently I learned of large denominational groups practicing steeple jacking, or church stealing. Another less flattering term that is becoming more prevalent today is the term "Hostile Take-over." It is sad that during a time in America when the American Church needs help in the area of church revitalization and renewal that such negative practices are scaring churches and church leaders away from even considering church revitalization and renewal. A new ministry strategy has been proposed by some emerging younger churches to actively consider Steeple Jacking as a viable strategy tool. Such vulturine advances are not welcome with any hope for the declining church. These take over strategists run the risk of harming the cause of Christ within the community. It presents church planters as the ones willing to euthanize the old church participant in order to provide a cheap place for the young new and cool church plant.

Now, it is true many churches are plateaued, declining, or dying. It is true many will be unable to support their facilities. It is true other churches in the same communities could make good use of vacant or underused church properties according to Schultz. It is not surprising that leaders of once large congregations face the painful picture of a shrinking number of congregants and a sea of empty seats, dormant, that were once overflowing with souls hungry for the gospel message of salvation. Many of these churches, without help in church revitalization, will be forced to close their doors in the near future. The best strategy in my view is the restart strategy over the takeover strategy.

Where Did this Strategy Originate?

National ministry organizations advise local pastors to target declining congregations and overtake their properties. It's like a Churchfield foreclosure and eviction process as the ambitious ones attempt to acquire buildings at little or no cost. "All for the sake of the Kingdom," they say. Once in a while, all ends well. Both the overtaking and the undertaking congregations find ways to meet their challenges and simultaneously serve their communities and honor God. They find win-win solutions. Both see their years of faithfulness, hard work and sacrifice developing into something valuable and durable.[214] But there are times when the practice of steeple jacking develops into an unnecessarily conflict-ridden and caustic activity.

The Strategy Behind the Takeover

Most of us in the field of church revitalization have seen young leaders of younger churches communicate in less than loving ways with a pastor of a struggling and rapidly declining church. These young leaders boast of their attendance numbers and tout their plans to establish churches that meet in many places all over the landscape. That is never a wise strategy because it makes the church that has been doing the work of the Lord for a long time feel like they are second class to the church plant and the church planter. These young leaders often attempt to intimidate the older declining church into surrendering their keys to the church and property or "face the possibility of closure." Some even go so far as to encourage members of small groups to join a church, for a

---

214 https://churchleaders.com/pastors/pastor-articles/163374-thom-schultz-steeplejacking-churches-is-foreclosure-a-legitimate-mission-strategy.html/2.

season, in significant numbers so that they can bring before the business floor the idea of allowing their former church to take them over. A group of individuals identifies a declining church and moves people in to become members. Once this new group outnumbers the original members they can call for a Congregational Meeting, change the bylaws, change the name of the church, change the doctrine of the church and become the owners of the church's assets. When that happens, it is called a "Hostile Takeover". Here are some descriptors of these negative terms in restart of churches:

Hostile Takeovers – Hostile takeovers are those situations when a weak church is aggressively swallowed by a larger church. That is not a concept most people think about with regard to churches, but it transpires every week. This is usually done by pressure either from a new wave of church members within the declining church or by much larger churches which seek to expand their ministry signature. Those churches which seem to be more susceptible are often elderly populated, single family controlled, singular language, and monoethnic churches. Sometimes a new pastor comes to a church communicating they he is of the same doctrinal stance as the membership but in reality, he has a different faith agenda. Sometimes the takeover occurs by the new pastor. When that happens, it creates chaos and a church split. There are times when a larger church desires a broader appearance of multiculturalism and desires to merge these ministries into their own footprint, often it is for the desire to help the larger church appear more in line with the transformation of community.

How Takeovers Happen - Takeovers happen in different ways in different locations: Sometimes, as one pastor relates, they begin slowly and move along subtly. For example, a lay leader with a strong personality comes into the church and starts sowing seeds of discord. He may begin to hold private meetings to convince individuals that the truth is not being proclaimed in that church. He gives liberally and offers to serve. People within the church begin to trust him. He becomes a Sunday School teacher, a deacon, and chairman of various key committees. He may quietly assemble followers. Other new members may join the church with the same hidden agenda to align with him. Some church members may see through this scheme early-on, but others will not believe them and will criticize them, even as he and his group begin to sow discontent and manipulate the nomination and election processes for future church positions. Then the pastor leaves to go to another church, and the group of crusaders begins to manipulate the replacement process and to stack the pastor search committee with people who will vote to bring in a like-minded pastor. Many Para-Church groups have taken over churches this way and redirected former missions' monies to their individual causes. New members, often bearing a hidden agenda, join the church and quickly voice their support of the new pastor's viewpoint, while helping him to intimidate people who raise any objection. Often, they are told to leave the church or stay home if they disagree. Conspirators call committee meetings and fail to invite those who might disagree.

The End Result - The disgusted and disillusioned members begin to leave the church, "and new ones come in as fast as the older ones leave," said one former member of a hostilely taken-over church.

Positive Strategies in Restarting

Just like there are negative terms in restarting churches such as steeple jacking and hostile takeover, there are some positive terms in restarting strategies as well. Here are some positive terms in restart of churches:

Multisite – Is when a church embraces in a mutually inclusive way another church and they begin to journey together with a new strategy of one church in two locations or more.

Multi-ethnic – Is a church that embraces the changing community around the location and begins to be more inclusive to multiple language groups either by new ministries or by utilizing a "Church Within A Church" strategy.

Adoptions – Sometimes a small weaker church needs to be embraced by a larger one to keep it alive. When that happens, a church might formerly seek to adopt the church as one of its ministries while seeking to re-strengthen it and to eventually release it for service, once it again returns to be self-supporting, self-sustaining, and self-propagating.

Church Merger – While this is often a strategy utilized by larger churches, it has positive as well as negative implications. The negative implications have already been considered. The positive impact is when a strong church merges with a weaker church in order to strengthen the work. Remember though that 150 + 75 seldom equals 225! In reality it looks more like 170.

Watchcare – Is when a struggling church asks another church for help and it enters into a covenant relationship where for a time the weaker church is embraced by the stronger one in order to help it regain its footing. Sometimes the weaker church is released in about three years fully able to continue doing ministry. Other times it is released by the stronger church because it has become a burden to the stronger church and two churches trying to grow from a single budget could cause both to decline.

There is a risk with any of these methodologies certainly, yet in reality the declining church is already at risk of closing due to apathy or neglect. There is a risk that some well positioned lay people within the church will come to such a place of desperation that they will stage an internal overthrow and grab the first church that makes any overture toward them and the result is they take over the church and all of its assets. The eventual journey is that a once faithful church to its spiritual roots and biblical heritage is led away from the doctrinal stance the church was established upon. Churches that have a declining attendance below one hundred people at the primary worship service each week are at risk. If the age of your membership is high and many are in senior care centers you are at risk. If you are dropping ministries because you cannot develop sufficient volunteers to do the essential ministries of the church you are at risk.

Three Views of Church Mergers

In working with churches all over the country you get to see all types of merging of churches. Let me tell you of three churches in the south which were trying to merge. Church "A" saw Church "B" as highly vulnerable and sought to take it over by means of a hostile takeover. Church "B" knew they were in trouble but were unwilling to simply walk away from the long-time work in the community. Church "A" wanted it for a multisite and was only willing to bail out the church if they handed over the property lock stock and barrel. Church "C" came in to meet with Church "B" and told them immediately up front they did not want their building or property but were willing along with the revitalization leader they were working with to help them seek a mutually agreeable partnership where two churches become one and the Lord get the victory. As the result of Church "C's" willingness to advise, pray, and protect the vulnerable church, in a few months Church "D" came on the scene which was selling their facility and looking for a partnership to continue doing ministry in the area. Church "B" was without a pastor and Church "D" had a young and vibrant pastor who was willing to seek the Lord on the possibility of merging together. In the net ninety to one hundred and twenty days both churches worked out an agreement and the church that sold property joined the church that was vulnerable. These churches were about the same size, by the way. They each had about 70 participants. The day they merged that seventy plus seventy which seldom adds up to the total number, miraculously added up to 180 and the church has never looked back. It is blowing and going and a blessing to all who attend.

There was another church in which the church planter was somewhat of a celebrity who tried to merge with a downtown church and take it over. This church planter said that the declining church would be required to turn over property and facilities in a downtown metro area to the church planter if he was to merge his growing church with them. They balked, and it was a good thing because about a year later the church began to see the stirrings of revitalization take place, and today it runs just below three hundred in worship. The planter was seeking property where the church was seeking a way to survive and continue to bless the downtown community it had loved for so long.

Invasion from Outside Groups

Many a conservative church has been encroached by a group from another spiritual faith tradition. I currently know a group of individuals who have split a revitalization church to about two thirds remaining. The third, who left because they did not get their way, actually called my office to see if we had a church "they could help." What they sought to do was take over a declining church's facility and then move it to become an independent church. They wanted a way to steeple jack the facilities so they would not have to pay for purchasing property and constructing a building. Not everyone wants to be an independent church. There are wonderful faith traditions in Baptist, Lutheran, Presbyterian, Methodist, and others that people enjoy. Laying aside our faith traditions might not be the best thing for a community.

I know of a Baptist church with property exceeding a million dollars not counting the buildings on the premises that a group tried to take over and extort the declining church's assets. Currently it is in court, and yet to be determined is the future of the church. There is a church in the southwestern portion of our country that has a rather large investment account but lacks very many participants. One church planter has sought to take over the church by attending and embracing the remaining few. Immediately there was a change of financial supervision so that the former members who were accountable to the board and the church body of members were dismissed and ones more in line with the new church planter were put in their place. The constitution has been ignored as well as the bylaws of the church. This church currently is seeking counsel about how to remove the new pastor. Had the church done a better job of vetting the candidate, most of this would have been avoided. Then, there is a church in the northwest where a candidate told the search committee they needed to move fast if they wanted him as their pastor. They did, only to find out later that his track record for sabotaging other churches was well-documented. Through intimidation he ran most of the stalwart members away until he had a vocal majority and then made sweeping changes to the church, some of which placed him and his wife as the owners of all of the church's current assets. There is a church in the southeastern portion of our country that had a vibrant pastor full of the Lord. He was a great Bible preacher. The church refused to follow the pastor and revealed they only wanted someone who would proclaim the Word of God strongly, but not place any substantial responsibilities such as evangelism and outreach upon them. He continued to preach that the membership must be out reaching those who need the Lord and in response to his scriptural call to be a witness they dismissed him. Here is something even more bizarre: There is a church where the pastor really couldn't be bothered by their church's by-laws. Now that sounds like most of you does it not? This church encountered a hostile takeover by non-church members who had been placed on various boards of the church. They one day decided to follow a new emerging leader within the fellowship and in a matter of days changed locks, dismissed staff, eliminated board members and pushed everyone who was not following the new emerging leader out and actually asked them to stay home if they did not like what was going on. In the northeast I learned of a church where the pastor died and the entire property and assets were held in his name. Currently the church is in a legal dispute because the remaining family says they own the property and should be paid for the facilities if the church desires to continue. As you can see, I offer no legal advice but merely horror stories of things that have happened in steeple jacking events all across the land. Sometimes it is an individual while other times it is a faith-based agency that has found themselves in the middle of such a mess. But might I also warn you that sometimes your church gets in trouble with your loan institutions because you fail to pay your bills. When that happens, you have not only hurt your church's reputation but have damaged the cause of Christ as well. Pay your bills and retire your loans as a church.

The Perils of Steeple Jacking

As you can see from my words of warning, steeple jacking is happening all over North America. Declining churches are vulnerable to such takeovers. Not all churches that encounter such challenges need closure, leaving them never to be raised from the decline again. Here are the primary perils of those individuals and organizations that are in the steeple jacking business:

P – Places pressure on weaker church to succumb to larger churches' desires.

The pushy church planter or para-organization seeking to intimidate you as a declining church is unbiblical. Prematurely forcing a vulnerable church into making decisions it is not ready to make is hurtful. It is better to give your assets away to a local association which will utilize the facilities for the planting of new churches, or utilizing your facilities as an outreach center for the work of missions. In the day where people are choosing the smaller church over the larger ones, allowing for three or more churches to meeting at the mission's center weekly is a far better way to honor all of the commitments and sacrifices of past generations which have supported the work from that church. Never allow a church to place pressure on your remaining members to sign away their faith heritage to some cooler and unattached independent organization that is not part of your spiritual heritage and journey.

E – Endangers the autonomy of individual churches.

Your church is an autonomous religious entity and not supported by a large organization that has agreed to the perpetual support of your congregation. One of the dangers currently in the steeple jacking realm is when a denomination headquarters declares it will take care of the dying church only later to find out that if you have not become successful in a limited time that all of the assets revert to the headquarters for their use. There was a church in Atlanta taken over by its big brother. The church planter was growing the church and things were getting good once more. About four months before the end of the second year of the revitalization effort, the headquarters decided that the church planter was not growing the church fast enough and dismissed him. They sold the facility to a mega church and pocketed the resources. He pastors a growing church on the west coast of Florida now and is very successful. The shame of it all is that the revitalization effort was becoming successful with over one hundred weekly attenders. It is those individuals for which my heart bleeds because they bought into the vision of restarting their church and were well on their way. You are your church and you are autonomous. Do not give that away to some national entity that only views you from afar.

R – Raises the distrust that weaker church participants have towards outsiders.

Dying churches are often distrustful of outsiders who have never walked with them in any way. Remember your local mission's association has been there for you for a long time and has the necessary skill sets to help you face the challenges. Your local director of missions or area missionary strategist has been available and will always be available for your church. When organizations thousands of miles away say they understand your issues, do they really? Probably not. Steeple jacking has caused weaker churches and its members to be leery of outsiders who have no boots-on-the-ground presence.

I – Increases the danger of organized groups developing a concerted strategy for stealing smaller churches.

With the rise of hostile takeovers, the dying or declining church has never been more vulnerable. Church revitalization should always be about restoring the church of the Lord Jesus. Seldom does it have anything to do with a strategic plan to steal a church from a group of Christ followers. We have allowed this dilemma to grow because we have been unwilling to defend Christ's church. One pastor I worked with was so excited when a group of individuals began worshipping and joining his church. He noticed that they were a unified group and seemed to congregate only with the new participants in the church. They became active on every committee, especially those that were part of the church's governance. For six months it was a breath of fresh air. Then it happened. In one very divisive church business meeting the new group turned out in full force. They voted to close the church in two weeks and the original membership, of which the majority stayed home or were no longer involved, were powerless to stop the overthrow. At the same time the group made a motion to place one of the ringleaders as church planter, and before they knew it the church had seceded from its heritage and was relaunched as an entirely new church. Within the next six weeks the church had become an entirely different church, the former members were asked to either embrace the new thing or leave. In less than a year the church had moved from a denominationally aligned church to an independent church. While it had many more participants than it had had previously, it left a stain on the church and the older community avoided any connection with the new fellowship. Organized church planting clusters are a danger to the struggling declining church. You may not need a relaunch. You probably need a restart. A word of warning should be given, that any church in need of renewal needs to be cautious.

L – Limits God from a miracle of reinvention.

The Lord is still in the miracle business. We see it almost every day in the field of church revitalization and renewal. God has a plan for displaying His glory through the salvation and revitalization of declining churches. It is so wonderful to walk into a church which was formerly dead only to see that now it is full of vibrant possibilities and people. There is a renewed vigor and willingness by the laity to do the work of ministry. The former sour and hopeless attitudes have been replaced by an expectation that the Holy One is once again in the House of the Lord guiding, prospering, and blessing the flock. It is amazing that when we are at the end of our ropes as church members, God is at his best to show us that it is never too late for a miracle. The scripture declares that: *"Unless the Lord builds the house, those who labor, labor in vain."* That is so clear in the work of church revitalization and renewal. Churches that are becoming revitalized actually are expecting a miracle because the Lord has declared He would never leave them nor forsake them! In the early days of every revitalized church, the effort is blessed by an incredible commitment of the church revitalization team to pray until they see a breakthrough. That is the excitement about revitalizing a church. Participants wake up every day asking and expecting the Lord to do a miracle for their tiny church. Though revitalization is an all-out effort, often the membership feels like they are up against incredible odds. You do not know what to do except to seek the Lord. That is enough if you faithfully seek him continually. That is where the peace of the Lord comes in as you are in the midst of great challenges. Revitalized churches place a high premium on seeking the face of God daily. You have heard it said many times, I am sure, "that nothing happens unless it first happens in the place of prayer." I have heard so many testimonies from members of revitalized churches that prayer was the gateway to revitalizing their church. Prayer reshapes a church's life. It starts with a singular individual and permeates the membership of a renewing church. Real prayer, heartfelt prayer, deep prayer. Prayer reshapes the churches life. Expecting the miraculous from the Lord is part of the reinvention of the work in a local church. Do not limit god from the miracle of reinvention.

S – Sends the message that the only way out for smaller churches is a merger.

Not every declining church needs to be saved by a larger one. Sometimes a church must go through the death throws to purge itself of the sin that has been consuming the Lord's house. Those plateaued or declining churches that jump at the offer from a larger church to take them over might in the end realize that their worship now looks more focused upon the entertainment evangelism forms prevalent in those churches. Smaller churches are being revitalized all over North America. More are being revitalized through individual church efforts and not larger churches taking over smaller ones. While church mergers work, it is not the cure all for a declining church. One church planting group in the north central states has done many a successful church revitalization effort by embracing the declining small church for a time and once they are large enough to be let go, they do so.

Wrapping it Up!

The work of restarting a plateaued or declining church is challenging. There is fear in the small church that is facing possible closure. Remember, Jesus said that he would build his church and even the gates of Hades will not prevail against it. Although we recognize that the Church of the Lord Jesus will last it does not mean that every congregation will last. Scripture records some remarkable local churches that history tells us no longer exist. The Church of Jesus Christ is not an organization, it is a living organism; the body of Christ. Organisms do not live forever, they are born, mature, and (most often) procreate and eventually die. Church Revitalizer, read your Bible. Pay attention to the Lord Jesus. Be still and pray. Be grateful for what we have. Fear not. Think upon the things of God. Listen to the voice of God. Do not worry nor weary. Be at peace with all of those in your congregation. Continue to reach out to the lost and evangelize even though the future might be unclear. Be generous. Let your light shine. Do not judge. Practice the gift of grace. Boldly speak the truth in love. Forgive early; do not be the last but the first to forgive others. Major on the majors. Love one another and serve them. Trust in the Lord with everything you have. If you are facing the challenges that lead you to consider a restart do not be afraid. Rather, be strong and courageous. God has led you this far, and God will never forsake you. Remember that just as a seed has to die in order to bear much fruit, so death and change can lead to abundant life. This can be just as true for the life of a congregation as it is for individuals. God's assurance to Joshua as he faced an unknown future is still God's guarantee to us: *"Be strong and courageous; do not be frightened or dismayed, for the Lord your God is with you wherever you go."*[215] God was declaring the end of an era, but also the perpetuation of the promise he had made to Moses, the same promise of a place and a people that he had made to Abraham, Isaac, and Jacob. God's brutal honesty with Joshua can be a lesson for all of us. God's people have always had great responsibilities. We do not have the same tests or responsibility that God gave Joshua, but we do have a charge from God, and we will face challenges. Like the people of Israel, we can also become discouraged and fearful, thinking that we cannot succeed. Nothing should be of greater encouragement when we face these responsibilities than the assurance that God will help us accomplish them. The lessons Joshua received from God about the challenges he would face can be relevant for us today. Having received instructions and reassurance from the Lord, Joshua began to prepare his people to cross the Jordan into Canaan for the very first time. He commanded the officers to instruct the people in the camp to prepare provisions and be ready in three days to cross the Jordan and go into the promised land. Joshua told his people to get

---

215 Joshua 1:9.

prepared and be ready to move forward. There was a promise by Joshua made to the people. The place of the preacher was that of preparing his followers for the journey. The conclusion was that in three days God will deliver you across the Jordon River into the promised land. These same lessons can apply to us as we examine the health and viability of our own congregations. If you are part of a congregation that is fearful and apprehensive about their future, consider the story of Joshua on the verge of the promised land. Could God be pronouncing the end of one era, but also continuing his promise in a new way through a restart? Perhaps so. There is life after death so walk not in fear of restarting one's church.

Chapter Fourteen
The Importance of a Proper Launch: The Art of a Proper Launch

Forget about what's happened; don't keep going over old history. Be alert, be present. I'm about to do something brand-new. It's bursting out! Don't you see it? There it is! I'm making a road through the desert, rivers in the badlands.[216]

Les Brown once said, "You don't have to be great to get started but you have to get started to be great." How enormously true that statement is. The proper start or launch will determine the greatness of the restart church. The beginning doesn't have to be flawless, but it must be sincere and motivated by a high calling from God.

Guy Kawasaki writes in his book *The Art of the Start,* "THINK BIG. Set your sights high and strive for something grand. If you're going to change the worlds, you can't do it with milquetoast and boring products and services. Shoot for doing things at least ten times better than the status quo."[217] Of course Kawasaki is referring to starting a new company, however, the same should be said about the launch of a new church. Starting a church from nothing is difficult to say the least. It is even more difficult to close a church and restart a viable and fruitful church from nothing as well. It could be described as an art in the sense that it takes special skills and commitment because the launch of a new church is most often accompanied by the lack of funds, people and staff. It is necessary that the restart pastor have the skills and commitment to develop a strategy for fundraising, team

---

[216] Eugene H. Peterson, *The Message: The Bible in Contemporary Language* (Colorado Springs, CO: NavPress, 2005), Is 43:18–19.

217 Guy Kawasaki, *The Art of the Start* (London: Penguin Books, 2004) 10.

building and effective ministry such as worship, evangelism and discipleship.

Before the launch takes place there must be an honest look at the cost of commitment, finances and manpower. Of course, this is not to be the determining factor of going forward with the restart, because if God has ordained the process then He will take care of the incidentals. However, the Bible says we are to count the cost. Luke 14:28-30 says, "For which of you, intending to build a tower, sitteth not down first, and counteth the cost, whether he have sufficient to finish it? Lest haply, after he hath laid the foundation, and is not able to finish it, all that behold it begin to mock him, Saying, This man began to build, and was not able to finish."[218] One must always remember, however, that in a God ordained and led restart, He is in control and He is doing a *new thing*. Isaiah 43: 18-19 says "Remember ye not the former things, neither consider the things of old. *Behold, I will do a new thing;* now it shall spring forth; shall ye not know it? I will even make a way in the wilderness, *and* rivers in the desert."[219] You can be sure that any new thing that God does is going to be a good thing. He will ensure the future even if there is involved a wilderness and or desert journey. He is still the Master even of the wilderness and the desert.

The fact is, God has a plan for the restart church. God loves the community where the restart will be much more than the restart pastor does. Nelson Searcy in the book *Launch: Starting a New Church from Scratch,* says "Launching a new church that impacts the community positively, reaches the lost, grows rapidly, helps people mature in their faith, and

---

218 Luke 14:28-30 KJV.

219 Isaiah 43: 18-19 KJV.

then starts more new churches nearby and around the world is entirely possible—with God!"[220]

Francis of Assisi said, "Start by doing what's necessary; then do what's possible; and suddenly you are doing the impossible." The insinuation of his words is that when we strive to do the will of God the impossible becomes possible. This is so true of the task of restarting a church. An anonymous writer once said, "Starting over again is not that bad. Because when you restart you get another chance to make things right."

Many people in the past have been credited with the quote "anything worth doing is worth doing well", but anything worth doing is worth doing right, not just well, especially that which God orders to be done. In this chapter we will discuss the importance of a proper launch. To put it another way, we will shed light on the right way to properly launch a new work for God in the form of a restart church. Here are some major steps in a proper launch.

First Things First – Form a Launch Team

There are a multitude of ideas as to who should make up the launch team of a restart and how they are to effectively help in the launch. Some revitalizers advocate for individuals that have been reached in the early stages of the restart. I believe this is a mistake because launching a restart calls for some specific qualities and abilities on the part of the launch team. Others advocate for a group of outsiders handpicked and trained by the revitalizer to make up the team. This is without a doubt the best scenario because you can control the direction of the team better and it makes for a more cohesive team attitude.

---

220 Nelson Searcy and Kerrick Thomas, *Launch: Starting a New Church from Scratch* (Grand Rapids: Baker, 2017) 34.

You can launch a restart without a building, without finances and without equipment but you cannot launch properly without a well trained and equipped launch team. So, the first and most strategic step in launching a church restart is securing that launch team. This team can make or break the launch and or the entire restart. A team at Exponential did a study about issues that church planters face. In that study titled, "Top Issues Church Planters Face, *building a launch team* was third as one of the church planter's major challenges. Don't confuse a launch team with a core group. A launch team is focused on the aspects of launching specific to their assignments and responsibilities. Their job is to get this church off the ground, and their part is to train and prepare for the launch."[221]

This team must be comprised of people with leadership qualities who are willing to make an unquestionable commitment to the restart. They must be teachable and visionary. This team must be made up of team players. A "lone ranger" mentality will stop the work of the team quickly. After the team is in place, they must be properly instructed in the purpose of the team, the work of the team and the operational parameters of the team by the Church Revitalizer.

Furthermore, the team must know the purpose for which they were formed and the role each will be playing. For instance, in a very successful restart in eastern Georgia, the team that was formed was credited with the reason behind the success. That team was made up of a retired banker, retired educator, a retired and highly successful pastor and several very committed laypersons who had been leaders in their churches. They were "all in" for the long haul to get the

---

221 Ed Stetzer, "Building Your Launch Team," *The exchange,* March 8, 2016, accessed January 10, 2019, https://www.christianitytoday.com/edstetzer/2016/march/building-your-launch-team.html.

restart up and going to become a viable and productive church fellowship. The result was a launch Sunday audience of 167 and a leveled-out audience of 145. The church that closed was averaging 17 on Sunday. It was a great success, but it could not have happened without the launch team. Anyone serving on the launch team should exhibit "servant leader" qualities and abilities.

Answer the Critical Question

The number one question that must be answered as you consider a new church launch in the North American church culture is, "What are people looking for in a church experience?" When considering this question, one must understand the community where the church is located. However, there are a few absolutes that must be taken seriously when determining how to reach the community. There are five core things that people are looking for when they go to church. All of these are intertwined into an experience that causes seeking people to sit up and take notice.

First, statistics show that most people who are truly seeking a beneficial church experience, especially in North America, *almost always prefer a Sunday morning service*. There are those critics of the Sunday morning, church building worship service that say it is too institutionalized   They believe that the true purpose of church has been minimalized. I think, to the contrary, these critics have forgotten some basics of worship and fellowship. The argument that the church, in a large group setting, is too impersonal, is not a valid argument. I would argue that *the house church is too intimate and personal for some* and they will not attend because of it. Some unchurched people are not ready for that kind of intimacy. Because of that fact, house services could deter the growth of the "church." I would argue also that *most house churches are a "turned inward" group*. Little or no evangelism takes place in the house church movement and there seems to be an exclusive atmosphere that permeates it. They tend to attract only people that have the same likes and lifestyles without any consideration of the bigger picture of going to the whole world with the Gospel. The bottom line is that the average seeker sees the Sunday morning worship service as a more structured church setting, and a more legitimate concept of church.

Tom Rainer states it well when he says that the rise of non-Sunday worship services is only slowly progressing. He says "Churches with multiple Sunday morning services will soon be in the majority. This trend, once more common with larger churches, is now taking hold in congregations of all sizes." He further states that, "The 11:00 am worship service is no longer the designated time for most churches. The so-called sacred hour of worship is not sacred in most churches. This change started slowly, but it is pervasive now." He goes on to say, "The most popular worship times start between 9:30 am to 10:30 am. This mid-morning worship time attracts attendees to churches with both single and multiple worship services."[222] His stats come from a survey his organization did with over 1700 churches. The preferred time for worship is Sunday morning. Right or wrong, whatever your opinion might be, in our North American culture the Sunday morning worship service in a church building gives legitimacy to the church being a church.

Second, is the *quality of preaching* in the church. There must be good Biblical preaching in a new church launch. "Now when people evaluate churches, they might evaluate them based on many things. But there's only one that really sets the tone. The single most important reason to choose a church is the nature and character of its preaching and

---

222 Thom Rainer, "Seven Trends in Worship Service Times," https://thomrainer.com/2015/05/seven-trends-in-worship-service-times/, (May 25, 2015).

teaching. Where you have strong biblical preaching and teaching, everything else tends toward strength. Where you do not have strong biblical teaching and preaching, everything else is weak and tends toward shallowness. Preaching sets the tone in the church, and proclaiming biblical truth is essential."[223] One of the several functions of a New Testament church is to preach the Gospel and if it falters in this aspect of church the church will have little or no impact on the community.

Third, is the *quality of the music.* Churches across North America have gone through what has been coined "worship wars." While music is a vital part of worship, it is not worth fighting over. Music is a matter of one's own personal preferences. Any Christian music can be an avenue to enhance and carry one into a time of worship. However, the average church visitor is looking for something a little bigger than mediocre. They are looking for a message even in the music and song. I personally believe the words of a song is what matters. It is not the beat, the loudness or the softness of the music but it all hinges on the message, the words of the song. So, in the first service of a relaunch and every service afterward the music must be focused on the message of the Gospel, not on whether it causes you to tap your feet.

The fourth quality *is the overall worship experience.* Many who attend a church for the first time come looking for a worship experience that is different, challenging, encouraging and Holy Spirit led. A dead dried up approach to worship probably had something to do with the death of the previous church. You certainly do not want to repeat that scenario. Most dying and dead churches have failed miserably in their worship experience. People in these times will not sit in a

---

223 Grace to You, *The Responsibilities of the Church: Preaching, Part 1,* accessed January 2, 2019, https://www.gty.org/library/sermons-library/90-143/the-responsibilities-of-the-church-preaching-part-1

morgue to worship. Neither will they listen to a mediocre sermon or tepid music that has no Biblical message

Fifth, is the *quality of preschool, children and youth ministry.* As a pastor for 32 years, I can say, without any doubt that the number one thing that most families look for when they visit a church is the nursery, children and youth programs. Parents now expect the very best out of the church as it ministers to their children. They will forgo comfort for themselves in order that their children may have the best church experience possible. It is important to have rooms well equipped with furniture, games, clean safe toys, learning aids etc. Parents expect the best of the well-trained workers in those areas as well. Second best will not work in this area. If these areas do not meet the parent's criteria, they simply will never return, and they will find a place that does suit them.

Finally, is the *appearance of the facility.* It is imperative that the church building be well kept. It does not have to be a modern and up to date facility, but it must be clean and comfortable. In fact, more and more research is showing that millennials are not necessarily looking for a modern structure as much as they are seeking a nostalgic setting that is clean and inviting. It is, then, imperative that the building inside and out be inviting. Parking lots should be kept up and well lighted. Landscaping should be inviting and neat. Everything should say to those who may visit, "Come on in we would love to have you worship with us today!"

Four Crucial Observations

There are some very important elements that should demand our attention be paid to them prior to the launch. Here are some of those crucial observations about the importance of the launch.

Observation #1: You are *launching a new Life Cycle.* The life cycle of the church has been discussed at length in a previous chapter so I will make this section short as I refer you back to these chapters. Every church goes through a life cycle. Most churches don't understand that cycle until it is too late. The restart, of course, is the result of the previous church coming to a fatal end in the cycle.

Every church begins out of a God-given dream and vision. That dream expands into a church's phase of developing strategy, programs and direction. This leads the church to a point of maturity, but then, that maturity phase causes the church to begin to lose momentum and it goes into a "death spiral" and dies. When a restart occurs, the church must launch with a new dream and vision. It must develop new programing, convictions, systems and direction. It cannot remain the same as it was at the point of death and expect the restart to be successful. The launch team is responsible for the development of that dream and vision for the design of the future program and direction of the restart. This new life cycle will insure a fresh new start with a new direction that will inspire a new hope for the future.

Observation #2: It is imperative that you *launch with a new DNA*. *"One of the biggest advantages a church plant or new church has is the opportunity to start fresh; design things from scratch, eliminate the "sacred cows" and create DNA."* [224] As a result of the launch of a new life cycle there must be new DNA built into the restart. Greg Wiens said in his work, *Dying to Restart,* when writing about the restart having new DNA, "Dying to restart is not about re-creating a better version of the past but rather, something qualitatively different."[225] He goes on to say, "As a church begins to emerge from death, it's obviously in a very fragile state. This

---

224 Brad Ransom, *Retool, Refocus, Relaunch: How to Reset, Reimagine and Restart a Church,* accessed January 5, 2019, http://ncfwb.org/wp-content/uploads/2017/06/Retool-Refocus.-Relaunch.pdf

225 Greg Wiens, Dan Turner, *Dying to Restart,* (Exponential, 2018), 68.

is a critical time to start accepting the new DNA that God wants in infuse into the resurrected church. The DNA must be built into the foundations of the new church. In studying churches that have died to find new life, we have discovered some common practices to help ensure the survival of the new, healthy DNA."[226] This new DNA must have some specific elements if the restart is to be successful.

The main particle of DNA that must be present in the restart church is a fresh, different and clear approach to *missions*. Most churches that die, do so because of a lack of missionary zeal in its DNA. No church can be considered a New Testament church without a healthy approach to missions. Its approach to missions should include evangelism and discipleship. This new DNA should be the catalyst that drives the church to be involved in every aspect of missions in its Jerusalem, Judea, Samaria, and to the ends of the earth. This missional DNA will prove to be the unique motivation that will launch the restart into a great growth cycle. Any church that is without a strong mission's emphasis will not stand for long.

Every restart church that will survive will instill, as part of their DNA, a new clear *God-given vision*. Almost every church I work with that is in desperate need of some sort of revitalization has no clue about ministry vision. Some years ago, I asked a pastor of a dying church, "What is your God given vision for the church you serve?" The pastor thought for a minute and looked me in the eye and said "I would have to say that my vision is for survival. I was shocked at that answer. In fact, I responded inquisitively, "What do you mean...survival? Please explain this to me because I don't understand what you are saying." He replied, "My survival and the survival of the congregation." When survival becomes a part of your churches DNA you are in a death spiral and death is very close!

---

226 Ibid, 70.

Any restart must have a fresh vision built into its DNA. That vision is born out of the needs that are present in the church community. The vision DNA of a restart church will be much different from that of the church that chose to die. Vision is the driving force that catapults the church into success. It determines how effective the church will be in changing lives and meeting needs.

This new DNA will also manifest itself in a *new healthy philosophy of ministry*. This new DNA will always replace old failing systems, ministries, and broken approaches with new, vibrant and enthusiastic ministry. The ministry in the church that has been replaced, obviously, was not healthy or the church would still be in existence. The DNA of a restart must possess a transformational approach to ministry. Its main objective is to transform the community it resides in. The dead church focused its energy of ministry philosophy on simple survival. In the restart the philosophy is focused on seeking Kingdom results as it evangelizes and disciples those around it.

Furthermore, the DNA of a restart is *not self-serving*. Dead churches are dead because they were self-serving. Everything this new DNA calls for is to meet the needs of others. Teaching, training, budgets, programs and systems should reflect the new DNA of servant ministry.

Observation #3: The launch should have *little or no room for failure*. Improper planning can cause failure in the launch. By this time everything should be falling into place. Here is a check list that can be used to give a bit of assurance for success:

- A one-year plan for ministry and formulation with goals and priorities.
- A new constitution and bylaws with basic doctrinal beliefs spelled out.

- A determination as to what kind of worship service the church will have - blended, contemporary or traditional.
- Musicians and worship leaders should be in place for the launch.
- Children's workers should have been background checked, trained and in place.
- Youth workers should have been background checked, trained and in place.
- A nursery with well trained workers and well-equipped space should be in place. They should be background checked as well.
- Media techs should be trained and in place.
- Sound systems, monitors, etc. should be purchased or rented and in place.
- Podium area should be well decorated and set with proper furniture, etc.
- Any teaching/training materials and equipment should be available for those attending.
- Finances should have been acquired by the launch team.
- Dignitaries, denominational leaders etc. should have been invited by now.
- The preacher and special music should be well prepared for the worship experience to be the best it can be.
- A method of securing contact information from those attending should be set up.
- A welcome center should be placed in the most likely place people will enter.
- Greeters should be in strategic points in the building.

- Qualified adult teachers for small groups should be in place.
- All of this must be saturated with PRAYER!

There is nothing that can guarantee a perfect launch, but you can alleviate many problems by simply being prepared. Preparation will give the greatest sense of hope because it is a natural form of reassurance and encouragement.

Observation #4: The launch should seek to *rebrand the church*. When the subject of branding or re-branding arises, we usually think of businesses and not churches. However, any church can benefit from rethinking its message and methods as it seeks to reach out to a given community. Every church is always communicating a message to the surrounding area. To rebrand will refresh and or reestablish that message and will reach a much broader audience that the dead church was reaching.

The *Senior Pastor Central* website gives a great explanation about rebranding the church. It says "Rebranding is much more than creating a new logo – it involves identifying <u>who you're trying to reach</u>, positioning them as the hero in your church's story, and aligning everything (logo, font selection, color pallet, signage, etc.) to speak to them."[227] The question is asked, "Why rebrand a church?" The answer is simple, especially for a restart. Your church's brand always speaks of the church's reputation. When churches die, they always leave a reputation and many times it is a bad reputation. So, the church needs rebranding. It is sort of like starting a new identity with new vision, strategy and purpose. Rebranding puts the church in a better position to impact the community because it has separated from the old dead past.

---

227 Senior Pastor Central, *10 Steps to Rebrand Your Church,* http://seniorpastorcentral.com/4185/10-steps-rebrand-church/.

To rebrand the church, its leadership must know the direction the ministry is going. This direction is determined by the knowledge the leadership has of the church community and those it will be ministering to. The good news about branding is that you can give the right impression, directly influence what your community thinks about your ministry, and do that without compromising your message."[228]

Prerequisites for Preparation to Launch

These four prerequisites must be present in the early stages prior to the restart launch. It will make or break the effectiveness and success of the restart! Preparation for the launch is as important as the launch itself. What you do in preparation and how effective that preparation is will determine the success of the restart. There are many early steps to a launch that have been discussed previously but I am listing four of the most important prerequisites. Without these the restart will fail.

Prerequisite #1: *The presence of Fervent and Zealous Prayer.* This, of course, has been discussed already in this book but it deserves another visit. The restart must be confidently founded in prayer. There is not one part of a restart that is humanly attainable. The entire process must be bathed in prayer. Prayer obtains the vision from God to establish a restart. It opens our hearts to the plan of God and gives the direction to proceed into unknown territory. It obtains the power of God through the Holy Spirit. In the absence of prayer there will be no power from on high. Without prayer we are not connected to God in order to find His will, plan and direction. The importance of prayer is seen in Philippians

---

228 Daniel Thrilfall, *Church Marketing Basics – How to Brand Your Ministry (Part 1),* accessed January 8, 2019, https://www.sharefaith.com/blog/2010/10/church-marketing-basics-brand-ministry-part-1/.

4:6. It says "Be careful for nothing; but in everything by prayer and supplication with thanksgiving let your requests be made known unto God."[229]

Prayer must never become an addendum to the process, it must be the power that drives the process to success. This dependence upon prayer must be instilled into the DNA of the restart but it must begin with the revitalizer and the launch team. Prayer, for the restart, should become as natural as breathing. Prayer builds fellowship between us and God and between the members of the launch team. The more time the team spends with God in prayer the more relational the process becomes. The key element that is present in the concept of prayer is that as we pray, we begin to learn the heart of God about a matter.

Robert Velarde in his article, *Prayer Has It's Reasons,* asks, "Does God need our help?" No. He is all powerful and in control of everything in His creation. Why do we need to pray? Because prayer is the means God has ordained for some things to happen. Prayer, for instance, helps others know the love of Jesus. Prayer can clear human obstacles out of the way for God to work. It is not that God can't work without our prayers, but that He has established prayer as part of His plan for accomplishing His will in this world." We don't pray because God needs us to accomplish a task. We pray because we need God to accomplish His will in us. The restart launch **MUST** be born out of consistent, fervent and dynamic prayer!

Prerequisite # 2: The Presence of a *clear heart for Evangelism*. Apart from prayer, this is the most important prerequisite to the launch of a restart. Again, this must be built into the DNA of the new church. Obviously, the previous church died, and it probably died because of a lack of evangelistic involvement. If the restart is to be successful it

---

229 Philippians 4:6 KJV.

must commit to real evangelism. If it does not have that commitment it will simply be occupying the same space as the previous failed church and it will never be the church God intends for it to be. In fact, it will probably die an early death. Prayer is the life line of the church, but evangelism is the life blood of the church. No restart will be successful without a commitment to reach people with the Gospel. It is essential to the permanency of health the restart needs. The church will never have a prosperous ministry without the process of going into the community and sharing the love, mercy and forgiveness of God.

The restart pastor, core team, and launch team must be totally committed to changing people's lives with the Gospel. Evangelism must be integrated into the God–given vision by which it operates. Everyone in the new church must see and know that the process of winning souls is inflexible. Every member of every team and the congregation must be committed to winning souls!

Prerequisite #3: The presence of a *sound and single-minded fellowship of believers*. In church planting, whether it be a traditional plant or restart, there is always the element of loneliness. Restarting a church is difficult! It is not easy work and it gets lonely at times. Even launch teams, because of the difficulty of restart, gets discouraged and complacent. There must be a singlemindedness built into the launch teams and the new congregation. The team must be committed to each other as well as the task and it must be experiencing camaraderie. Because of the nature of the task of restarting a church, the launch team will be spending a lot of time together. That time calls for mutual trust and understanding. The team must exemplify cooperation and fellowship for the new church to buy into this fellowship. This too, must be incorporated into the DNA of the new church.

This kind of fellowship always fosters good communication and good communication among the fellowship usually brings peace. The Greek word for fellowship spells out the importance of fellowship in a new church. That word is "*koinonia*." The word simply means "to hold something in common." It is mandatory that the new congregation hold to a common faith, ministry and purpose. This fellowship is vertical as well as horizontal. The church must cultivate vertical relationship (fellowship) with God and maintain a horizontal relationship (fellowship) with those around it.

This fellowship of believers must be single-minded in its approach, message and ministry. It must have one thing in common…a desire to bring people to Jesus Christ by the proclamation of the Gospel.

Prerequisite #4: The presence of a *clear promotional strategy*. I don't particularly like the concept of marketing the church. I prefer to use the term promotional. The question is how do you promote the new work that God has entrusted into your hands? How can you get the message of a new church out to the public? There are many different strategies. Some are good and others are not so good. However, there are a few things that are effective in promoting the new work.

First, the use of i*nvitation cards* can be quite effective if the new congregation will utilize them. An invite card is just as it sounds. It is a small card (there are various sizes) that has all the pertinent information about the restart and is used to invite people that crosses the path of a congregational member. It should have location, contact info, times and the restart pastor's name. These can be used in any setting as they are given out randomly wherever the contact is made. It can be used in a mall, laundromat, sidewalk, or restaurant…anywhere to invite people to the launch of the new church.

Second, is the use of *postcards*. The use of EDDM (Every Door Direct Mail) is the best mass mailing process. Mass mailings with the local post office can be expensive and sometimes not nearly as effective as personal contacts but it is one way of getting the news out to people in an area. You should choose a zip code or zip codes to send the mailer to. The most efficient mass mailing should be made up of a postcard with all the pertinent information about the launch included. With this method there are no addresses required. The post card will be dropped at each residence in the chosen zip code area. It is impersonal but it does get the information into the hands of a lot more people.

With EDDM you can target age groups, income or even household size. Mailing time for this is usually 7-14 days. It is designed only for flat mail such as postcards, brochures, etc. You can mail up to 5000 pieces per post office per day.

A third method is the use of *banners and "giveaways."* There are many companies that can produce *pens, magnets, calendars and door hangers* and other items to use as "giveaways" at a very reasonable price. You name it and it can be used to promote the launch. The banners can be used inside and outside of the church. They should be used at the entrance of the parking lot and along sidewalks leading to the entrance of the building. Other street side signs can be placed on roadsides to promote and or direct people to the launch service. Ink pens, magnets etc. can be used to randomly give to people but they should have all pertinent information about the launch on them.

Fourth, *use technology* to get the message out. There are at least three tech outlets that can be used effectively.

The new church should have a dynamic **web presence**. A well designed and well-kept website will be well worth the investment. In this technological age, the computer is a major means of communication and should be used to its fullest in promoting the work of the new church. The website should focus on the vision and ministry of the new church. It should communicate core values and the mission of the new work. In our technological age a website is not optional. Statistics show that 8 out of every 10 people who visit your church will have already visited your website. The website gives you an uninterrupted opportunity to showcase your ministry to all who visit the site. When developing a website, it would be wise to pay a webmaster to construct and maintain the web site.

Also, the restart should use the **power of social media** to promote the launch day. It cannot be denied that social media is a force to be reckoned with in our culture. Again, stats show that approximately one half of visitors under the age of 40 have already looked the church up on social media and knows the good, bad and the ugly about the church. There are literally hundreds of social media sites available, but the church needs to stick with a few major sites to advertise through. Facebook is another social media outlet that can be used effectively for the effective launch of a new church and by the young church to get the message out about events etc. Facebook and twitter have the potential to reach thousands of people in your area.

Everything in Its Place – Launch Big

Again, nothing can take the place of preparation. The reality is that anything new seems to draw larger crowds. People are naturally curious about new "anythings", especially churches. Often people who are genuinely looking for a meaningful worship experience will visit on launch day just to check things out to see if it meets their spiritual needs. They are looking for a worship time that will be meaningful and motivational. You must be prepared to receive these seekers and give them the best church experience they have ever had. Where do you start? What are the main things that need to be prepared in order to give that experience to the seeker? Where do you focus your attention for launch day and thereafter?

One of the important areas you should pay close attention to is in the *parking area*. There should be an abundance of parking attendants who are committed to moving people from outside the facility to inside safely. If it is raining some attendants should have umbrellas and escort people into the building to keep them dry. If the parking area is large or disconnected from the existing worship area, a shuttle may be necessary. This is an important time for first impressions. As the attendants park cars and relate to the people in the parking lot, a lasting impression will be developed. It must be a good impression.

Once the attendee has moved into the facility there should be *greeters* present to register, give assistance to and direct the attendees to the proper location in the facility. There should be initial greeters that stand at the door and make the second impression on the attendees. They should be people with joyful personalities. They should have a smile on their face and willing to shake hands and show love and kindness. Then there are the secondary greeters. They are the ones who stand behind a registration counter to greet a third time and register the person and give direction concerning meetings in the building. The third level of greeter is the "runner" that, if needed, will personally escort the person or persons to the place of the meeting. Again, this leaves a lasting impression on the newcomer.

Another important preparation to be made is the presence of *clear and professional directional signage.* Nothing can take the place of good signage in the facility. People want to be able to find rest rooms without having to ask. Moms expect clear directional signage to the nursery and children's departments in the church. Every room should be marked clearly in order to make it easier for new attendees to navigate the building without constantly asking directions.

There must be a manned welcome center at the main entrance of the facility. It should be manned with very capable and knowledgeable people. They must be familiar with the building and its lay out. They must have firsthand knowledge of what is taking place in the church that day. This is a very important step in greeting the new attendees. At this point, information for future use should be acquired. The record gathering and keeping this information for future ministry begins here. The registration form should have a place for name, address, phone and email info. This is invaluable for the pastoral team and the visitation team as a follow up for the service. It gives info that will help disseminate future information to anyone who has attended the church. They must keep good records.

At the point of the launch service the *best nursery and child care workers* should be enlisted and trained. These workers must be personable and friendly as they proceed to take care of the most prized position of a parent…their baby or child. This part of the process must not be taken for granted. It will make or break the success of the launch and the future of the church. A system should be in place that will pair babies in the nursery with diaper bag and formula and parents. There should be a way for the parent to properly and quickly claim their child from the care area. A system of reaching the parent during a worship service is also important in case there is some type of emergency concerning the child. This is imperative. People will not tolerate second rate service for their children.

Then comes the reason everyone came for…*the worship experience*. If this fails, the church will be in trouble from the start. We discussed some of this previously, but it cannot be stated too much. A mediocre worship experience may bring some back. An unenthusiastic worship experience will bring no one back. However, an exciting, well planned, dynamic worship experience will be sure to gain a following and bring people back next Sunday. Announcements should not be a part of the main worship time. They should be placed at the end of the service. Music must be at its best. The preaching must be spot on. This service should have a strong element of evangelism incorporated into it. Then people will sit up and take notice and the restart will be up and going for the Kingdom.

The final element in the launch service should be a *meet the pastor time*. The pastor and his wife should retire to an adjacent room and be available to meet and greet those who desire to gain more information about the church and its ministry. This is good public relations and will help people make up their minds about returning to the next service.

Conclusion

How did you measure the success of your launch? Paul Andrew, lead pastor for Liberty Church in New York City, spoke about his launch in 2011: "I didn't have a particular number in my heart for our launch, but I did dream of the venue feeling full and an electric atmosphere of faith and celebration. Having a great launch is so important, but don't neglect your plans for the hundreds or thousands of Sundays after it! Launching strong is good but launching strong and then staying strong is even better." [230] To be honest, only time will tell how successful the launch really was. What happens in the future will be evidence of a real successful start.

It is important to say that many restarts will not have the finances to do all that has been discussed but it should strive to do all it can to accomplish success. **Do what you can, and God will bless your efforts**.

---

230 Scott Marshall, "Outreach Magazine," *Church Planting, Part 1: Picking the Launch Date,* March 20, 2015, https://outreachmagazine.com/features/4668-picking-the-date.html.

Chapter Fifteen
When the Death of a Church is a Good Thing!

*To everything there is a season, and a time to every purpose under the heaven: A time to be born, a time to die.*231

It is a fact that the death of a church can be as much a success as it is a failure! It is true that some churches need to die. The big question is "How does the congregation know when it is time to close the doors? How do they know when it is time to die?" The answers to these questions lie in the people who make up the existing congregation. People tend to drift and stray after years of being in the church. Commitment seems to subside after years of service and church seems to take a back seat to many. So, the people who make up the congregation allow and even sometimes, initiate the death of their church.

King Solomon said in Ecclesiastes 3, "To everything there is a season, and a time to every purpose under the heaven: A time to be born, a time to die;"232 and Jesus said in John 12:24, "Verily, verily, I say unto you, except a grain of wheat fall into the ground and die, it abideth alone: but if it die, it bringeth forth much fruit. ... Very truly I tell you, unless a kernel of wheat falls to the ground and dies, it remains only a single seed. But if it dies, it produces many seeds."233

David Olson asked in *The American Church in Crises,* "Why do churches close? In most cases, a process of decline leads to closure. Churches lose members, income, energy, vision

---

231 Ecclesiastes 3:1-2 KJV.

232 Ecclesiastes 3:1-2 KJV.

233 John 12:24 KJV.

and ability to minister in a changing world. Unless they can reverse those dynamics, death will inevitably occur."[234] Churches do close their doors every day in America. Some of these churches have been around for decades and some even over a century. Others are new plants that just could not make it. No matter how old or how young the church may be, the closure is usually for the same set of reasons. It may be that they simply were or became irrelevant to a community that has changed because of population or cultural shifts. Others die because of moral failure on the part of leadership and still others die simply because they lost their purpose and vision. As tragic as this seems, it should not and must not be the end of a church's influence because in such an instance a restart can bring new life, vision hope and witness to a needy and spiritually starving community.

Mike Regele says it clearly, "A decision is imminent, but is only a decision about how the church will die. Death is inescapable. We cannot and will not avoid it. The institutional church will either choose to die or it will choose to die in order to live."[235]

In past chapters the infamous "death spiral" was discussed. When the church gets into a "death spiral" it more than likely will end in death and closure. What will be discussed in this chapter are the illnesses or the sicknesses that the church that is in a "death spiral." Usually by this time in the life cycle of a given church it is too late for general revitalization tools such as retooling, renewal, or refocus. The only hope for the future of this type of church is a restart. When I hear of a church in this condition, I get heart sick. I

---

234 David Olson, *The American Church in Crises* (Grand Rapids: Zondervan, 2008), 120.

235 Mike Regele, *Death of the Church* (Grand Rapids: Zondervan, 1995) 20.

never thought I could get to the point that I would admit that the death of a church would be a good thing.

Some General Observations

Some churches need to die because *they bring dishonor to the King and the Kingdom.* Malachi 1:6 says, "A son honoureth his father, and a servant his master: if then I be a father, where is mine honour? and if I be a master, where is my fear? saith the Lord of hosts unto you, O priests, that despise my name. And ye say, Wherein have we despised thy name?"[236] That is a question our churches need to be asking themselves… "How have we despised your name, oh God?" That question can be answered by asking and answering another question: "What are we giving to God?" This verse makes it clear that the people had been presenting to Him unclean offerings on the altar. In so doing they are showing disrespect and insult to the Lord.

The people were not bringing the best they had to the Lord. It was obvious that the people were bringing defective animals for sacrifice and the priests were accepting them as an adequate offering to God. That brings dishonor to the King and His Kingdom. This is much like the church today in America. We bring the defective parts of our lives. We bring the leftovers of our lives. We present to God that which we don't want or think we needed and that brings dishonor to God. We give the left-over time, talent and substance rather than the first and best of our time, talent and substance. Here is a news flash…God will not take from us our seconds and thirds. He expects our best. How could the people ask God for His blessing when they presented to Him their leftovers? What we as the church presents to God always reveals our

---

236 Malachi 1:6 KJV.

heart. The best we have, shows how much we love Him. The seconds, thirds and leftovers reveal how little we love Him.

Many Christians (who make up our churches) do not give what they give out of love and desire to please God but rather out of compulsion and habit. What are you giving to God? God is to receive the first fruits of our labor and effort not the fag ends of our days. We need to do things with excellence, not as our tired leftovers. The activities of the Lord need to take precedence over other things in our lives or the things of the world.237

When a church begins to hold back the best it has from God, it dishonors Him, and He removes Himself from that place. God warns us in His word in Revelation 2:5 when He says, "Remember therefore from whence thou art fallen, and repent, and do the first works; or else I will *come unto thee quickly, and will remove thy candlestick out of his place, except thou repent.*"238 We must understand that what God wants from His church is excellence not mediocrity; excellence in our activity, in our worship, in our service and in our praise. It seems that the world has taken over the hearts of God's people in America. Television, movies, electronic gadgets, music and fun have been substituted for a dynamic walk with God. If the Lord came into one of our worship services on any given Sunday would He tell us not to waste our time or would He rejoice in our commitment to Him? Would He see a self-centered, self-dependent and selfish congregation? When a church dishonors the King and the Kingdom it often ends in disaster. It begins a death spiral and ends in death and the only thing left that will salvage it is a restart.

---

237 Brent Kercheville, "Dishonoring God's Name," https://westpalmbeachchurchofchrist.com/old-testament/malachi/dishonoring-gods-name.html, February 4, 2007, accessed February 12, 2019.

238 Revelation 2:5 KJV.

Still other churches need to die because *they become a stumbling block to the world.* Mateen Elass says it best, "We, the half-hearted, half-converted Church, are often the greatest stumbling block to the appeal of the gospel, dull before the world not because of our holiness but our sin."239

The church at Pergamos had become a stumbling block. Revelation 2:14 says, "But I have a few things against thee, because thou hast there them that hold the doctrine of Balaam, who taught Balak to cast a stumbling block before the children of Israel, to eat things sacrificed unto idols, and to commit fornication." 240 Matthew Henry's commentary says, "There were some who taught that it was lawful to eat things sacrificed to idols, and that simple fornication was no sin; they, by an impure worship, drew men into impure practices, as Balaam did the Israelites."241

Barnes notes says, "And to commit fornication - Balaam taught this; and that was the tendency of the doctrines inculcated at Pergamos. On what pretense this was done is not said; but the church had regarded this in a lenient manner. So accustomed had the pagan world been to this vice, that many who had been converted from idolatry might be disposed to look on it with less severity than we do now,

---

239 Mateen Elass, *When the Church is a Stumbling Block to the Gospel!* Mateenelass.wordpress.com/2018/05/03/when-the-church-is-a-stumbling-block-to-the-gospel/, May 3, 2018, accessed February 11, 2019.

240 Revelation 2:14 KJV.

241 "Revelation 2," Matthew Henry's Commentary, accessed February 18, 2019, https://www.biblestudytools.com/commentaries/matthew-henry-complete/revelation/2.html

and there was a necessity of incessant watchfulness lest the members of the church should fall into it."[242]

The church at Pergamos had become a stumbling block because of the distortion of truth and active sin. There are many churches today in America that are preaching partial truth and sometimes no truth about the scripture. When a church deserts the truth of the Word of God, it needs to die because it becomes a stumbling block to those who need desperately to hear and respond to the truth of the Gospel!

Furthermore, other churches need to die because *they simply are not modeling a New Testament Church!* The New Testament church is our model. It is God's model, not man's! What we find in the Bible about the church is God's design for His church. It seems that the church has been perverted in many instances to meet the needs of the people who attend. It is not mine or yours to redesign or to remake. It is His church!

An anonymous writer said it like this, "In other words, watered-down, oversized, uncommitted, spectator church is much like a pasture filled with Astroturf—to a sheep it looks amazing, but there's not much to eat. Much of today's sheep are lost not because they wandered off, but because their unfit shepherds simply led them astray."

So, the big important question that must be answered is, "when is the death of a church a good thing?" Some churches get so sick that there is nothing left for them but death. However, often when death does come…new life can be realized through a restart.

---

242 "Revelation 2," Barnes' Notes, Accessed February 18, 2019, https://biblehub.com/commentaries/barnes/revelation/2.htm

Twelve Diseases that Kill a Church

Desertion Disease

The first sickness is what I call the Desertion Disease. This is when the church is consistently losing members and leaders and visitors never return a second time. These departures are often young people who were brought up in a Christian home in the church and has simply lost interest in the faith once professed. It could be a leader who leaves because they see nothing is happening that will advance the Kingdom of God or maybe they were not given an opportunity to make a difference in their work for the Lord. Or maybe it is a person who has suffered great loss, and no one came to their aide to help them in a real time of need. These and many other instances make up those who are departing the church, probably to never return. Church Revitalizers have compiled lists of those who seem to be leaving the church.

The newest category of those who are leaving the church are the *"Dones."* This is a term that researchers use to describe the individual that walks away from the church for various reasons. It may be because of the evidence of hypocrisy in the church, infighting in the church, the irrelevance of the church or simply no desire to be in church because of preoccupation with the world. They are clear that they are done with church. They may not necessarily say they are done with God or spiritual; things…just the church. Most of the "Dones" were once a part of the church and some were in leadership roles of the church. But, in the process of time they became dissatisfied with church as an institution. They see the local congregation as an entity that they have no need for. This seems to be a fast-growing category of unchurched people in America.

Then there is the category of the *"None's."* This is a group that will state clearly that the present-day church structure is not working for them, so they remove themselves from the organized religious group to do their own thing spiritually. Statistics show that one fourth of the population of the U.S. now identifies with the "None's." They refuse to identify with any given religion or religious group. Furthermore, 40% of those under the age of 30 identify as a "None." That is a frightening statistic because of the ramifications that places on a void of future generations of Christian leaders.

Like the "Done's" most of the "None's" grew up in church. In fact, statistics show that 78% of the None's grew up in the environment of a local church. What caused this to happen? Why have so many young people walked away from the church? What could be bad enough in the local church that would cause someone who grew up in church to want to walk away from it? Some stats show that the church is not helping them find solid answers to life's tough questions. Some say that they see and experience the hypocrisy in the church. Furthermore, it seems that the church has not stressed a relationship with Christ as much as it has stressed a set of rules and regulations. Still other stats say that these dropouts have not been properly connected to the church and its true message.

Much of the make-up of the "Done's" and the "None's" are millennials who have their own set of expectations and desires that affect the church. In most cases the church has made a dire mistake about what will lure these people back to church. Some churches have completely changed their music to ultra-contemporary with lights and a stage show that often dwarfs a secular rock concert. They seek to change everything about the church to bring those back that have departed.

In an article written by Rachel Held Evans (a Millennial herself) titled, *Want millennials back in the pews? Stop trying to make church 'cool,'* it says these many changes are sort of deflated. She says, "This, in the view of many churches, is what millennials like me want." She describes what churches are doing to lure the millennials back, **"Bass reverberates through the auditorium floor as a heavily bearded worship leader pauses to invite the congregation, bathed in the light of two giant screens, to tweet using #JesusLives.** The scent of freshly brewed coffee wafts in from the lobby, where you can order macchiato and purchase mugs boasting a sleek church logo. The chairs are comfortable, and the music sounds like something from the top of the charts. At the end of the service, someone will win an iPad." She goes on to says, "In response, many churches have sought to lure millennials back by focusing on style points: cooler bands, hipper worship, edgier programming, and impressive technology. Yet while these aren't inherently bad ideas and might in some cases be effective, they are not the key to drawing millennials back to God in a lasting and meaningful way. Young people don't simply want a better show. Trying to be cool might be making things worse."[243]

What are these who have departed really looking for? They are looking for authentic Christianity not hypocrisy. They are looking for a place to be taught authentic Christianity that makes a difference in their lives and the world around them. They are looking for a fellowship of believers where they can serve and live together in peace and harmony. Finally, they are looking for a place that is transparent and real.

---

243 Rachel Held Evans, "The Washington Post," https://www.washingtonpost.com/opinions/jesus-doesnt-tweet/2015/04/30/fb07ef1a-ed01-11e4-8666-a1d756d0218e_story.html?noredirect=on, April 30, 2015, Accessed Feb.11, 2019.

When a church is plagued with the departure syndrome often the only good solution is to die and restart!

Dissimilar Disease

The second illness is when the church is plagued with the *Dissimilar (Not-Like-Us) Disease.* This usually occurs when the church refuses to reach the community because it has changed, and the people are different from the membership. When this becomes reality, the church should close its doors and allow a restart to take place where the community will be loved and cared for.

In some cases when the community changes, the changes occur in cultural and racial ways. Sometimes its changes are age related or socioeconomic in nature. Usually when this takes place people begin to move out of the area or become reclusive and cease relating to neighbors and/or community. Most often when this occurs the church fails to transition with the community, and it becomes irrelevant and uncaring. When the church might reach out to the community it is usually through an invitation for the community to come to them instead of them going to the community, and the attempt to connect fails. At other times, when some segment of the community seeks to connect with the church, they feel unwelcomed in the church by the "people who are not like them."

Many churches in this syndrome are more concerned with protecting their way of doing things and their way of life than they are in reaching people who may be different than themselves. The results of all of this is that the church becomes void of a heart and ministry for the community and the church becomes ineffective as well as irrelevant to the community and is left to die a slow death. But it does not have to end this way...It should die with dignity and allow a restart church to develop in order to reach the community with the Gospel. When a vibrant, restart church begins it looks out for the interest of the community and not itself. This results in the community learning to once again trust the local church and find hope in the message that it preaches.

When a church refuses to reach its community with the Gospel, the death of that church is a good thing!

Aging-Out Disease

The third deadly illness of a church is when the church realizes it is experiencing the Aging-Out Disease. This is when the congregation ages to the point of uselessness. The people begin to die out because the church has failed to reach out to the community.

According to the Statistics of the U.S. Department of Health and Human Services' Agency for Aging, the population of the United States is aging at an enormous pace. Projections are that by the 2030 72.1 million people will be older than 65. That is double the number at that age in 2000. Furthermore, according to recent stats, the "Baby Boomer" age group is becoming the largest and oldest population group in America. The "Baby Boomer" generation seems to be living longer and more productive lives into old age than any other generation in American history. This is taking a toll on the local church. It seems that these aging groups, even though they are in good health, are relinquishing leadership and activity in the local church. Many are even deserting the church for retirement, travel and other activities. At any rate, they seem to simply end, in many cases, their role as a servant and leader in the church. This has been disastrous for the local church. Many churches are realizing the closure of their church because of the aging out of the congregation. Still, this can end with a great success if the church will die with dignity and allow a restart church to enter the picture.

The sad results of any church aging out is difficult to deal with but when it dies it can become a good thing if another church becomes a reality!

Looking Back Disease

The fourth and likely a fatal church illness is the "Looking Back Disease". This is when the church is constantly living in the past. It is when the church thinks more about how things used to be than about how things should be now. This church is not interested in living in the present to reach a needy world but is stuck in the past in likes, methods and programing. This is a time when the programs of the past that have ceased to be effective are continuing to be used with the same failed results. When a church gets stuck in the past it will surely experience certain death.

This syndrome is realized more in the church that has had real success in the past but for some reason the success has diminished and now the church is in decline. Usually, in this setting, the leaders are more apt to be stuck in the past. The dominate voice of this kind of church is, "we need to go back to the way things used to be." The sad reality is that it is not possible to go back to better days. All the church has is the present and the future. The past is forever gone! The past is dead and if the church is not careful the past will kill any future the church might have for the Kingdom.

What churches fail to realize is that when certain programs and efforts worked in the past they worked because at the time is was the right program. Conditions in the church, as in any living thing, change regularly, sometimes, almost daily. What worked in the 50's and 60's may not and probably will not work today. Culture is different. People are different. Times are different and it calls for a different approach and methodology.

Churches tend to fall into the "tradition" trap. The "we've never done it that way before" trap. But it is not necessarily the older and more traditional church that only falls prey to this illness. Even newer, more contemporary churches can become so traditional and so set on looking back at their beginning that it can become fatal.

A few years back, as a consultant, I was asked by the lead pastor of a church satellite system to visit one of his satellite churches. It seems that the church was not bringing enough tithes in to sustain itself and the lead pastor wanted me to see why. I visited the church two Sunday mornings and it became obvious as to what the problem was. The idea of tithing and giving had become an afterthought to the church. It was hardly mentioned in the worship time and the only time to give was at the end of the service as you were leaving. It seems that a box was placed at the exit door and you were simply told if you wanted to give you were to place the gift in the box as you leave the building.

I reported my findings to the lead pastor, and he asked me to come to a staff meeting where all the satellite pastors would be meeting so I could share my findings with them. When it came time for me to share the findings, I noticed at the other end of the table was the pastor from the satellite I visited. As I shared my findings, he became quite agitated. When I finished, he stated very loudly and pointedly: "You don't seem to understand that we are not a traditional church. We don't have the same old tradition of taking an offering during the service. It has become an offense to some people!"

Then I responded, "Yes, you are a traditional church that has developed its own tradition that will kill your church if you do not change it soon!" Of course, he argued his point and then I concluded the conversation by stating, "You have made your church a traditional church in the sense that you have created a tradition of not taking the offering but tacking it on the end of the service where there is no significance placed on giving." The lead pastor said, "How true. It seems that no matter how hard we try we all end up steeped in tradition."

You see, there is no real problem with "tradition" in the local church unless your tradition begins to govern how you will do church even if it kills the church. It is true that most churches who live in the past will not have much of a future. Sad to say, looking back and hanging on to tradition has killed many churches.

This is a very unnecessary condition for any church to put itself into. A church should focus on the future and the will of God - not the past. There are some churches that become so preoccupied with the past that they have no desire to look to the future. When this happens, it is a good thing when that church dies.

Insolvent Disease

A fifth terminal illness that can destroy a church is the Insolvent Disease. This is when the finances of the church (checking, savings, etc.) are all but depleted and the tithing has dropped because of a retired congregation. The simple fact is that Church financial issues can cause the death of a church. Sometimes the lack of funds comes because of a scarcity of people. It can come because of the congregation aging out and or losing personal income. It can come because of some people who withhold their giving because of anger with leadership and disagreement with church programs. At other times giving is not what it ought to be because the pastor is afraid to preach biblical messages about tithing. No apologies should ever be made for preaching the truth of God's Word. In fact, we have a mandate as preachers of the Gospel to do so. But whatever reason that may be present, it will kill the church.

In my experience as a consultant I have worked with churches where the giving was down to the point that the church could not pay its bills. After some investigation and digging, I have found that some people quit giving because they did not trust the leadership of the church for some reason. Pastors and leaders that cannot be legitimately trusted should be dealt with for trust to be restored in the fellowship.

At other times, I have found that people quit giving when they see that the budget is not followed and the spending in the church is out of control. There must be accountability while making and executing a church budget. This will build trust on the part of those who give and will insure them that the money is being spent as it should be. Sometimes people quit giving because too little of the budget is used to reach people, through evangelism, the community around the church, and other mission fields.

There are other times when finances fail in the church because the church takes on too much debt by building buildings they do not need or hiring additional staff that is unnecessary. This can be devastating to the financial wellbeing of a church and could cause the church to die because of a financial deficiency.

This is an unfortunate situation for a church to find itself in. The desire and the hopes of the people must surely be crushed by the reality of failing finances. It is, however, a time that the church can find solace in the fact that the death of their church could be the beginning of a good thing if another church is given the opportunity to take over. The death of that church could be a good thing for the Kingdom.

Sacred Cow Disease

The sixth deadly disease some churches face is the Sacred Cow Disease. This is when the church places certain things, ideas, buildings and programs etc. on a higher plain than the pure Gospel and service to God. These things become sacred cows or idols. The church during this time erects imaginary idols in their hearts to these sacred cows and consider those things untouchable and irrevocable. When this occurs, the future of the church is in jeopardy and will probably end in death. These idols or sacred cows take all kinds of shapes and identities. Thom Rainer says, "Sometimes they are called idols. Though the sacred cow terminology has its origins in Hinduism, it is commonly used in churches to describe those facets of church life that are given undue (and sometimes unbiblical) respect to the point that they cannot be changed."[244]

What are these sacred cows? What are these Golden Calves that really keep us from worshipping God and truly knowing Him? What are the things we worship or idolize? The idols can take almost any shape or form. They can be tangible in nature like objects and buildings. Pews, choir robs, musical instruments and even rooms in a building can become sacred cows. A major sacred cow in many rural churches is the cemetery. Often more money is spent on keeping up cemeteries for the dead than is spent on reaching the living with the Gospel.

They can take the form of intangible programs, procedures, meetings or even services. Worship styles, worship service times, the order of worship and even the hymnal used in worship can become idols in the church.

---

244 Tom Rainer, "15 Common Sacred Cows in Churches!," August 27, 2018, accessed February 18, 2019, https://thomrainer.com/2018/08/15-common-sacred-cows-churches/

Committee structure and how each should function can become an idol.

They can take the form of personal attitudes of likes or dislikes, expectations and traditions. Rainer refers to tradition as "those extra-biblical customs that become a way of life for many congregations. A tradition is neither inherently good nor bad. Its value or its distraction in a given church really depends on how members treat the traditions."[245] We humans have a knack for idolizing almost anything around us if it suits our personal self-centered wants and desires.

Some of the subtler idols can take the shape of various religious practices. This is seen often in using Jesus as insurance or a lucky rabbit's foot. This is all self-focused and far from being God centered. There are some theological idols or ideological philosophy that becomes idols. A good example is idolizing one translation of the Bible over another. One ideological idol that is prevalent in the more contemporary church today is the idea of tolerance and inclusion and still another is the concept of consumerism in the church. Both concepts are self-centered and usually with the exclusion of God from the equation.

People can become sacred cows in the church as well. This is seen in the sacred cow of the patriarchal or matriarchal family. They have risen to the roll of power broker in the church. Usually in these situations the church will not attempt anything the power broker does not want to attempt. Thus, they become an idol, sacred cow or golden calf in the church.

How do you break from sacred cows? How do you destroy these idols? There must be a change in the heart of the local church if it will survive. However, it is said that "the

---

245 Ibid.

only people who want change are babies with wet diapers." How true that is in many churches. In fact, many of them would rather die than change and die is what they should do!

Often these sacred cows, these idols have been erected long before some members ever attended, so how do you deal with them? It is for sure that a "bull in the china shop" approach will not work. There must be respect for the history of the church and there must be patience to overcome the past. However, it is tough to face the truth that most churches will not change, instead they choose to die, and the death of that church can become a blessing for the future as another church can step in and reach the community.

Rut Disease

A seventh illness is the Rut Disease. Some people call it the "we've never done it that way before syndrome." This is when the rut (route we travel) becomes more important than the will of God. The late great evangelist Vance Havner said, "Many people are in a rut and a rut is nothing but a grave- with both ends kicked out." So, it is for the church. It must be clearly understood that a rut is a place of death for the church!

"Rut living leads to rote religion. If you don't know what else to do, you resign yourself to checking the box and going through the motions. You're stuck. You can't go back to your pre-Christian life and securing victory seems impossible."[246] The danger of being in a rut is that it can lead to death.

---

246 Rick Thomas, "Four People Types Who Get Stuck In a Rut," *Rick Thomas Net.,* accessed February 18, 2019, https://rickthomas.net/four-people-types-who-get-stuck-in-a-rut-and-cant-get-out/

Sometimes the rut the church finds itself in was a long time in the making. Some "religious" practices seem to foster living in a rut. Notice I said "religious" not Christian practices. I am convinced that the rut of religion is the most dangerous rut the church faces. Our religious forms and practices (even though sometimes not even Christian in nature) often hamper the growth and wellbeing of the local church.

Jim Bell says "Instead of seeking to get out of the rut, we just say, well others are in the same rut. It can't be us, because they are worse than we are in numbers and we take some pleasure that other churches are suffering like our church and argue that it is not our fault and that it must be attributed to this "new generation" of millennials who have no sense of dedication or commitment. Our refusal to get out of the rut we're in as churches is what the new generation is seeing."247 The church must decide that it and the heart of its ministry must be in sync with the heart and will of God. When a church gets stuck in a spiritual rut, for whatever reason, it can be disastrous.

Sometimes the church can get stuck in the rut of religiosity to the point of forgoing community and spirituality. Young adults today are not looking for religion. They see it for what it is: hypocrisy, self-centeredness and mere rhetoric. They refuse to get in that rut. Their desire is to follow Christ not some form of religion.

The history of the Christian church in the 20th century was full of great success. Christianity was booming and churches were filled in every Sunday service. Because of the great success, the church began to overhaul its program and

247 Jim Bell, "Churches Stuck in a Rut," Jim Bell's Jottings, May 26, 2015 accessed February 19, 2019,
 https://pastorjimbell.wordpress.com/2015/05/26/churches-stuck-in-a-rut-or-transformed/

its structure. It began to look more like a business than a place of worship. Some churches even employed Business Administrators who often had more to do with the day to day functions of the church than the pastoral leadership. The church became more organized into denominations and took on the appearance of an institution. Everything became professional about the church. This is what the youth of our day see when they look at the modern church. They see a church that is stuck in an institutional rut that it is having a difficult time getting out of. The church that cannot find a way out of that rut will surely end in death and that may not be a bad thing.

Churches must get out of their rut and be transformed and become transformational. They must seek a new vision and mission from God. They must begin with new purpose and meaning. Their mission must not be solely the maintenance of a building, programs or polity but evangelism, discipleship, and missions must take priority. The church must get out of its rut and begin to once again connect with the people in their community and area. They must once again seek to carry out the mission and calling of Jesus Christ that has been placed on it. Paul said in Romans 12:1-2 "I beseech you therefore, brethren, by the mercies of God, that ye present your bodies a living sacrifice, holy, acceptable unto God, which is your reasonable service. And be not conformed to this world: but be ye transformed by the renewing of your mind, that ye may prove what is that good, and acceptable, and perfect, will of God."[248] That is the Word of God for the church that is in a rut today! The institutional church of our day must not remain stuck in a rut. If it does it will surely die and maybe that is not a bad thing.

---

248 Romans 12: 1-2 KJV.

Purposelessness Disease

The eighth fatal illness a church can die from is the Purposelessness Disease. This is when the church has no spiritual direction. It no longer understands its mission, or its purpose and it wanders aimlessly in its existence without a vision. A vision from God for the church can be defined as God's plan for a church at a particular time. We have discussed the importance of a clear, God given, vision in past chapters, but it is important to understand that without that vision, purpose and mission, the church is deathly ill. Dr. D. W. Ekstrand said, "Many churches are barely surviving today because they have no vision – they've lost sight of their purpose. Over the years I have had the opportunity to consult with several churches in varying degrees of dysfunction, and I am often reminded of the need for church leaders to keep their eye on the goal. The work of ministry can easily distract us from the priorities of ministry, and when it does it can overwhelm us. What each of us needs to do from time to time is "refocus" on the things that really matter."[249] He goes on to say that the three great priorities/purposes of the church are: (1) Love God – Up reach, (2) Love the Church – In reach, and (3) Love the World – Outreach. If the church tries to exist without these three purposes, it will never succeed.

Understanding the purpose and mission of the church gives substance to the work of the church. It gives direction to the leaders and the congregants. It provides the enthusiasm that is necessary for a church to attempt and accomplish great things for God.

---

249 Dr. D. W. Ekstrand, *Purpose of the Church,* "The Transformed Soul," accessed February 19, 2019,
http://www.thetransformedsoul.com/additional-studies/miscellaneous-studies/purpose-of-the-church

In reality, a very high proportion of those attending church on any given Sunday have forgotten or have never had a clue as to what it is all about. Church seems to have become "old hat" to many who attend. They attend out of habit, not purpose. They come for tradition not mission. Many would have to admit they do not understand the purpose or mission of the New Testament church. "Week by week they attend services in a special building and go through their particular, time-honored routine, but give little thought to the purpose of what they are doing. The Bible talks about the "the bride of Christ" but the church today seems like a ragged Cinderella. It needs to reaffirm the non-negotiable, essential elements God designed for it to be committed to."250

Instead of being driven by a purpose, mission and vision, the church seems to be more isolated than ever before in history. All the modern technological amenities the church possesses today has helped to isolate the congregation from the world and the purpose and mission has been turned inward to meet the needs of self-absorbed members who have no sense of real Christian community. Often the church has sold out to theatrics, rather than real worship. In many instances, this has painted a picture of the church to the surrounding world as an exclusive club that cannot be penetrated by the average sinner needing a savior. When a church gets to the point of trying to live with no real purpose or a distorted modernized worldly purpose, it is destined to death. It may be later rather than sooner but the church without a Biblical, spiritual purpose will die and that is a good thing.

---

250 Phil Layton, *What is the Purpose of the Church?*, "Faithlife Sermons," January 20, 2008, accessed February 19, 2019, https://sermons.faithlife.com/sermons/70902-what-is-the-purpose-of-the-church.

Systemic Sin Disease

The ninth and one of the deadliest illnesses the church can contract is the Systemic Sin Disease. This is when systemic sin has taken over the church fellowship and becomes a thing to tolerate rather than something to correct. When this happens, it may be time for that church to die.

Jack Wellman says in his blog, "When a church begins to look the other way when there are members within the body living in serious sins, such as adultery, corruption, drunkenness, drug abuse, violence in the home, or any other such thing as these, then that church has failed to follow Jesus' admonition for church discipline. In Matthew 18 we read about the church for the very first time and it's regarding church discipline."[251] When sin is identified in the church body, it must be dealt with or it will fester and cause an illness that is often irreversible. It's much like an infection in the human body. If not treated it will affect the entire body and can even result in death.

A perfect example of this is found in Acts 5 when Ananias and Sapphira lied about what they had given after they sold some property. Peter said they lied to the Holy Spirit and the scripture records that when they lied each fell dead. There is example after example in the Bible about sin and the tolerance of that sin in the church. Just as the church in the New Testament dealt with known sin in the fellowship the church today must not disregard sin when it is detected. The motivation for dealing with the sin should always be restoration and repentance.

---

251 Jack Wellman, *What Causes Churches To Die Or Close?* July 3, 2017, accessed February 12, 2019,
https://www.patheos.com/blogs/christiancrier/2017/07/03/what-causes-churches-to-die-or-close/

It is a dangerous thing for the church to ignore "sin in the camp" because it will usually have disastrous results. E.L. Bynum writes, "One drop of contaminated water will contaminate a whole reservoir of pure water, but one drop of pure water will not purify a reservoir of contaminated water. One deadly cancer cell can be disastrous to an entire body of healthy cells. "A little leaven leavened the whole lump."252 This seems to be a real problem in the modern-day church because of the overemphasis that has been placed on tolerance in our culture. However, when sin is tolerated and even condoned in the local church, the church is falling head long into a death spiral which will be next to impossible to escape from. The Bible has high standards for the local church and when these standards are ignored God will take His hand off the church in question. God will withdraw his hand of blessing from a church that tolerates known sin.

Some statistics show that there is a moral crisis taking place, not only in our country, but also within the confines of the local church. Dale Robbins says it this way, "Across our land, many professing Christians are practicing shameful lifestyles that are little different than those of unbelievers. Sins of adultery, fornication, drunkenness, drug abuse (just to name a few) are rampant among those who claim to be followers of Jesus."253 He goes on to say that much of the tolerance for sin in our churches are magnified because of a lack of preaching against sin from our pulpits. When a church fails to speak out against the sins of our present-day culture, it

---

252 E. L. Bynum, *Sin in the Church and What to do About It,"* accessed February 20, 2019,
http://www.beaconmbc.com/articles/sininthechurch.htm

253 Dale A. Robbins, *When Sin Persists in the Church,* accessed February 11, 2019, http://www.victorious.org/pub/sin-persists-church-168.

seems to compromise its standards and as a result the church becomes powerless to confront the world as it is.

It seems that our churches are inundated with people who profess to be Christians, but they live in a continuous state of immorality, perverse lifestyles and sin. Let's be honest, those who live like there is no consequence to their sinful lifestyle simply may not be Christians at all. Jesus made that clear in Matthew 7:21 when He said, "Not everyone who says to me, 'Lord, Lord,' shall enter the kingdom of heaven, but he who does the will of My Father in heaven."[254] Those are some straight forward words that the church needs desperately to heed. One anonymous writer said it this way "The Church can exist in a world of sin, but it cannot prosper when a world of sin is brought into the Church. A ship in the water is fine, but water in the ship can be disastrous."

When a church contracts the illness of Systemic Sin in its fellowship it is headed for certain death and it should die before it brings dishonor to the King and the Kingdom.

Coup Disease

The tenth illness that plagues some churches is what I refer to as the Coup Disease. This disease takes place when a hijacker tries to take over that which belongs to someone else, to use it for their own ends. Cars get hijacked. Businesses get hijacked. Airplanes get hijacked. Ships get hijacked. Even churches can get hijacked. This is when the people hijack the church from its original purpose and govern by human intellect rather than by Gods wisdom. In actuality, the people steal the church from God! How is that possible? The church has been hijacked by a culture that is more occupied with self-interest than worship of a Holy God. It

---

254 Matthew 7:21 KJV.

has been stolen by the philosophy that people must be entertained in order to feel like a part of the church.

A funny story I read about the Lone Ranger and Tonto depicts how subtle these hijackings can occur. "The Lone Ranger and Tonto went camping in the desert. After they got their tent all set up, both men fell sound asleep. Some hours later, Tonto wakes the Lone Ranger and says, "Kemosabe, look towards sky, what you see?" The Lone Ranger replies, "I see millions of stars." "What that tell you?" asked Tonto. The Lone Ranger ponders for a minute then says, "Astronomically speaking, it tells me there are millions of galaxies and potentially billions of planets. Time wise, it appears to be approximately a quarter past three in the morning. Theologically, the Lord is all-powerful, and we are small and insignificant. Meteorologically, it seems we will have a beautiful day tomorrow. What's it tell you, Tonto?" "You dumber than buffalo chip. Someone stole the tent."

Jesus said in Matthew 16:18, ""I will build My church, and the gates of Hell shall not prevail against it."[255] These words of Jesus are clear indication that anyone who tries to hijack the church is in for a rude awakening. Still, it is an alarming fact that in many church settings the church has been stolen! Who has stolen the church? Those who have decided that they know more about the nature, work and purpose of the church. Those who have decided that human wisdom and human intellect trumps the wisdom and will of a Holy God who gave His Son to die for the church. We must understand clearly that the church is not ours. It is not a matriarch or patriarch's or any powerful family's possession. It is Gods church, and no one will ever take it from Him.

Many churches have been taken over by people who have made it their own. They see themselves as possessors of

---

255 Matthew 16:18 KJV.

the church. It has become theirs because of family ties or longevity of membership. They see it as theirs because of the financial investment they have mad in it in the past. One instance of the church being stolen from God is seen in a church that I worked with to help get a pastor. The church is in a country setting and has very few people to draw from. It is a typical "family chapel." The controlling family was the family of the former and now deceased pastor that had been there for 42 years. The matriarch and clear ruler (not leader) of the church was the former pastor's wife. She called the shots. She made all the decisions. She controlled the finances and she decided who would preach in the pulpit. However, they asked me to help them find a pastor. The young man I recommended to them passed the matriarchs scrutinizing and he became the pastor. He began to preach the Gospel and people began to be saved. Baptisms were up and the matriarch began to lose her power. She was finally outnumbered and decided to leave and all but one of her family members left with her. The one who stayed behind began to work hard to take possession of the church and he ultimately took over. In a final meeting of the church as the pastor was being ousted the pastor recommended that they seek answers to the problem in the church over control from the Bible. This power broker declared…" We are not going to bring the Bible into this discussion." The pastor resigned and left.

In the days following the congregation that had been grown from 20 to 65 members under the pastor's leadership was now down to 12. The power broker had stolen the church from God, but God wrote Ichabod over the door posts and the church died a painful death.

This same scenario is taking place all over the church world. It is happening in small and large churches. It happens when the truth of God's Word is distorted to contradict the teachings and life of Jesus. It happens when men's personal egos get in the way of Gods ultimate will for his church. It happens when a personal agenda replaces the agenda of God in the church and one's personal interests take the place of the plan of God. It happens when someone or a group of people think they know better than God and refuse to follow Gods plan and instead make the church a human organization rather than a blood bought body of believers. When the church is stolen by anyone…it will not have long to live and rightfully so.

Abandonment Disease

The eleventh illness that can plague a church and become fatal is the Abandonment Disease. This is when the church abandons the truth of the Word of God and begins to allow human teaching, intellect, ideas and ideals to take over the local body of believers rather than focusing on the Word of God for its direction and insight. When a church leaves the true Word of God it leaves behind all the basics and principles of the Christian life. When the Bible is neglected or negated principles of evangelism, discipleship and any other Christian principles are in danger of being left behind. "Church leaders and members must ask themselves, "Why would God keep a church alive that does not preach the Bible and does not evangelizing?" I can't come up with a good answer to that, but churches that do not "Go!" (Matt 28:18-20), typically do not grow. Churches that don't rely on expository, verse by verse preaching, for the most part, neglect to unleash the power that is in the gospel."256

---

256 Jack Wellman, *What Causes Churches To Die Or Close?*, "Christian Crier," July 3, 2017, accessed February 18, 2019, https://www.patheos.com/blogs/christiancrier/2017/07/03/what-causes-churches-to-die-or-close/

Our modern American culture is slipping further and further away from Christian principles. The pressure to abandon Biblical truth is coming from many directions. This is a growing problem and the pressure will grow greater and greater against the church that holds to Biblical truth and will not waver. Many churches, that for decades, held a high view of scripture seem to be acquiescing to pressure to step away from scripture. Standing on truth is mocked and even scorned in this present-day culture and some churches are falling into the trap of compromising the Word of God. Lifestyles that are immoral and unscriptural are becoming more prevalent and public and this has brought pressure on churches to be more tolerant even to the point of compromise. There seems to be a tendency in some churches to try to reach the youth of our day at the expense of the truth. Some churches are even taking the position that the Old Testament teachings are no longer seen as relevant for the individual life or the life of the contemporary church.

The frightening thing that seems to be missed by those who are abandoning the Word of God for the cultural norms is that this demand is demonic and ungodly. The pressure to be a relaxed Christian who does not take the Bible seriously is mounting in our society and is affecting many churches. Those who believe and seek to live by the truth of God's word are considered the dangerous people in society. The tragedy is that this could possibly lead to persecution of those who seriously seek to be Christian.

A real element that is present in this abandonment of the Bible is seen in the fact that many younger Christians who, I believe, really do love Jesus, have not been taught a high view of the Bible and they see much of it as insignificant. This view of Scripture has been instilled in them by the culture and educators who do not believe in the validity of the Bible. Amid this dramatic cultural shift, the church must remain committed to the Word of God as the ultimate truth to live by. If it fails to do so, it should die before it becomes a stumbling block to a lost world.

First Love Disease

The twelfth and final illness that is affecting the church is the First Love Disease. Jesus said in Revelation 2:4 to the church at Ephesus, "But I have this against you, that you have left your first love." 257   This is when the church has replaced their love for Jesus with their love for themselves.

The Bible makes it clear that our love for God should take precedent over any other love we might have. But when we leave our "first love" we divert that love from the main object of our affection (God) to some secondary entity and that entity takes the place of God in our lives. A church can leave its "first love." The Bible makes it clear that we must Love God with all our heart. We must love Him with all our soul. We must love Him with all our mind. There can be no substitutes.

When a church leaves its "first love" the Word of God and the importance of prayer seem to be lessened. The churches existence depends on the instruction from the Bible and the times it spends in prayer seeking the face of God. However, when the church leaves its "first love" those basic activities are no longer that important to the body.

Furthermore, when a church leaves its "first love" people forget the rich blessings that God has showered on them and their commitment to giving of themselves, their time, talents and money become unimportant. As believers in the church we understand the grace of God and the demands that our walk with God places on our lives. We understand that grace has been given to us, but grace must also be given

---

257 Revelation 2:4 KJV.

by us to others. When a church leaves its "first love" it usually places a greater importance on receiving approval from our broken world rather than being approved of by God. Churches that have left "first love" scoffs at rejection by the world and would do anything to be accepted by the world.

Jesus gave a remedy to that church. He said "remember." Remember where you wee as a church and where God brought you to. He said "repent." Tell Him of your sin. Agree with Him about your sin. Confess it and turn from it. Then He said "return." Return to where you fell. Go back to the beginning. Go back and begin again. What great advice! But what happens if you fail to follow His warning? He says he will "come unto thee quickly, and will remove thy candlestick out of his place, except thou repent."258 He will take His hand off the church and it will die!

Conclusion

All these illnesses in the local church can be deadly and most often are! Some churches are plagued with more than one of these diseases. Some have many of these diseases. In fact, some of these diseases may result in other of the diseases being contracted.

It is not a happy thought to think about a church dying, but sometimes, it becomes a necessity for the Kingdom of God to be advanced. It becomes a necessity for a new church to take the place of the sick church so that those affected by the church can be given the hope that is found only in Jesus Christ as they are confronted by His Gospel.

---

258 Revelation 2:5 KJV.

Chapter Sixteen
Birthing a Legacy for Restarting Churches

Do nothing from selfish ambition or conceit, but in humility count others more significant than yourselves. Let each of you look not only to his own interests, but also to the interests of others. Have this mind among yourselves, which is yours in Christ Jesus, who, though he was in the form of God, did not count equality with God a thing to be grasped, but emptied himself, by taking the form of a servant, being born in the likeness of men. And being found in human form, he humbled himself by becoming obedient to the point of death, even death on a cross. Therefore, God has highly exalted him and bestowed on him the name that is above every name, so that at the name of Jesus every knee should bow, in heaven and on earth and under the earth, and every tongue confess that Jesus Christ is Lord, to the glory of God the Father.259

When the Lord comes to take you home to glory, how would you like to be remembered? As a Church Revitalizer what will others say about your willingness to revitalize churches. What are the words you would like to have engraved on your memorial stone? Before his death, Thomas Jefferson—the third president of the United States—gave instructions on what he wanted on his grave site. Jefferson wanted an obelisk with the following engraved on it:

> Here was buried Thomas Jefferson
> Author of the Declaration of American Independence
> Of the Statute of Virginia for religious freedom and
> Father of the University of Virginia.

Very few Church Revitalizers will have such grand notions that we will have a memorial stone with such grandiose words being said about us. Think about this as your final reminder of service to the Lord:

---

259 Philippians 2:3-11(ESV).

> Here lies a Church Revitalizer
> A man who was devoted to the saving of declining churches
> The world never knew him but the Church thanked him.
> The Lord called him to the hard task of restoring His chosen work
> Loyal to the community, fervent in his message, zealous for the church.
> He left an indelible legacy. Always faithful.

Would not that be a wonderful statement about the legacy you made as a Church Revitalizer working in restarts? It would represent as a minister and Church Revitalizer an ordinary life lived well with the grace of the Lord and what a difference one's life made in a community. Some pastors are more concerned with avoiding leaving a negative legacy than with creating a positive one. Churches all over the United States are beginning to catch the call of the Lord to leave a legacy through restarting. What are the words you would like etched on your memorial stone? I pray that all over North America and the world for that matter, there will be tens of thousands Church Revitalizers who have saved the church through revitalization and have left a legacy of saving churches. I seek to inspire you and help you to become more intentional in your church revitalization efforts.

Five Initial Ways to Leave a Legacy

Great church leaders ten years ago are now often viewed a decade later as a passing fade. That is such a shame but shows just how fickle we are as individuals. Even great churches may not remember very long your results as a Christian leader, because next year there's always another goal for the church to reach regardless if you are there or not. We live and work in an atmosphere of "what have you done for me lately" church environment. Church revitalization is a demanding career choice. It is a potent reminder that leaving a legacy as a Church Revitalizer takes intentional effort. I believe that great legacies are left through these individuals you have poured your life into as a minister and they have responded in ways that have been a blessing for the church you serve. Your legacy initially is who you have equipped, trained, and deployed for the work of the Lord. Your legacy will not be big budgets and bigger buildings.

Have you ever thrown a stone into a lake and watched it cause a circular ripple that went out from its epicenter? Think about the legacy you could leave as a Church Revitalizer and the positive impact it could make. Your ripple as a revitalizer goes far beyond your time of service. Far beyond the countless hours of inspiration and service. May your ripple cast a graceful shadow on the mission of revitalization you have given as a leader. Legacies are lasting ripples which continue on forever. It is something we do not initially set out to accomplish, and yet during our journey - if we are lucky - we create such a positive legacy that others are blessed even after we are gone on to glory. Here are five legacy ripples you can take initially:

Place People Above Bottom Lines

Many lay church leaders emphasize the financial bottom line as the church begins to rapidly decline believing that if they could just get rid of their present pastor and replace him with a new one that their troubles would be over. That is simply not true. In fact, though most lay leaderships in dying churches will never admit it, they should be shouldering a large portion of the blame for the current state of their church. Unless your pastor has been exposed for grievous sin and has hurt the reputation of the congregation, usually the state of the church has more to do with the members unwillingness to get to work for the Kingdom of God. Yet, if you as the church restarter are going to lead your church to renewal through a restart, you must place a high emphasis on relationship with the present participants while developing further connections with future ones. The results are critical but far too much focus has been placed by declining churches on nickels, numbers and noses. Interestingly enough, if you do a good job as the church restarter in this one arena, your membership and your revitalization team will not remember if you achieved your entire list of revitalization goals. A thousand-day journey is a long time to scrutinize every little it and tittle. What the renewing church will be able to recall with fondness is how you connect to them, and how they responded to your care and ministry. The *"how are you doing my friend?"* leader achieves more in a restart.

Go Do Not Call

So many pastors live in a disconnect world today. They have locked themselves in an office and have hunkered down so the rank and file member who needs them feels they are inaccessible. Many a pastor of a dying church has told me just how often he has called his church members with no success. I have one in the area I serve that intentionally builds barriers so as not to get involved in his membership's lives. His church has declines from one hundred and thirty to about forty-five. He is always saying at least he tried. Finally, in frustration one day with our conversation I asked if he ever went to visit his members and his response was that he sees them every Sunday so it is not needed. Church members in a restart need their restarter to connect with them in person. No matter where you live across our country, the pace of our world is accelerated. Pastors do not intentionally slide into the electronic touch world, but it is happening. Some I justified, most is not. You will never leave a legacy as a Church Revitalizer if your ministry is supported by a barrage of emails to your membership with little or no connection to prospects and members face to face. We live in an experiential world and that means you must go and not call. Your positive legacy can only be perpetuated by positive human interaction with your community.

Exemplify the Behavior You Desire for the Future

Personify the behavior and conduct which you desire for the future of the church restart. The church restarter needs to model any and all behaviors he desires to become part of the revitalized church. It is the only way these behaviors will last. Church leaders and church members learn more from seeing you lead than they do hearing your lead. That is why revitalizers need to get out of their offices and into the streets making connections with members and potential prospects. How you act in business meetings or deacon meetings will display proper behaviors you want to last. Church restarters intentionally model the behaviors they would like to see the membership embody.

Dictate Less, Train and Empower More

Lead your lay leadership to embrace risk in a church restart. What do you really have to lose? Revitalizing a dying church takes a degree of speculation and improvising along the way. Leading a restart requires the Church Revitalizer and lay leadership to hold their possessions lightly. By that I

mean they are willing to open up the church to new
ways and new ideas even when they are not the norm
for the older lay leader. The restart needs to control
less and empower the membership more. Become the
ministers of "yes" over remaining the ministers of
"no," the work of renewal will become more
enjoyable if you do. Additionally, you will
demonstrate to your leaders that trying is preferred
even if we fail together. Creating a climate where
members risk for future life is commendable. Allow
them to make decisions without you. While that is
scary you might find they break up your ideas and
make them better while dividing the actions steps
among themselves and in the end, you just lead.
Would not that be wonderful? Teach your lay leaders
to make intelligent gambles and improvise along the
way.

Be There and Make the Investment in Them

I have a group of church revitalization leaders in
which I invest monthly. Additionally, I have a group
of seven men I pour into weekly for the purpose of
raising up strong leaders who could take over what I
do when I no longer can do it. There is a growing
group in which invest in through our national church
revitalization magazine, *The Church Revitalizer*. This
large group seems to be doubling every two years and
stands right now about thirty thousand subscribers.
Thirty of the nation's best leaders in church
revitalization write for the magazine. They are also
making an investment. Here is the point we are there.
We are not phoning it in but in the trenches right
with you. Every Church Revitalizer must do the same.
The church restarter must be there and make the daily
investment in the revitalization team they are leading.
You must help them grow into better leaders,

disciples, and begin setting the example for others to visualize how they also might leave a legacy. Help you members become more successful as teachers, and leaders. Disciple them and help them explode with possibilities. You being there now will allow them to leave a legacy later. Impacting the church at large for the benefit of revitalizing churches is why we are there and you are there. If not, it should be. Those investments in others will allow the legacy to be carried further into the future. I invest in men who want to develop in ways I have a passion. I am not investing in them with things someone ese could do and should do. Because my time is valuable and my schedule crammed full, these individuals I am investing are smart enough to never waste my time. They realize the investment being made and they appreciate the sacrifice and the investment in them. But in reality, someone did that for me some thirty years ago and I am paying it forward just like they did. Leave an enduring legacy through your church restart.

Your legacy which you pass on to others is all you have got. It is the one thing you will give freely to others for the betterment of the Christian world. I love to write. While authors might dream of riches and fame deservedly so, writers must write. A true writer longs to leave behind a piece of themselves, something that withstands the test of time and is passed down for generations. That is what you are doing as a church restarter and revitalizer. Think about how you would like to be remembered by other believers within the church you restart. Now get busy and act on those thoughts. Give the devil a run for his money by creating something meaningful in your church restart that will outlive you as the restarter. The embodiment of influence is to leave a great legacy that lives on after you are gone. Christian leaders as well as churches feel better in the face of death if they are a part of something that will live on after them. Having a

positive impact on future generations can help fulfill that
need.

Churches Leaving a Legacy Through a Restart

Some churches wait too long before they will
consider working in the area of church revitalization and
renewal. Once critical mass has been lost and has dwindled to
below fifty adult active members it is very difficult to develop
the necessary momentum needed to begin the process of
revitalization. Stephen Gray and Franklin Dumond in their
book *Legacy Churches* state: "One of the main factors limiting a
church's growth potential is age. Both the ages of the
congregants as well as the age of the church itself play a role
in its limitations. Research supports the fact that the longer a
church is around and the older the average age of a
congregation gets, the more it settles into a routine and loses
steam."260

When this happens usually one of two things happen.
The first is that the church gets mad and looks for someone
to blame while wanting to hang on a little longer in hope of a
miracle. Those stiff backs stand up and defy someone to help
them unless they do it their way which currently is not
working. The second and the best way is to deed over the
church and its facilities to the local association of churches
which can put either a Church Revitalizer or a Church Planter
in place. Obviously, the better solution is to save the former
church over merely taking over the facilities by a church
planter who will not keep a legacy but close everything down
only keeping the facility as a real estate transfer. Actually, it is
steeple jacking but we have talked about that in a previous
chapter.

---

260 Stephen Gray and Franklin Dumond, *Legacy Churches* (Chicago:
ChurchSmart Resources) 2009, Pg.31.

A restart leaves a legacy for future generations. Think about it for a moment that there are hundreds of saints who through the ages sacrificed for that church to be located in that community. They attended regularly. They tithed to the church. They followed the ministers the church called to lead them. These godly Christians were making a legacy and leaving a legacy. It is shameful when a church is not remembered for all that it has done for the decades of service. It is a best practice to have a closing of the church and deeding the property over to the association service which allows for a dignified closure and transition from rapidly declining church to new church revitalization effort. There are some groups which will place a church planter into the mix and want you to deed your facilities over to a national agency, which just might later sell it to recouped its cost of investing in your church for three years. The preferred choice is giving it to the local association which can put a restarter in place or place multiple plants into the property and therefore leave a legacy for the former church. One such church is right in Orlando which had declined to about sixteen people. It gave the facilities over to the local association and today it is known as the Greater Orlando Baptist Association *Rosemount Outreach Center* with three churches meeting weekly in the facilities and around two hundred people now on campus each week.

Does your church need to consider and recognize that the existing ministry is approaching an end? There is a procedure that will allow you to start down a new path of church revitalization and renewal to have lasting impact and reach your changing community. This Leaving a Legacy Church Revitalization Model may be the very next step for your church to consider. What looks to be a crisis can really be an opportunity provided by God to allow your church to do something glorious for the Kingdom of God.261

The Church Restart Legacy Synopsis

We all want to leave our mark on the Christian world and to know that our life really mattered. The legacy synopsis is that of contributing to future generations while putting a mark of the future. Church members desire to leave a legacy because they want to feel that their life mattered. Here is a quick overview of a legacy church revitalization model and the conditions for it to be considered:

> To be considered for a Leaving a Legacy Church Revitalization model the local church will allow a Church on Site Assessment to be conducted in order to determine the feasibility of such an agreement.

> The potential Leaving a Legacy Church will agree to a change in leadership and decision-making makeup.

> The Leaving a Legacy Church will approve by vote of the church in an officially called business meeting to deed over all properties and assets to an Association or church revitalization network for the purpose of placing a Church Revitalizer into the revitalization project.

> The Leaving a Legacy Church Revitalization model will call for the local church to allow the revitalization association or network to develop a Church

---

261 If you have come to the realization that it is time to consider a restart for your church, we have a plan and want to talk with you about a process for planting a new church right in your community. To explore this Leaving a Legacy Church Revitalization Model, contact Dr. Tom Cheyney, Founder & Directional Leader of Renovate National Church Revitalization Group at Tom@Renovateonference.org.

Revitalization Assistance Team which will work side by side the Church Revitalizer for the purpose of support and counsel during the revitalization project.

This model is in most cases a last-ditch effort to allow the church an opportunity to seek revitalization and renewal before it collapses and loses its ability to maintain critical mass. Many a church simply waits until it is too late and can only use this model for an effort of revitalization. If you and your church are in this state of rapid decline please take the time to contact us at the Renovate Group and allow us to come along side of you for the purpose of leaving a legacy for the Lord through the effort of restarting your church fresh and a new.

Building One's Legacy as a Church Revitalizer

For the Church Revitalizer, leaving a Christ honoring legacy is possibly the most powerful thing you can do in ministry because it allows you to have influence well into the future, even after you are out of the pastorate and into retirement. I have many pastors who though they are retired still provide great assistance to the work of revitalization. Your willingness to sacrifice for long term viability of the local church, allowed for it to regain strength, continue to be productive for the Lord as a witness in the community, and more prized to the Lord than it was previously by being in decline. That old church about to die has been replaced by a glorious turnaround as it has become a new and fresh example of a growing church. For the Church Revitalizer, by thinking legacy it enables you to see the long-term view over the short term thus helping the church to regain its anointing and power. Paul the apostle, says:

> *Do nothing from selfish ambition or conceit, but in humility count others more significant than yourselves. Let each of you look not only to his own interests, but also to the interests of*

others. Have this mind among yourselves, which is yours in Christ Jesus, who, though he was in the form of God, did not count equality with God a thing to be grasped, but emptied himself, by taking the form of a servant, being born in the likeness of men. And being found in human form, he humbled himself by becoming obedient to the point of death, even death on a cross. Therefore, God has highly exalted him and bestowed on him the name that is above every name, so that at the name of Jesus every knee should bow, in heaven and on earth and under the earth, and every tongue confess that Jesus Christ is Lord, to the glory of God the Father.262

What will be your legacy as a Church Revitalizer when the Lord calls you home? It was **Benjamin Franklin who said, "If you would not be forgotten as soon as you are dead, either write something worth reading or do something worth writing."** A legacy is what you leave with the church members and individuals you are closest to after you are gone. It is what survives after you die. How will you be remembered? It is the impact you made in this life while you were here.

Every Church Revitalizer Leaves a Legacy

The question is not if you will leave a legacy as a pastor and Church Revitalizer, because every one of us will leave either a positive or a negative legacy. The question is what kind of legacy you are going to leave. Have you ever considered your legacy? Whether you realize it or not, you are writing one with your life. Have you ever considered how you will be remembered when you die? Because you will be remembered. How will you influence others? Because you are an influence. Have you ever taken a moment to consider the legacy that the Lod Jesus left after he departed from this

---

262 Philippians 2:3-11(ESV).

earth? Let's look at the one man who left the greatest legacy of any man that has ever walked this earth, our Lord Jesus.

Characteristics of Jesus' Legacy

In the Epistle to the Philippians, Paul was speaking to the church which was in Philippi. He was giving them instances of how they were to live and particular characteristics they were to have. He explained the reason we are supposed to do this is because these were the characteristics that Jesus had in His life. They were the things that caused Him to leave the legacy He left. *Humility* was one of those things that molded Jesus' legacy. Paul declares;

*"Do nothing from selfish ambition or conceit, but in humility count others more significant than yourselves."*263

This is the biblical definition of humility. It is the foremost characteristic the Scripture calls us to. It is regarding one another as more important than ourselves. As a Church Revitalizer and church restarter regarding others above our desires and wishes is often hard because we were raised to win at all costs. Yet, the Scripture is calling us to be the exact opposite. We are called to consider others more important than ourselves. There are many in the ministry today who have false humility. In public they are not prone to take credit, yet in the quiet confines of the pastoral study, when they are honest many really want the credit. That is not humility. Humility is when you look at other people and actually consider them better than yourself.

Not only was humility one of those things that molded Jesus' legacy. *Caring for Others* is another

---

263 Philippians 2:3 (ESV).

thing that caused Jesus to leave the legacy He left. The Bible says *"Let each of you look not only to his own interests, but also to the interests of others."*264 Another distinctive is for church restarters and revitalizers to be leaders who do not just care for themselves, but care for others as well. Do not get so caught up in all the things we do in revitalization that we make the church our idols. When we're busy living life, it's hard to always care for others and put their interests first. We are called to care for our church members interests, to love them anyway, often in spite of how they treat us as their minister. God is calling us to be church restarters who care for the interest of others.

We See the Lord Jesus' Example

Our Lord gave of himself and then he kept on giving. Paul reminds us here in the text: *"Have this mind among yourselves, which is yours in Christ Jesus."*265 We are to walk as Church Revitalizers in humility. We are to care for others. Not to look at just our own interests, but to the interests of others. That is what Jesus did. He lived out these values. Paul states:

> *"Who, though he was in the form of God, did not count equality with God a thing to be grasped, but emptied himself, by taking the form of a servant, being born in the likeness of men. And being found in human form, he humbled himself by becoming obedient to the point of death, even death on a cross. Therefore, God has highly exalted him and bestowed on him the name that is above every name, so that at the name of Jesus every knee should bow, in heaven and on earth*

---

264 Philippians 2:4 (ESV).

265 Philippians 2:5 (ESV).

and under the earth, and every tongue confess that Jesus Christ is Lord, to the glory of God the Father."[266]

Jesus was a man who did not live for Himself. He lived for the benefit of others. The glory of God and His legacy, Jesus' legacy, will be seen and felt forever. At the end of our lives, there is only going to be one thing that lives behind you. It is what you do for Jesus.

Wrapping it Up!

The question is not will you leave a legacy, it is what legacy are you leaving? Hundreds of years from now, if the Lord tarries, nobody is going to remember my name as a Church Revitalizer. Let us live our lives for the only thing that hundreds of years from now will still matter. Stephen Gray and Franklin Dumond speak to the challenge of restarting and leaving a legacy when the discuss the fact of loss of the lower ages in a dying church. They say, "One of the main factors limiting a church's growth potential is age. Both the age of the church itself and the age of the congregants play a role in its limitations. The difficulty for churches in this situation is the realization that few, if any, children and teens remain to sustain the church in the next generation. Even well-known mega-churches throughout the United States are scrambling to re-engineer themselves due to the problem of aging."[267] As a Church Revitalizer the only thing that will last is what you do in this life for Jesus. That's the legacy you want to leave. But a legacy of faithfulness, love and service will matter a long time after you're gone.

---

266 Philippians 2:6-11 (ESV).

267 Stephen Gray and Franklin Dumond. *Legacy Churches*, (ChurchSmart Resources, 2009) , pg. 30.

I recently heard Christian speaker and author Patrick Morley talk about a very interesting and challenging subject. He asked the question, "Who is going to be crying at your funeral?" After moments of pause he went on to say, "These are the people you should be spending time with right now in your life." What a provocative thought! Let me ask you today that same question, "Who is going to be crying at your funeral?" Those are the people you should be spending time with right now in your life. When people are on the death bed some remarkable confessions are made. However, no one on their death bed says, "I wish I would have spent more time at the office." What kind of investment are you making right now to the future of your family, your church and your friends? Billy Graham the great evangelist for the Southern Baptist Convention reminds us all when he says, "Our days are numbered. One of the primary goals in our lives should be to prepare for our last day. The legacy we leave is not just in our possessions, but in the quality of our lives. What preparations should we be making now? The greatest waste in all of our earth, which cannot be recycled or reclaimed, is our waste of the time that God has given us each day."268 Do you realize the only true and worthwhile investment that pays the biggest dividend is when you invest your life in people, especially the ones who will be crying at your funeral?

One day in 1888, a wealthy and successful man was reading what was supposed to be his brother's obituary in a French newspaper. As he read, he realized that the editor had confused the two brothers and had written an obituary for him instead. The headline proclaimed, "The merchant of death is dead," and then described a man who had gained his wealth by helping people to kill one another. Not surprisingly, he was deeply troubled by this glimpse of what his legacy might have been had he actually died on that day. It is

---

268 https://www.goodreads.com/quotes/159535-our-days-are-numbered-one-of-the-primary-goals-in.

believed that this incident was pivotal in motivating him to leave nearly his entire fortune following his actual death eight years later to fund awards each year to give to those whose work most benefitted humanity. This is, of course, the true story of Alfred Nobel, the inventor of dynamite and the founder of the Nobel Prize.

King David made a very large investment in the future of the world. In fact, his life at the end can serve as a model to us about where we should invest our life so we will leave something behind that is of value. David passed on a vision to the people of Israel. He challenged them to do something great and glorious. In his letter to the new believers in Thessalonica, Paul reveals three characteristics that produce a long-lasting spiritual legacy: faith, hope and love. When these are at the very core of who you are, you will display works by faith, labor by love, and endurance by hope in Christ. It is only when the legacy of Christ changes our character that we can begin to live and leave a lasting legacy. The legacy we leave behind can have lasting value.

A Parting Word of Conclusion
What Now?

The Legend of the Trading Ship Octavius

The legend begins "in 1761 with the *Octavius* docked in the port of London to take on a cargo destined for China. This majestic sailing ship left port with a full crew, the skipper, and his wife and son. They arrived safely in China and unloaded their cargo. They headed back to sea once she was loaded with goods destined for British shores, but as the weather was unusually warm, the captain decided to sail home via the Northwest Passage, a voyage that at the time had not been accomplished. This was the last that anyone heard of the vessel, her crew, or her cargo. *Octavius* was declared lost.269

The legend goes on to say that in the year 1775 another trade vessel stumbled upon a ship that seemed to be just drifting around in the frigid waters of the Arctic. The legend says that as the crew from the trade ship boarded the Octavius it found the Captain still at his desk with pen in hand frozen in time. The last addition to his logbook dated 13 years prior to the discovery. All the people aboard were found in their bunks, all frozen where they lay asleep. It seems that the ship Octavius was a floating crypt, inhabited by a frozen crew and passengers. In my experience as a church revitalizer that sounds much like many churches I see. They are like that floating, frigid sepulcher where leadership and congregation have lost their way in ministry and seem to

---

269 Ian Harvey, "The Mystery of the Octavius," *The Vintage News,* October 30, 2016, accessed February 28, 2019, https://www.thevintagenews.com/2016/10/30/the-mystery-of-the-octavius-an-18th-century-ghost-ship-was-discovered-with-the-captains-body-found-frozen-at-his-desk-still-holding-his-pen/

have no purpose. Like the Octavius they drift with no authority at the helm and no direction on the compass.

But there is hope! No matter how futile it may seem there is hope for churches on this ecclesiastical journey, but that hope is only through **Jesus Christ**. That hope lies in the fact that the church is His body and He declared in Matthew 16:18 that the "gates of hell would not prevail against it." We totally understand that verse and we understand that the church, **the bride of Christ**, will be victorious in the end. However, that really doesn't mean that some local congregations will not die. The truth is that between 6,000 and 10,000 churches die and close their doors in the United States every single year, and that means that more than 100 will die this week alone.[270]

William Barclay in reflecting upon the church of Acts 2:42-47 says that that church was: a learning church, a fellowshipping church, a praying church and a reverent church. It was a church where things happened and there were great expectations. The participants shared with each other. They worshipped the Lord in that church. This church was a happy church and it was a winsome group of participants.[271] The healthy revitalizing church is a healthy church full of diverse individuals but sad to say there are some churches that are full of people that have remained as infants, Biblically. It should be a maturing church but without diligent encouragement from the shepherd, the church will lapse into unfaithfulness.

---

270 Michael Snyder, "Between 6,000 and 10,000 Churches in the U.S. are Dying Each Year," *Intercessors for America,* December 6, 2018, accessed February 19, 2019, https://www.ifapray.org/blog/between-6000-and-10000-churches-in-the-u-s-are-dying-each-year/

271 William Barclay, *The Acts of the Apostles,* Revised Edition, Philadelphia: The Westminster Press, 1976, Pgs. 30-31.

We believe that it is the Lord's will that churches survive and prosper. The local church is to blossom and flourish. Biblical, healthy churches keep on ministering to the communities they have been placed in. Yet, some churches will die. They are not supposed to die but some will. Furthermore, those of us working in the field of church revitalization struggle with the reality that many churches in North America are in a slippery slope of decline. While the invisible church of the Lord, those who give their heart to Jesus, keeps growing; the visible church, down the road, appears to be in decline. Statistics concerning church closures are staggering but no church should have to have bleak statistics. All it takes is for the pastor and or lay leaders to decide that they will revision and refocus their church for the future. Refusal to do so will certainly end in a disastrous situation for the church.

The Christian faith is all about resurrection. Our savior was resurrected on the third day to ensure that all would have the opportunity to be saved. Jesus said of himself in John 11:25, "I am the resurrection, and the life: he that believeth in me, though he were dead, yet shall he live:"272 Because He is the "resurrection and the life" there is wonderful hope for the stuck, hurting church. There is hope that it can be revitalized, renewed, or restarted for His glory. The simple fact is the church is not stuck, because of forces outside the church, as we would like to believe. The church is usually stuck because of forces within such as a lack of commitment, self-centeredness and a real lack of concern for the lost. For any rebuilding to take place, the pastor or lay leaders must take some action to intercept any sign of failure and death for the church. Thom Rainer says, "A leader must rise and be willing to lead the church toward radical transformation

---

272 John 11:25 KJV.

regardless of the personal costs to him."273 John Kotter, in his book *Leading Change*, says it is vital that in a turnaround you make sure that new hires are not screened "according to old norms and values."[274] A restart is simply not possible if new hires are swamped in the methodologies of the past. Old ways are often opposed to the new ways of revitalization and restarts. How can a leader rise to this occasion?

Here is a Plan of Action

Heed the Call to Urgency

There is not much time left for many churches. **The pastor and lay-leadership must take the proverbial "bull by the horns."** You cannot play around any longer. Time is wasting. People are lost and your church is dying! What will you do? It is a simple answer yet so difficult to swallow…There must be change in the leader's heart and in the hearts of the people in the congregation. There must be a sense of urgency or your church will die a slow, painful death! It is time to do something!

Without a sense of urgency on the part of leadership, the church will die. How desperate are you for God to do a "new thing" with your church? Are you willing to put yourself aside to let God reveal to you this "new thing?" What cost are you willing to pay for this "new thing?" A "new thing" calls for action. It calls for getting out of your comfort zone. It calls out the best in the leader. It demands that we act in God's

---

273 Thom Rainer, "6 Radical Steps for a Dying Church to Find Life," *Facts & Trends,* May 22, 2017, accessed February 21, 2019, https://factsandtrends.net/2017/05/22/6-radical-steps-dying-church-find-life/

274 John Kotter, Leading Change (Boston: Harvard Business Review Press, 1996), pg. 155.

Will and not our own. How desperate are you for God to change your churches direction?

Accept the Call to Revitalize

Sometimes it is necessary for **the pastor to get out of the way!** Not every pastor is willing or capable to undertake such a task as revitalization. At the risk of being too blunt…that pastor should get out of the way and let someone else take control of the future of the church! If you, as Pastor, are determined to stick it out, and you believe you have a call of God to lead the church in a revitalization effort, then there are certain things that you must consider. 1 Peter 5:2 says "Feed the flock of God which is among you, taking the oversight thereof, not by constraint, but willingly; not for filthy lucre, but of a ready mind;"275 The big question is "are you willing to get out of your comfort zone to become the leader that God can use to revitalize your church? Are you willing to make some hard decisions about the future of your church? Revitalizing a church is hard work. It calls for the best you have to give. It demands an unwavering commitment to the plan of God at the cost of relinquishing your own plans. Will you accept that call?

Acknowledge the Call to Relinquish Control

There must be a new sheriff in town. Most pastors I know do not want to hear that statement because of the personally conceived idea that they are in control of the future of the church. Nothing could be further from the truth. When a church needs revitalization there is no authority or power that can accomplish the task other than the power of God through the Holy Spirit. There must be empowerment from the Holy Spirit and leadership and wisdom from God to bring a church back from the brink of

---

275 1 Peter 5:2 KJV.

destruction. So, pastor or leader stop being a control freak! There is only one power that can fix the problems we face in the church today and that is the power of Holy God through the presence and anointing of the Holy Spirit. We are to be the vessels through which He does his work, but we must remember it is His work! The salvaging of a dying church can only come through wisdom from on high and not man's wisdom. Man's wisdom is what kills the church in the first place. So, if you will take the "bull by the horns" you must give up the power and "LET GOD" have control.

Affirm the Call to Seek Help

"I need help!" These words are seldom heard by the church revitalizer. This is the hardest thing for any pastor to admit. It seems that pastors are seldom willing to say they need help from someone else in ministry. I am convinced this is an attitude of pride and the Bible says that pride "goeth before a fall." Here is some friendly advice…get over yourself…admit that you need help! Be willing to seek the kind of help that 93% of our churches need today. God has gifted many church revitalizers to help churches get unstuck, but they cannot interfere with a local church unless they are asked to get involved. Asking for outside help does not reveal weakness or failure on the part of the pastor or leader. On the contrary it shows a great deal of wisdom. If your car breaks down and you are not a mechanic, do you drive your car into your garage and start taking it apart, all the time not knowing what any of the parts really do? No…you take it to a mechanic. You take it to someone who knows how to fix cars. Furthermore, if you try to fix something that you don't know how to fix, you could make a bigger problem with the mechanics of the car. Then you really do have a larger problem.

If your church is dying, put your pride aside and ask for help. If you don't you may be presiding over the funeral of your church very soon.

Yield to the Call to Die with Dignity

In many cases the church finds itself on life support and death is knocking at the door. Maybe your church has all the symptoms and outward signs that it is dying. What are you going to do? Will you sit by and watch it die so slowly that its testimony is ruined in the community? Will you continuously adjust the life support to keep the church hanging on but knowing that death is eminent? My advice is to **plan for a funeral**. Get yourself and your congregation prepared. Take some of the trauma out of the whole process. The worst thing a pastor can do is to let a church linger on the brink of death while the church community looks on and sees its failure. If they must die, then allowing dignity amidst the sadness is recommended. But clearly hear both authors shouting to you that dying churches have potential and we must give them a chance to succeed once more. They are worthy of our effort and deserve our total attention. If the church is dying seek and honorable death. Plan the funeral and die with dignity. When you plan for the death of the church you can also plan for a "new beginning."

Consent to the Call to Begin Again

It is the wise pastor who recognizes the church is dying and determines in his heart that it will live again by the power of God. The pastor who determines in his heart to help the church **begin again** by doing a restart is the pastor and congregation that God will honor. So, it is a noble thing to help the dying church die for it to live again. Here is a true account of how God gave a new beginning to Immanuel Church in South Georgia. It is the account of the death, burial and resurrection of the church.

For many years Immanuel Church was an exciting and enthusiastic congregation that held a high view of evangelism and discipleship. Every Sunday morning 500 people crowded into that beautiful facility for worship and Bible study. It was one of the most talked about church in the area. It had a great reputation. It focused on missions at home and abroad and gave financial support to several missionary organizations. Then something began to happen in the church. The founding pastor was loved by the Christian community as well as the secular leaders in the community. Through a series of small conflicts a few very powerful people in the church began to oppose the pastor and became determined to push him out and put a new pastor in his place. Of course, because of his long tenure and being the founding pastor, this caused a major division in the fellowship and over a period of around 2 years of bickering and infighting the church finally split. Almost half of the 500 regular attenders either followed the trouble makers to another site to form a church but many of them, because of their disappointment in the church leaders, left and scattered all over the area.

Over time, those who remained after the split began to get spiritually fatigued and burned out as more and more people began to drop out. During this time, they were being led by a transitional pastor who decided he wanted to take the church full time, but the congregation was divided over him being their full-time pastor. That conflict brewed for several months and the transitional pastor left angrily and caused another split in the church. This split left 75 people to keep the ministry going. That is when I was asked to get involved as a church revitalizer.

When I began to survey the situation, it was clear that they could not make any more mistakes and if they did, they would close their doors. They were at that time on the verge of death. The money was very tight, and workers were few. After a time of bringing stability back to the few who were still attending, I began to train the search committee and they began their search for a new pastor with the understanding that they would allow me to work with them through the process. After about 5 months of searching they settled on a young man from another state. I helped them investigate the young candidate and immediately saw red flags in his past ministries. I shared the concerns with the search committee, but they refused to listen. It seems the young man had been in his present church only 13 months and with a little further digging it was clear from things in his past that he had a major anger problem. Nevertheless, the committee refused to listen, and they called him anyway.

In the very beginning he seemed to be doing well. He began a new evangelistic thrust in the church and grew the church from 75 to around 120. Everything seemed to be going well until one Sunday afternoon I received a call from the chairman of deacons requesting a meeting with me and declaring that their pastor was leaving. Thirty minutes after speaking to the chairman of deacons the young pastor called to inform me of the situation and to let me know that he was leaving the pulpit that day and moving back to the state he had come from.

It seems that there had been a disagreement between him and the deacons about an issue that was to be brought up in the business meeting that Sunday morning after worship. The chairman of deacons wanted to speak to the issue, but the pastor refused to allow him time to speak. The chairman left his seat and went to the pulpit where an altercation ensued, and a physical fight broke out in front of the entire congregation. Well, I suppose you know the results of that. People got up and walked out. The next Sunday they had 34 in attendance.

Of course, this killed any remaining good reputation the church might have had in the community. I was asked to step in again and help bring some semblance of life back to the church. That was an impossible task. Instead, after a period of time working with the few leaders that were left, I suggested that a complete restart be considered. There was no other option. It was either restart or dissolve and sell the property. Upon the recommendation to do a restart, others left, seeing the situation as being too far gone to help. To make a long story short…the restart was a great success. The first Sunday the church reopened under a new name, new leadership and a new identity there were 176 people in attendance. God blessed and is still blessing that church to this day.

This is a great restart success story but not all turn out that way. Sometimes some churches wait too long to be brought back to life and even in this situation, it would have been much easier had they been willing to do the restart before they called the young preacher.

This can and should be a story to be repeated over and over again if pastors of dying churches would sense the urgency to revitalize by making a personal commitment to a restart or getting out of the way for someone else to lead. If pastors would commit to seeking help when the signs of death are seen and be willing to relinquish the power, they have to the Holy Spirit to salvage their church, many churches could be salvaged. This would allow their church to die with dignity for it to live again.

Conclusion

In the day in which we live the tragedy of dying churches does not have to be a reality. **There are solutions**. There is help. The church does not have to drift in the frigid waters of death populated by people who have tragically lost their sense of purpose. It can live again! It can experience a spiritual thawing! It can become a viable body of believers again!

Pastor, are you willing to pay that price? Are you willing to be the man that God can and will use to reignite the flames of success in the church you serve? If you can't be that revitalizer, will you get out of the way to let God put someone there who can get it done? If so, then now is the time to act. Don't put it off. Be the change agent in your church to assure that it has a future! What God needs is not more pastors and church leaders...He wants more willing vessels who will be a part of something new in the church. Are you that person? Are you that pastor?

ABOUT THE AUTHORS
Dr. Tom Cheyney
Founder & Directional Leader
Renovate National Church Revitalization Conference
The Renovate Group
RenovateConference.org
ChurchRevitalizer.guru
tom@renovateconference.org

Tom is the founder and directional leader of the RENOVATE National Church Revitalization Conference, The Renovate Group, Executive Editor of *The Church Revitalizer Magazine*, and founder of the RENOVATE Church Revitalization Virtual Coaching Network where he mentors pastors, churches, and denominational leaders in Church Revitalization and Renewal all across North America. He serves as the National Host of the weekly *Church Revitalization and Renewal Podcast.* Dr. Cheyney has written over 5,000 print, audio resources, guides, or books for Church Revitalizers, pastors, church planters, and lay leaders. His most recent books include *The Seven Pillars of Church Revitalization and Renewal, Practical Tools for Reinventing the Dying Church*, *The Church Revitalizer as Change Agent, Thirty-Eight Church Revitalization Models for the Twenty First Century*, *The Nuts & Bolts of Church Revitalization and Renewal,* and *Preaching Towards Church Revitalization and Renewal, Church Revitalization in Rural America: Restoring Churches in the Heartlands, Slaying the Dragons of Church Revitalization and Renewal: Dealing with the Critical Issues which are Hurting Your Church.* Cheyney has written along with his friend Rodney Harrison *Spin-Off Churches* (B&H Publishers). Tom is a nationally recognized conference speaker and a frequent writer on church revitalization, church planting, new church health, and leadership development. Others have label Tom as the *Father of the Church Revitalization Movement* as his influence has stretched across multiple denominations and countries. He leads a monthly training lab for all those desiring to see their churches brought back to life.

Dr. Steve Sells
Founder & President
Operation Transformation
jstevesells@gmail.com

Steve is the Founder and President of Operation Transformation, a church revitalization group based in Salisbury, North Carolina. Steve has served in North Carolina and Georgia as a local church pastor for 31 years and a Director of Missions for 12 years. Dr. Sells is the co-author of the book **With Greater Power: The Secret to a Spirit-Powered Life** and is a regular contributing writer for *The Church Revitalizer Magazine.* Steve has written numerous guides, resources and programs to be used in local church revitalization. He has developed special ministries designed to help plateaued and declining churches in all areas of revitalization and church restarts. He is a member of the Society for Church Consulting and is a Certified Church Health Consultant. He has led in planting churches in India, Romania, South Africa and Haiti. The ministry of Operation Transformation transcends denominational lines and seeks to help churches of all denominations and sizes experience new health and growth.

www.ingramcontent.com/pod-product-compliance
Lightning Source LLC
Chambersburg PA
CBHW062356090426
42740CB00010B/1293